Women

in

Television

News

Revisited

Judith Marlane

Women

in

Television

News

Revisited

Into the Twenty-First Century

UNIVERSITY OF TEXAS PRESS, AUSTIN

Requests for permission to reproduce material from this
work should be sent to Permissions, University of Texas
Press, Box 7819, Austin, TX 78713-7819.

(∞) The paper used in this publication meets the
minimum requirements of American National Standard
for Information Sciences—Permanence of Paper for
Printed Library Materials, ANSI Z39.48-1984.

LIBRARY OF CONGRESS
CATALOGING-IN-PUBLICATION DATA

Marlane, Judith, 1937–
    Women in television news revisited : into the twenty-
first century / Judith Marlane. — 1st ed.
        p.   cm.
    Includes bibliographical references and index.
    ISBN 0-292-75227-X (cloth : alk. paper). —
ISBN 0-292-75228-8 (pbk. : alk. paper)
    1. Television broadcasting of news—United States.
    2. Women in television broadcasting—United States.
    3. Women television journalists—United States—
Interviews.   4. Television news anchors—United
States—Interviews.   I. Title.
PN4888.T4M365   1999
070.1′95—dc21   98-48678

TO RON—

with my love

CONTENTS

ILLUSTRATIONS

FOREWORD

In reading Judith Marlane's *Women in Television News Revisited: Into the Twenty-first Century,* my own mind revisited a ten-day trial in August 1983. Christine Craft won her breach of contract lawsuit against Metromedia, Inc., in which she charged she had been dropped as an evening anchor from its Kansas City, Missouri, station because the general manager and his male bosses believed her "too old, too unattractive, and . . . not sufficiently deferential to men."

I covered that trial as a TV columnist for the *Los Angeles Times,* and later rejoiced with the "elderly" Craft (who was then in her late thirties) over her deserved victory and the five hundred thousand dollars in damages awarded her by the jury. The celebration was short-lived, for the verdict was subsequently thrown out by U.S. District Court judge Joseph E. Stephens Jr., who ordered a new trial. That second trial, in 1984, also resulted in a verdict for Craft, but one that she lost on appeal when it was later tossed out by the Eighth Circuit Court. Go figure.

When the U.S. Supreme Court refused to hear Craft's case, her long, frustrating day in court had ended. Yet her nationally publicized struggle against antifemale bias and stereotyping in television news was powerfully symbolic. It became a shining Bethlehem Star that was followed by other women journalists who rejected being defined and pigeonholed as "cupcakes" because of their gender. In losing a painful skirmish, Craft had helped revitalize an offensive that began even before her arrival on the scene—one that, as Marlane's latest interviews affirm, continues even today.

In *Women in Television News Revisited,* Marlane skillfully returns to the TV trenches she slogged through in her former interviews, which were first published in 1976, speaking to many of the women she previously questioned, measuring earlier career dreams against new ones, while adding many interviewees and expanding the dialogue to some key male journalists, too. Relying mostly on their words, she has shaped what they have reported into an exhaustive and profoundly illuminating update that spreads an equally intense, but much broader beam across the battle plain where Craft was mired in the early 1980s. Even though the going is certainly much easier than it was then, that battle plain still exists. Yet why have some careers bloomed brilliantly, while others have not? Is it all due to differing abilities? We learn from Marlane and her subjects that much has changed in a positive way for women TV journalists since those earlier days when barrier after barrier was deployed against them. And we learn that too much has not changed.

When you think about it, the progress made by some of the women in the field has been simply stunning, if late in coming. After all, one of the globe's most famous and best-paid journalists today is a woman. Christiane Amanpour's rise to VIP loftiness at CNN came not from reading copy from a TelePrompTer in a comfy studio but from doing serious hard-news reporting and risking her neck as a foreign correspondent in dangerous hotspots where many male cupcakes fear to tread. Other females have joined her, from Bosnia to the White House, in being entrusted with some of TV's most perilous and most important news beats. Some of them now find themselves dodging shrapnel instead of their boss's archaic attitudes, and the highest rungs of TV journalism are increasingly being occupied by women, giving hope to young aspirants just starting the climb.

Meanwhile, the impenetrable age ceiling that so many females in the business once feared awaited them because of their gender has come crashing down, with Leslie Stahl of CBS and Diane Sawyer and Connie Chung of ABC having joined the fifty-and-over crowd, as have some of the less well-known working journalists interviewed most recently by Marlane. And ABC's Barbara Walters, revered by many of her progeny as the grandam of TV newswomen, pursues her high-profile interviews as ferociously as ever despite being on the far side of sixty. In contrast, of Marlane's original interviewees, only the late cotton-mopped Pauline Frederick of NBC was past fifty in an era when men were seen still as aging with gray grace and distinction and women, poor things, subject to extreme gnarling as they grow older.

Lest we get giddy about how far we've come, though, it's good to recall that as this is written, Stahl remains a virtual matriarchy of one on manly *60 Minutes,* and that only Walters (briefly in the 1970s) and Chung (briefly in the 1990s) have infiltrated that exclusive men's club, otherwise known as nightly news anchordom, on the big-three networks. The symbolism of this is striking. Meanwhile, although more women than ever have access to journalism's executive washrooms, all of the top jobs in TV news remain in the hands of men, none of whom appears excited about the prospect of relinquishing control.

On October 16, 1997, Andrew Lack, president of NBC News, and a number of his executive producers gave a conference telephone interview to promote a project of the news division that was to ambitiously cut across all of its programs. Although the project's title was "The Sex War: The Tension between Men and Women," everyone on the phone talking about it for NBC was male.

HOWARD ROSENBERG
Los Angeles, 1998

PREFACE

Two decades have passed since the publication of my first book, published by Columbia University Press, *Women in Television News*. This pioneering effort received the Broadcast Preceptor Award in 1976 for excellence. When I traveled to San Francisco to accept this award, I found myself sharing the stage with Alex Haley who was being honored for his masterful work *Roots*. This was a meaningful juxtaposition since most of my professional life was devoted to issues related to women and minorities. At that time, I was the head of a small television production company that specialized in documentary and public affairs programming. I had entered that entrepreneurial venture because prospective employers in the television business had told me that I was "overqualified" and a "threat" since I had recently received my doctoral degree. It was pointed out to me that the only person who was not stigmatized by a doctorate in the television industry was Frank Stanton, former head of CBS.

As I did the research for this book and revisited the women I had met over twenty years earlier, I relived my own life and the changes the years had made. As I wrote their history, I was writing my own. I had raised two daughters and ended a long-term marriage. At WWOR-TV in New York where I wrote and produced weekly public affairs programs and news specials, I was the victim of sexual harassment. A vice president and general manager bluntly asked me, "What are you willing to do for me?" When I did not provide the desired answer, I found myself without an office and not in line for a raise. This was the same man who rushed down from his office into the newsroom screaming when he viewed two women anchors delivering the noon news. Illness had created a last-minute crisis and there was no male anchor or correspondent available. "Never again will two women appear together as anchors on any of my news shows," was the shouted command. He was ultimately fired but not for grievous sexism, or incompetence, but rather because he kept firearms in his private bathroom and a disgruntled former employee (male) discovered it and brandished one of the guns directly at him.

Soon after this episode I was recruited by California State University, Northridge, to be the first female to head the Radio Television Film Department and its first female full professor. Since I believed it was of critical importance to continue to open doors and to help break down barriers, I moved to the media center of the entertainment industry, Los Angeles.

Women of achievement are always standing on the shoulders of those who preceded them. Together, we must sustain and help support the women who will follow in our footsteps. While traveling from New York City back to Los Angeles, I met a young woman with whom I worked while at WWOR-TV. She was now the executive producer of the *Montel Williams Show* and she thanked me for serving as her role model: "You made me realize what I wanted to be and that as a woman, it was possible." It was a wonderful feeling of acknowledgment. But I must note that she flew first class, while I sat in coach; when we landed, she was met by a driver and a limousine. I carried my own luggage and went home by Super Shuttle.

This new history, *Women in Television News Revisited,* is all of our stories. It is about sacrifice and successes, problems and pleasures, aggravations and attainments. Most of all, it is about the ability to make choices and have options—and the need to follow your dream wherever it leads.

Author's Note: In a project of this breadth, given the dynamic and volatile nature of the television industry, bear in mind that in the time between interview and publication, there will have been changes in assignments, promotions, retirements, illnesses, and deaths. Nevertheless, this study marks a turning point in the continuum of the history of women in television news: the conclusion of the century of the birth and infancy of the medium and the threshold of the twenty-first century.   J. M.

ACKNOWLEDGMENTS

My sincere thanks to the women and men in television news broadcasting who spoke to me with candor and insight about their professional careers and personal lives. They made possible the basic research for this book. I also owe a debt of gratitude to their dedicated and hard-working staffs who helped arrange the time and place of the interviews within the constraints of pressured schedules and mind-boggling logistics.

From my world, I offer special thanks to Gayle Sharlow for her endless patience and secretarial skills; Sue Young for her precise transcription help; Chris Martin at ABC's headquarters in Washington, D.C., for providing a comfortable place to wait between interviews and airplanes; Theresa May and Jim Burr at the University of Texas Press for their understanding and support of this project from its inception.

No expression of appreciation is complete that does not acknowledge the love and strength given by my family. I am grateful to my daughter Sari for her sense of humor and her basic computer skills, to my daughter Debra, who never fails me in the crunches, most especially to my husband, Ron, who sets the standard for compassion, wisdom, and unconditional love—and finally, to Nicholas, Douglas, and Scot, who will join the fearless leaders of the twenty-first century.

Women
in
Television
News
Revisited

1
Design
and
Detail

Being a woman is a terribly difficult task
since it consists principally in dealing
with men. JOSEPH CONRAD (1857–1924)

Over a quarter of a century has passed since the Federal Communications Commission added women to its equal opportunity ruling that originally applied only to social and ethnic minorities. Television stations grudgingly learned to reach out and hire women in a mandated attempt to implement affirmative action policies and to end the discrimination against women in broadcasting.

Every television station in America felt the need to hire one female newscaster. Often they would seek out a minority woman and thereby satisfy tokenism in one fell swoop. A small but growing number of women began to appear in positions equal with those held by men on local and national newscasts around the country. They became known as "the class of '72."

It was at this point that I first began to document the background, contributions, and struggles of women in television news. Thirty women reporters and correspondents working in New York and Washington, D.C., on network and local news formed the sample for my first study. This pioneering effort provided an inside look at how women were then entering and working successfully in the male-dominated profession of television news.

Twenty-five years later, I became ready to reexamine and revisit the world of television news and the role that women were playing. I was eager to learn what changes had occurred in the personal and professional lives of women who were now working in television news broadcasting—those who were part of my original study and others who were not.

Over a period of nine months I conducted in-depth interviews with eighty-five of the leading women and men who are working as anchors, correspondents, and bureau chiefs, as well as many who hold key management positions in the network news divisions. Seventy women and fifteen men make up the basic sample and provide the research material for this book. Interviews were held in person and by telephone in New York City, Washington, D.C., San Francisco, Los Angeles, San Diego, Connecticut, New Mexico, Florida, New Jersey, Toronto, London, Paris, and Jerusalem.

The volatile nature of the news business made the task of speaking to these broadcasters challenging, exciting, and frenetic. The number of letters, faxes, and telephone calls necessary to secure a definite date and time were prodigious. The vast majority of those interviewed were cooperative and pleased to be part of this effort. A few were not.

It was especially meaningful to meet with those women with whom I had not spoken for over a quarter of a century. It was a time of introspection and discovery for all of us. The physical changes were present—added pounds on some, fewer pounds on others, and the remarkable evolution of those who appeared even more attractive in their mature years than when they were younger. The experiences of illness, even death, marriage, and divorce that are part of the passage of years and the stages of one's life became documented, discussed, and digested. As we shared and explored events, there emerged a special bond of understanding and friendship—one that does not require constant contact or renewal, but rather remains as a feeling of warmth and mutual respect that is a thermal layer on the fabric of a life.

Each interview lasted between thirty minutes and three hours, based upon the availability of the person and the current demands of their work schedule. Several interviews were interrupted only to be completed at a later date. Interviews were conducted in offices, private houses, apartments, restaurants, hotel lobbies, studios, and running down the streets of New York and Washington, D.C. Times, dates, and locations were often changed to fit deadline pressures. I spoke to people at all hours of the day and night, seven days a week; whenever they were available, so was I. It often became a logistics nightmare to locate and speak to a correspondent stationed half-way around the world, busy on assignment covering a war zone.

Once I was caught in rush-hour traffic on the busiest freeway in Los Angeles when the call came in from Christiane Amanpour, in Paris, that she was ready to do her interview with me. Never before or since have I driven so recklessly to get to a destination. On another occasion, I missed a reunion dinner in New York with two lifelong friends who live in different parts of the United States in order to accommodate Barbara Walters who was forced to change her interview time with me. She was completing the editing necessary on her television interview with Lyle and Erik Menendez.[1] As she got up from her desk to show me out at the end of my evening interview with her in her 20/20 office, she apologized for being so difficult to see. She said she regularly receives at least two requests each day from people who are writing books. She went on to say how pleased she was that I was so persistent. Her comments hold special meaning for me. She was the pinnacle of the television news world twenty-three years ago when we first spoke; she remains one of the most respected and revered women in broadcasting.

While on this same trip to New York City, I met with and interviewed both Tom Brokaw at NBC and Dan Rather at CBS. Dan Rather was especially gracious with his time and spent almost ninety minutes with me. However, when I arrived at ABC for a scheduled appointment with Peter Jennings, his press representative, the late Arnot Walker, greeted me and told me how sorry he was but that I was "blown off" Peter's schedule due to a tobacco special that he was writing. As I was about to begin my interview with Kathy Christensen, then executive producer of *ABC World News Tonight,* Peter Jennings walked in, shirt sleeves rolled up, and declared he was about to close himself in his office for the next hour and a half to write. I was briefly introduced and while we shook hands, there was no indication that he realized who I was, why I was there, or that he had just canceled a confirmed interview that I had traveled three thousand miles to obtain—certainly, no apology was ever forthcoming. A telephone interview was promised by Walker as a backup, but it was never arranged despite my persistent follow-up calls.

The most uncooperative person I attempted to interview was Lesley

---

[1] Lyle and Erik Menendez were convicted of first-degree murder on March 20, 1996, for killing their wealthy parents in Beverly Hills. They are currently serving life sentences without the possibility of parole.

Stahl. She was part of my first study and I was eager to meet with her again. When I first attempted to contact her, I met with the understandable unpredictability of her hectic schedule. I continued to call; after six months she did call my office, without warning, ready to be interviewed. I was not there. This missed opportunity prompted me to begin checking in with her office on a daily basis to determine if she would be available. I did not want to miss this opportunity a second time. Her secretary repeatedly told me she never is aware of her schedule in advance. I kept calling.

On November 14, 1996, in Los Angeles, Lesley Stahl was the keynote speaker at Governor Pete Wilson's Conference for Women in Long Beach, California. I decided to attend. Just before her speech while she was seated alone at the dais I went up to introduce myself. Without a greeting, acknowledgment, or any other comment, she looked at me and said, "Don't call my office. Please, don't call my office." I was stunned. No other words were exchanged. I left her seated and walked away. It was firm, it was final, it was rude, and it hurt. I never did call her office again. I never tried to speak with her again. No interview ever took place.

During the course of this extensive interview process, I gained renewed respect for the profession of journalism and for the women and men who are working so effectively in it. They are an intelligent, articulate, caring, committed, and diligent group, who have achieved prominence in a career that is uncompromising and relentless in its demands.

Television remains the most powerful and persuasive medium of communication yet devised. Most Americans rely on television as their primary source of news and information. In a functioning democracy information is crucial for survival. This places an awesome responsibility on those individuals who choose to work in this profession. The aggregate skills of men and women working together are necessary to meet this challenge. Only through a broad range of expertise and opinion can television news expand its intellectual horizons and effectiveness.

The sample for this study consists of network women correspondents who, because of their on-air work and visibility, are able to serve as role models for women everywhere. Women in top management positions in network news divisions are able to influence the corporate culture and challenge the invisible barriers that keep women from obtaining responsible jobs that lead to substantial power in the executive suite. The men interviewed for this study all started working in journalism when women were a relative rarity. Their perspectives on the changes and gains made by women in journalism over the last twenty-five years provide important insights.

The network television news programs have always symbolized the pinnacle of the broadcasting profession. Only one woman of eminence appeared with regularity on network news before the 1960s. Pauline Frederick, NBC's United Nations correspondent beginning in 1953, was the exception, the first woman in television news. For much of her career, Frederick was the only woman broadcast correspondent present at news events. Her professionalism and success opened the doors for the acceptance of women in television and radio journalism. She was the first woman to win the Paul White Award of the Radio-Television News Directors Association and the George Foster Peabody Award. In 1976, Pauline Frederick became the first woman to moderate a presidential debate—the one between Gerald R. Ford and Jimmy Carter in San Francisco.

When I first interviewed Frederick in February 1973, it was shortly before her mandatory retirement from NBC in 1974 at the age of sixty-five. "If a man is old, he's called interesting," she said. "When a woman is old and shows wrinkles, it's terrible. She's finished. It's a double standard." She worked diligently to insure that her male colleagues treated her with respect and equality. She acknowledged the difficulty and discrimination she continually faced as a woman doing hard news. Much of the difficulty she blamed on the problem that people, even women, were said to prefer a male voice on the air. This is the voice "representing authority which is the male voice, the father, the husband, the lover, they prefer that to the female voice on the air."

Pauline Frederick died in 1990 of a heart attack at the age of eighty-four. Her pioneering efforts remain a distinctive legacy for so many of us. She will always be considered the first lady of television news.

With the passage of Title VII of the Civil Rights Act of 1964, which makes job discrimination for reasons of sex illegal, a growing number of broadcasters were encouraged to hire women. When Marya McLaughlin joined CBS News and Liz Trotta and Nancy Dickerson joined NBC news in New York, the *New York Times* headline read "Nylons Enter the Newsroom." When I first interviewed Marya McLaughlin in March 1973 she was a general assignment correspondent in CBS's Washington bureau, mainly covering the Hill and the Senate. She told me then that it was a very bad thing to have people say that women have

Pauline Frederick

made great strides when in fact "it's the other way around—it's the industry that has made great strides. I think they realize they have a resource they should be taking advantage of."

Marya McLaughlin left the CBS Washington Bureau in 1988 when her contract was not renewed. Many believe she fell victim to advancing years and the unforgiving gaze of the camera lens. She is now retired and still living in the Washington, D.C., area. When I contacted her for an interview for this book she was adamant about not wanting to talk to me. Sadly, she seemed quite angry and unwilling to discuss her former career.

At the time I was doing the research for this book, Nancy Dickerson was recuperating from a serious illness in a New York hospital.[2] Liz Trotta has recently written her own hard-hitting memoir of her career as a reporter and war correspondent, the first woman war correspon-

---

[2] As I completed this manuscript, I learned of the death of Nancy Dickerson on October 18, 1997. She was seventy years old.

dent stationed in Vietnam.[3] An irreverent and sexist New York news director told me in 1973 that women like Liz Trotta were being put on stories that were unsuitable for their sex. As a result, "they became masculinized. They lower their voices and try to imitate David Brinkley. You get these female-men on the air trying to look cool, look hard, and look knowing and do the thing that men have done." This was the same news director who, when I appeared for a job interview in his newsroom in 1968, told me that if I were a black woman I would have a job. When I asked him recently if he remembered that, he went on to explain that, "if you are a white male news executive and you have to hire minorities, a male minority is a threat. A female minority is much less a threat, they're more controllable than a man."[4]

Sex-role distinctions continue to plague the role of women in broadcasting. Ingrained attitudes and opinions about sexual role behavior is continually being reinforced by our society and reflected daily in the media. A survey of the top sixty-five prime-time situation comedies and dramatic series in 1995–1996 conducted by Dr. Martha Lauzen at San Diego State University shows that women remain underrepresented in these prime-time series.[5] These are her findings: 63 percent of all on-screen characters in this time period were male; female characters tended to be defined by their marital status while male characters were defined by their occupation; female characters were seen doing "women's work," such as being a teacher or homemaker, while male characters did "power work," including being a professor, business manager, landlord, or an athlete. The majority of female characters portrayed were in their twenties or thirties. Female characters were rarely seen on the screen after the age of fifty. Dr. Lauzen also examined behind-the-scenes representation in the 1995–1996 prime-time season. She found that women made up only 28 percent of all behind-the-scenes workers; 16 percent of executive producers were women, while 68 percent had no female executive producers; 18 percent of producers were women while 68 percent had no female producers; 11 percent of the directors

---

[3] See Liz Trotta, *Fighting for Air: In the Trenches with Television News*. New York: Simon & Schuster, 1991.

[4] Interview with Ted Kavenau, news director, WNEW-TV, New York, March 5, 1973. Today Ted is a news consultant living in New Jersey.

[5] Martha M. Lauzen, "Making a Difference: The Role of Women on Screen and behind the Scenes in the 1995–96 Prime-Time Season" (San Diego, Calif.: School of Communication, San Diego State University, August 1996, photocopy).

were women, and 22 percent of the writers were women. The study also reveals that when one or more women worked on a program as executive producer, producer, director, or writer, the female characters were more frequently seen speaking, introducing topics of conversation, and providing the last word in conversations. There is compelling evidence to suggest that more powerful female characters are visible on the screen when there are powerful women working behind the scenes to create them.

Other statistics confirm the gender disparity in the media. The Directors Guild of America (DGA) has reported that the number of women directing films has risen from 3 percent to 9 percent between 1983 and 1996. But in 1996, DGA reported a slight percentage decrease in the total number of days worked by women members (from 22.76% to 22.63%). Women working as DGA film directors make up 9 percent of the total membership. Martha Coolidge, first vice president of the Director's Guild, called the statistics "an embarrassment to our industry." [6] Within this same period of time, the Writers' Guild of America (WGA) stated that the number of women who received screen credit increased from 9 percent to 11 percent. WGA statistics for the period between October 1996 through September 1997 show that 26 percent of all working television members were women and only 23 percent of all working screen members were women. On screen, the world of women is not doing very well either. In a 1995 survey of distributors and executives conducted by the *Hollywood Reporter*, the global bankability of female stars was found to be at its weakest in the last five years while the survey named more than a dozen male stars capable of opening films worldwide on the power of their name alone; only three women made this "A" list.

The division between "A-Team" players and "B-Team" players is of major significance in broadcasting and in the struggle to reduce the obstacles that women face in the field. While the number of women correspondents expanded at the networks in the 1970s and 1980s, many experienced major frustrations and believed their ability to advance was effectively being blocked.

The network evening news has long been acknowledged as the flagship broadcast. A-Team correspondents would receive the major impor-

---

[6] Directors Guild of America, "DGA Annual Report on Women and Minority Hiring Shows No Trend toward Equality," press release, June 12, 1997.

tant beats and have regular visibility on the newscasts. Women found themselves relegated to the second-string, B-Team. This frustration and claim of second-class status was verified by research studies that began to appear.

For example, Joe S. Foote, a professor and dean of Southern Illinois University's College of Mass Media and Media Arts, discovered that between 1983 and 1984 women news correspondents composed 30 percent of the bottom thirty correspondents and only 10 percent of the top thirty correspondents. The existence of a "women's ghetto" was further documented in 1990 when a three-week sample of the network evening newscasts showed that women correspondents reported only 12 percent of the stories.[7]

In a more comprehensive study of the visibility of women correspondents on network evening news, Foote conducted a seven-year analysis between January 1983 and December 1989.[8] The findings show a static level of exposure for women correspondents throughout this period of time. There were 275 correspondents under review; 83.6 percent were men and 16.4 percent were women. In every year women registered high only in the lowest exposure category while the men were dominant in the highest exposure category. Overall, 27 percent of the women and 14 percent of the men placed in the lowest exposure category. Of the top fifty most visible correspondents, there were only four women who made the list from 1983 through 1989. All of these women were based in Washington, D.C. There was never more than one woman among the top ten correspondents until 1989 when there were three: Lesley Stahl at CBS, Andrea Mitchell at NBC, and Rita Braver at CBS. The study further documents that in none of the years analyzed were the majority of women correspondents among the top one hundred most visible correspondents. Overall, only 2 percent of the female correspondents numbered in the top ten. In 1997, Foote's annual media analysis revealed that for the first time in a decade there were no women in the top-ten tier of nightly news correspondents. Lisa Myers, NBC's chief congressional correspondent made the best showing for a woman with a

[7] D. Ziegler and A. White, "Women and Minorities on Network Television News: An Examination of Correspondents and Newsmakers," *Journal of Broadcasting & Electronic Media* 34, no. 2 (Spring 1990): 215–223.

[8] Joe S. Foote, "Women Correspondents' Visibility on Network Evening News," *Mass Communication Review* 19, nos. 1 and 2 (1992).

twelfth-place finish.[9] The conclusion is obvious: in the B-Team of correspondents who receive less-favorable assignments and little airtime, women are clearly overrepresented.

The television medium has a profound impact on the images and perceptions of women in our society. The network correspondent stands as the most visible symbol of the working woman in America. Only through effective representation of women in television news will it be possible to adequately address the wide spectrum of political, economic, and social issues that impact women's lives. Indeed, without the ability of women to share an equal voice in the news media, the freedom and future strength of our country is at risk.

Women are changing the face of America. Since 1962, more than one million women have joined the workforce each year. With 58.9 percent of women in the workforce in 1996, significant ground is being gained. More women than ever before are working in the news programs at the major networks. In 1997, of the 167 correspondents who worked on the ABC, CBS, and NBC nightly newscasts, 29 percent were women.[10] Never before have women played such a prominent role in the shaping and reporting of network and local news. In addition to the on-air positions, women are in jobs at all production levels: executive producers, producing editors, bureau chiefs, assistant bureau chiefs, even network vice-presidents. Yet, the growing numbers do not reflect a substantial shift in power. Clearly there is a dearth of women in the decision-making positions of the network news divisions. The news media elite is still composed mainly of white males. This situation parallels the role of women in American society at large.

In the United States no woman is president, vice president, or leader of either congressional chamber. In 1996, the number of women in Congress was at a record level—eight women served in the Senate (8% of the 100 seats available) and forty-eight served in the House of Representatives (11% of the 435 available seats). In all, women held a total of 10.5 percent of the 535 seats in both houses of the 104th U.S. Congress.

For the first time, the wives of both the 1996 Republican and Democratic party candidates were women with independent career accom-

---

[9] Joe S. Foote, "Women Shut Out of Top Ten Network News Slots," press release, University News Service, Southern Illinois University, Carbondale, January 21, 1998.

[10] Ibid.

plishments. Elizabeth Dole and First Lady Hillary Rodham Clinton each earned an Ivy League law degree. Yet the first lady was subject to loathing and even vilification by some members of the press and the public. Women of strength and achievement, for many, continue to represent an unwelcome threat. A measure of discrimination against women still exists in every newsroom in the world. This is merely reflective of the deep-rooted sexism that is pervasive in every country and stands as a barrier to the realization of women's equality everywhere.

2
Paradox and Perception

Whatever women do they must do twice
as well as men to be thought half
as good. Luckily, this is not difficult.

CHARLOTTE WHITTON (1896–1975)

The need to find an equitable role for women in society is reflected in the role of women in network television news. When their faces and voices are viewed in the public arena, reporting on issues of world significance, the ripple effects are felt throughout the country. The last twenty-five years have been witness to enormous social and economic change in lives of women in the United States. But a close look reveals that much remains the same.

My discussions with each of the eighty-five women and men in television news acknowledge the progress that women have made over the last several decades. But they voice varying degrees of concern about the gender biases and the difficulties women still face in the profession.

When I first interviewed Dave Marash in 1973 for my first book, he was the news anchor of the 11:00 P.M. news on WCBS-TV, Channel 2, in New York. He is now a correspondent on ABC's *Nightline* working out of the Washington, D.C., Bureau. Marash is still branded a workaholic journalist and remains bluntly outspoken:

Since we last talked there has been tremendous progress. But to me there has been at least an equal amount of backlash. We've gone two steps forward, we've gone two steps back, not one step. The opportunities for women are greater, particularly behind the camera. Overall, if you were a women on camera in 1972, you had a world of even greater opportunities. Behind the camera there were very few women in any position of power and even relatively few moving up that ladder. The great emphasis and the great progress in the twenty intervening years has seen the situation reversed. Now for women who want to be producer, who want to be management, who want to be shooters and editors, the road is open and even the glass ceiling eroded. I feel that in front of the camera, if anything, there's been stagnation and a retrogression. That is to say, the chick quotient seems higher than it was twenty years ago.

Linda Ellerbee is an experienced and outspoken journalist who now heads her own award-winning production company, Lucky Duck Productions. She spoke to me about the difficult early days:

In the beginning we were the dancing dogs. It wasn't how well the dog danced, it was that the dog danced at all. Their expectation of us was that we'd all screwed our way into our jobs and that therefore we didn't have a brain in our head. And they learned by getting stung by a bunch of smart women going in and asking smart questions and then printing or broadcasting the answers. So they don't do that anymore. . . . Probably the hardest thing for all of us was that in order to pass muster, to play with the big kids, you were expected to go out and you were expected to be aggressive and to not take no for an answer, and to pursue a subject or a story until it died an unholy death. You were expected to be strong, and you were expected to be ambitious. Then you were expected to turn around and come inside that station and be none of those things to your employers. And right away, I looked at this, and I thought one of two things is going to happen here. Either they're going to make me crazy, or I'm going to make them crazy, and if I've got a choice, I know which way this one's coming down.

Cokie Roberts holds a prestigious position as a correspondent and news analyst for ABC. She remembers being told "we don't hire women" and in every place finding herself the only woman who wasn't working as a secretary:

For a woman in any field, you have to work harder and be smarter. But as I tell girls, "that ain't hard, honey." But I do think that in television, particularly the television that I do (and for a long time, I was the only woman doing it, sitting there with the big boys discussing politics), a woman has to be very careful not to be pushy and aggressive and all those things. You have to let viewers get to know you before you assert yourself too much. Otherwise you are a pushy broad. You have to let them think that you really do have something to say. I was lucky because a lot of people had heard me on National Public Radio and felt I had something to say so they wanted to hear me on television. But you can't be a wallflower and not say anything because who needs you on television then—on the other hand, you can't just jump in there and interrupt the guys and be part of the mix. For awhile, you have to just say a few things, hold your tongue, wait awhile until everybody says, "Okay, she's one of the gang now."

One of the "big boys" that Roberts sits next to at ABC News is Sam Donaldson, a twenty-nine-year veteran of the network and a much-honored journalist. He candidly discussed the changes in women's roles over the years and the altering perception of their current status:

There's a strange little bubble that's happening and I think it's absolutely fair and that is that women in television have been discovered by the management. Whether through a desire to address the shameful record of the past or whether it's the awakened fact that the audience accepts women just fine. So women are coming to the fore and I hear some men grousing that they have been beaten out for a plum assignment or a plum spot by a woman. They're claiming it's reverse discrimination, yet I think it's absolutely fair. I work on a program called *PrimeTime Live*.[1] The executive producer is a woman, Phyllis McGrady. My co-anchor and clearly the person who has more influence than any other on the broadcast, except for the executive producer, is a woman, Diane Sawyer. I work here in Washington where the senior producer who runs this shop is a woman, Kerry Marash and her deputy, Helen Westwood, is a woman. If you came in on a business day here, you would say that Sam Donaldson and Chris Wallace and maybe two other guys were in the distinct minority and

---

[1] In September 1998, ABC combined *PrimeTime Live* and 20/20 into one program broadcast three times a week, called simply 20/20.

Cokie Roberts, ABC News

STEVE FENN/ABC

we'd better form a little enclave, if you're going to divide among gender. So I think, at the moment, women are making a big catch up. Now, having painted my little scenario, which is accurate, you could paint another scenario. There is no woman who is a major anchor of the commercial network newscasts. I'm simply saying there's a bubble now of women rising quickly to the fore, and a lot of men are grousing that they're being passed over. Well, so be it. How many hundreds of years has it been the other way around?

Andrea Mitchell is chief foreign affairs correspondent for NBC. She remembers creating a huge stir in 1967 when she tried to get an entry-level news job in the radio newsroom of Westinghouse Broadcasting. They did not want to have a woman in their newsroom. They finally agreed to make her a "copy boy" on the midnight to eight shift to see if it would work out and so she would be "less visible." Mitchell still acknowledges the serious problem women face and the fact that women are judged by different standards and expectations. She recalled the time the late mayor in Philadelphia, James Tate, refused to deal with a woman reporter and said to her face during a news conference, "Little girl, I don't have to answer your questions anymore."

Dan Rather, anchor and managing editor of the *CBS Evening News* admitted that women today face some prejudice in the workplace. He acknowledges that while "it's far better today than it was even eight or ten years ago and a light-year ahead of where it was in the early seventies . . . it's sure true that an overwhelming number of the major decision makers are male and there are no women in the ultimate decision-making positions in any one of the three networks."

One of the most respected men in the history of television news is the venerable Walter Cronkite. At eighty-five years of age, his career encompasses the history and development of broadcast news. In our interview, Cronkite spoke of the conspicuous effort to try to balance the genders on the air and the continuing problem that women have achieving a voice of authority: "I think there is a small and unfortunate disadvantage to women in the pitch of the voice. It is not quite to my ear, which is not a very good ear, I'll admit, but I've heard others comment about the same. The high pitch of women's voices are not quite as easily comprehended as the deeper pitch of a male voice." He noted that when he entered broadcasting "there was one brave young correspondent at the United Nations for NBC." He was referring to Pauline Frederick, who was frequently told as she fought for serious stories that she could not present the news on air because her voice simply did not carry enough authority.

The late Pauline Frederick knew how difficult it was for the male world to accept a woman doing hard news. She was, in her own words, "somewhat of a curiosity" because she was the only woman regularly broadcasting news on air. She would smile as she related her early efforts to enter the broadcasting profession:

> I remember asking an executive (not at NBC) what I could do really to broadcast news. I didn't want to go out and cover fashion shows, as they were having me do. . . . He said, "When you are broadcasting something as serious as news about the United Nations" (this, of course, was only radio—it was a long time ago) "listeners are going to tune out because, a woman's voice does not carry authority." And I always follow up this anecdote with the comment that I am terribly sorry I didn't have courage enough in those days to tell him that I knew his wife's voice carried plenty of authority in his house.

Although Pauline Frederick worked successfully to break down that barrier during her outstanding career in which she was the only reporter ever ranked among the ten most admired women in the world by a Gallup poll, vestiges of this prejudice remain.

Certain things refuse to change. When Judy Muller, an ABC news correspondent based in Los Angeles, was hired in 1982 by CBS to do radio commentary, she was the only woman in prime-time radio doing any commentary. The attitude still prevailed that one woman was enough because "women's voices weren't considered authoritative enough." She remembers Mike Wallace saying to her: "'Oh, you're the woman with balls in her voice that I listen to every day.' Of course that was supposed to be a compliment because I didn't sound like a girl. It's so patronizing, the more you sound like a man, the more valued you are."

The need to be one of the guys and to play the game has long been a fact of life in the male-dominated world of television news. Helen Westwood has been with ABC news for over thirty years, where she pioneered in a number of areas. Helen was the first woman on the television desk and then the first woman bureau chief for ABC News. At the time of our interview, she was a coordinating producer for *PrimeTime Live*. She recalls working very hard to be one of the guys:

> I knew women twenty-five years ago who were very talented, but were not promoted because they were too female. They dressed a

little too female, they giggled, they talked about girly things when they were supposed to be frowning and serious. And this was viewed as being too feminine, too girly to fit in.

Westwood admits the same is true today. Those women who are sober faced, serious, and more thoughtful are the ones more likely to succeed: "Those who are viewed as a little bit more like one of the guys are still the ones that I see get the promotions, and the others are still more easily passed over."

Jennifer Siebens has been the Los Angeles bureau chief for CBS for over ten years. Formerly, she was the first woman to be assigned by CBS to be its Paris bureau chief. She articulately observes:

> Television news is a team sport. So if you've grown up in a large family, it helps because you've had to elbow your way and fight your way and punch your way and kick your way and scratch your way, if you're a girl, through these rough spots. I always picked my fights with men well. I would say, you have to mix it up because there's still a lot of testosterone in the environment and you have to know how to deal with it. At the same time, you have to know when to back off. There's still some of the playing the girl and letting the guys think that. There's still this very subtle sexual politics that goes on. . . . No woman who is a success is there today because they carried her. Every woman is there because she fought to get there, in some cases assisted by men, in some cases hamstrung by men. But no news division is floating women on camera or behind the camera just to make themselves feel good about doing nice things for women. They are not a charity. These are Fortune 500 corporations designed to make money and operate in that environment. So lest anyone think that any woman in the business is there by the grace of some male being nice to her, that's not the case.

Lynn Sherr, ABC correspondent for 20/20, has been a personal witness to the positive changes that have helped to create a more equitable work place for women:

> There is much more acceptance and understanding. I would like to think that fewer deals are made in the men's room, but I'm not sure that's accurate. The good news is that there are actually some deals made in the ladies' room because there are so many of us that we get to decide things in our scope and on our turf from time to time. There

certainly has been a growing sensitivity and awareness of a lot of men, not by all men by a long shot, not certainly by all managers who are the ones who should know. I, frankly, think it's generational. I think that it's the younger men coming up, just as I see with my own kids, who are infinitely more attuned than my generation was. The young men around here don't see a lot of difference between men and women in terms of their ability on the air and their ability to get a story done. That's the good news. I don't think that we've reached critical mass. But there certainly are a lot of us now and a lot more of us on the way.

Sherr knows that these advancements have led to programming improvements:

I don't think there is any question but the evening news and all across the board, it's better rounded, it's more interesting, it's not just a bunch of white men's ideas of what's going on in the world. It's women's ideas. It's black ideas, it's green ideas, it's yellow ideas, and it also affected language. I don't know when the last time I heard on our air anything like "an attractive grandmother," when you're talk-ing about someone running for office, when you would never say "an attractive grandfather." We have opened the doors to more coverage of stories. I don't think you would begin to have the kind of cover-age of women's health issues, of stories about child rearing without women in the newsroom. I think we've done a lot of that. I love to do stories about women's issues, which are now stories about social is-sues. These stories that show how all the rules have changed, how nothing is quite the same as it used to be. But having said that, I'm here as a reporter first. I'm not here with an agenda. I'm not here to change the world. I'm here to find out what's going on in the world and to report it. Through my eyes, they get something they don't get from anybody else's eyes, male or female, we're all individuals.

Foreign correspondents and war zones have been traditionally in the male bailiwick. But in this arena, too, women have been tested and accepted. Christiane Amanpour, CNN's award-winning foreign corre-spondent, has recently signed an unprecedented contract to remain at CNN and also to contribute five pieces a year to *60 Minutes* on CBS:

It's the most incredible marriage and it's unprecedented. And I think that perhaps it says something that a woman was the first to do that.

It means that I can keep doing what I love doing, which is reaching a big international audience on stories of international significance and trying to reach a big American audience on stories of international significance and interest. I do believe that a country as powerful and significant as the United States of America needs to have a few more windows opened on the world. I think that's basic to future security, prosperity—and first above everything else.

Amanpour spoke candidly about the dangers she faces at work:

I think I have an impact, because I'm a woman doing what is ostensibly a man's job, going to war and I really mean going to war. When we go out, we go to the front, we stay for lengthy times on a story. I think I've covered Bosnia, for instance, much longer than any soldier is deployed there. Whenever I go, it's always men who say to me, "Wow, you're so brave." It's always men, it's not women. We know these are the dangers. We know what we're taking on. It's one of those unspoken realities. It would be great if we came back with this wonderful footage, and these great exclusives, and it would be great if we came back alive and uninjured. But sometimes we don't. I've had colleagues struck down all around me in Bosnia. My own camerawoman, Margaret Moth, was shot in the face by a sniper in Bosnia on our very first tour there in the summer of 1992. She's still doing her job. She was seriously wounded, and when you look at somebody like that, you realize the enormous risks we take.

Bettina Gregory, ABC News correspondent, acknowledges that there are no assignments she has not been allowed to cover during her extensive career in broadcasting, no matter how potentially dangerous:

As I say, ABC has always given me an equal opportunity to risk life and limb for the network. I do not feel slighted in that regard as a woman, not at all. For example, I have been under fire in covering riots in Northern Ireland before the British army was using rubber bullets as they do now. My sound man was hit with a couple of bricks and broke two ribs. I have been stoned in Boston when we were covering the busing and the media were hated. I have been in very tense and uncomfortable civil strife and unrest in this country. We were in Japan on the way to China, the People's Republic, with Joe Califano, who was then the secretary of health, education, and welfare, in 1979, when I read that my colleague Bill Stewart had been shot by

Christiane Amanpour, CNN

the rebels in Nicaragua. And I was shocked because that was my assignment. I had been slated to go to Nicaragua until they said suddenly, no. We'd rather have you go to China with Joe Califano, which was wonderful. But I was so shocked. I felt that it should have been me. I felt guilty in a way. Today I'm looking at our news file and I see that Hillary Clinton is dedicating a monument to all those fallen journalists. She mentioned the number, 934, I believe, who had lost their lives in the interest of covering news. I don't know if I would have reacted the same way as he did. I don't know if I would have been as much of a threat as he was as a man. I don't know what would have happened. But it is an eerie feeling when you see that somebody else gets killed on an assignment you should have had. This is a speech Hillary Clinton made at the monument to journalists who died in the line of duty, dedicated in Arlington, Virginia. She said, and I quote, "In the life and work of these 934 journalists, action and words are inseparable. Whether written, spoken, filed, or broadcast, their words are in themselves acts of courage and conviction."

She put it very well.

Ann Medina, now with the Canadian Broadcasting Company, is aware of the different atmosphere that surrounds women who are qualified and willing to accept overseas assignments. She describes the changes that she personally experienced:

When I was first sent to the Middle East, and probably specifically Beirut, I'm sure there was a feeling, in fact, I know one of the people who made the decision, "Wouldn't it be sexy to have a broad in Beirut?" As the stories we sent back won awards, sometimes all over the world, they began to recognize that maybe there was a way that newswomen could tell stories, and it wasn't just because they were sexy and for the ratings. I was always very interested in the grounding of stories. Take Lebanon, for example. Some people would cover the big officials, the assistant secretary of state, coming over to try to negotiate peace in Lebanon. What did that mean? So I would go to villages and just focus entirely on two villages with a history of hating each other's guts and killing each other. So that people would understand when the secretary talks about negotiating peace, he has got to find a way those two villages are not going to be going to war against each other and kill each other off. People at CBC initially said, "Oh, Ann's going off to do one of her people stories." And it was partly viewed, "Well, she's a woman, so she's going to do these little people stories." But slowly it started evolving. This was in '82. Now it's a part of the mandate. . . . But there is still the bimbos. There is still bringing in the cute, lovely girl. There is still, if a person is gorgeous and extremely bright in her twenties and thirties, she has to struggle to say, "Look, I am bright." And when there's a power struggle, as increasingly there is with the downsizing going on in news all over the world, or at least in the western world, women who are truly frontline on-air stars, are the first to get the shaft.

There are countries in the world where it is clearly more difficult for women to work. In fundamentalist cultures women are traditionally kept out of sight of strangers. Men in leadership positions will refuse to deal with a woman journalist. Sheila MacVicar is a foreign correspondent for ABC News based in London. She found it was possible to have her gender work to her advantage:

You sometimes are accorded what I would call Honorary Male Status. Where the women of the household will be kept out of sight preparing the food or the coffee for guests and where, if I were a local woman or an Arab woman, I would be expected to go and join them. Instead, I'm invited to sit with the men. You can use it to a disarming effect in places where there can be obstacles put in the way of your ability to do work effectively and efficiently. It's easier to present a woman as a leader of a team, for example, when you need to argue for something in the Arab world. There is no culture of argument with women. It can be very unnerving for people to have to deal with you in an adversarial way. And if you oblige them to deal with you, it sometimes can be more effective and efficient and you can get things done faster.

Kathy McManus is ABC's bureau chief in Jerusalem. She agrees that being a woman in a place with major cultural differences can be an advantage, especially if you are the boss. She spoke of the time she was dispatched to Saudi Arabia when the U.S. housing base was bombed. She was in charge of the satellite pool dish since it was brought in by ABC. The Saudis were not happy about letting the dish in and to have it operational. McManus describes the time Saudi officials came to give orders to dismantle the dish:

"Okay, you have to take down the satellite dish. Who is in charge?" I said, "I am," and they just took two steps back. They didn't know what to do. So the first night we had no confrontation. Then every night they wanted to take the dish down and every night we wanted to keep the satellite dish up. They finally said, after three nights of this, "What do we have to do to get the satellite dish down?" I said, "Well, you have to order me to take it down and then I'm not going to take it down because it's my job to keep the dish up and then you have to decide what you're going to do about the fact that I'm not taking it down." They stared at me again and said, "But you're a woman, and that sounds so violent." So it stayed up.

Kathy laughs when she remembers being referred to as Farah Fawcett. She stands five feet five inches tall and has blond hair. But with the impact of American television in their minds, she matched the image.

Susan Zirinsky, executive producer of *48 Hours* at CBS, has never been afraid to go to dangerous places or to travel to war zones around the world. She admits to being obsessed, even possessed and driven by the demands of her news life at CBS: "I craved it. I found it exciting. I wasn't fearful. I embraced it. I loved being part of the boys." She enjoyed relaying what happened to her in Saudi Arabia where she flew with Secretary of State George Shultz on one of his Middle East diplomacy swings in early 1990. There was to be a photo opportunity with Shultz and the king in the palace. Zirinsky was one of only two women traveling on the bus to the palace. The press attaché from the embassy told her nervously, "I don't know how to say this to you, but they don't want you to go into the palace." She replied defiantly, "You think I'm going to fly to Saudi Arabia and stand outside the gate? I don't think so." So they all drove in together and stood in the room where they did a body search on the reporters before allowing them inside. Zirinsky was first in line. The palace security officers dressed in the native white robes and head dress came over and as Zirinsky graphically describes:

This guard proceeds to a full frontal feel. I mean total. And everybody just shrieks with laughter. Somebody from behind me says, "Oh Akmeed, I thought they were grenades." It was unbelievable. I was so shocked and it was so fast, I looked around and thought, "Oh my God. They are all just alike. They can't control themselves." You could tell this guy wants to cut his hands off because he didn't know what to do. Then when we walked past to get into the photo op, I was stopped. They wouldn't even let me in the room. So it became this huge, sort of funny, pathetic kind of moment. On the plane back toward Israel, Shultz walks back and says, "I'm sorry" and he can't look at me, he says "I heard you were . . ." I supplied the word. I said, "felt up," and he said, "Well, I'm really sorry, I really apologize." And I said, "Well, it's not your fault, but if I'm going to give a sexual favor, at least I expect to get into the event." He laughed.

So while it is fairly well accepted that women reporters are found everywhere doing almost every kind of work, the cultural climate continues to affect how women are treated and the freedom they have to do their job. The women wear bulletproof vests, get shot at, get to slug it out in the mud, attract the same bugs and diseases the men do and are sent to cover the most brutal and nasty news stories on the planet. But the terrain is often tougher for women and they are continually being tested. In Saudi Arabia, women reporters may get wounded and bloody, but they are not allowed to drive themselves to the drugstores.

Diane Sawyer, co-anchor of the new *20/20*, at ABC, is one of the most celebrated and admired women in television news today. She routinely travels the world on assignments, often going into Islamic countries, African tribal countries, and even to some Eastern European countries where her presence has proved significantly disconcerting to some, simply because she is a woman. When Sawyer went to the Soviet Union during the coup attempt against President Boris Yeltsin, she was stopped when she got to the scene of the action:

> I wanted to get up into the floor where he was to meet me. Everybody was streaming out of the building because the tanks were supposed to fire on the building. The guards kept stopping me and saying, "no women are allowed in this building, no women are allowed." Finally, through an interpreter, I said, "Tell him, I'm not a woman, I'm an American journalist," I said, "We're not women." He sort of looked puzzled for a minute and then let me through. So it worked.

The need for a woman to be more clever and creative is clearly documented and acknowledged by those working in the news business today. Sawyer admitted:

> I do think that you have about six things to consider, where sometimes men have only two. It means that a lot of the things you do are more complicated. You do have these narrower margins between seeming too tough, and not tough enough. I think you're held to a little higher standard on some of these fine gradations of tone of voice

Diane Sawyer, ABC News

and "Did she wear the right things for the interview?" and "Is her hair looking good this day?" and "Oh, she looks a little tired," and "Oh, that color of lipstick!" So you do have sometimes, I think, about six report cards coming in at once, where men don't.

Al Primo, former vice president of news for ABC and now head of Prime News Service, is emphatic in his acknowledgment that women have a much more difficult career climb:

It's tougher for women always, it's just tougher for women. I am a great sympathizer in the sense that it's the old adage of the dancer Fred Astaire. He's doing great and his partner is Ginger Rogers. She's doing the same thing only she's doing it backwards. You had to work twice as hard to overcome what can only be described as the historic role of women in history which has been subservient to males. But I think that as we go along, women have had to fight this. They've had to get into the war. They had to fight to get out of the secretary's chair, and to do that they had to be much, much better and much, much more qualified to do the same jobs that were just simply given to men. So my sympathies are with women because they've had to work and struggle to get ahead. They have and they are doing it. I think eventually we'll see a woman as president of the United States. I think that will be a very good thing because there is a certain quality of struggle and toughness that they've gone through so they may be a little more open and a little more understanding of others.

Broadcasting does not exist in a separate sphere. It reflects the wider American culture. It will be no better or worse than the progression of events in that wider societal arena. The ebb and flow of opportunity and mistreatment that is the harsh reality for women in television news is a reflection of the gains and losses that women have enjoyed and suffered throughout our history. The struggle is ongoing and omnipresent.

The image of women in television is extremely important. When you turn on the television set and see a woman doing a responsible job on the world scene, a significant statement is made. The picture leaves a lasting impression.

Marjory Margolies-Muzvinsky, a former reporter for WRC in Washington, D.C., was elected to the House of Representatives from Pennsylvania in 1992. As a member of Congress she describes how she purposely chose to wear a fuchsia dress when she attended the State of the Union address:

I'm not a fuchsia person, and I walked in and every woman had a color on and most of them wear mostly conservative suits. But every woman in that chamber had color. They had the same reason. We really wanted to show people in a kind of a visual way as they turned on the television, that it just wasn't a bunch of suits. That we were changing the look of the body and there was something we wanted to say. People said it to me the next day, "It was so nice to see colors in Congress," and I know that sounds silly—when we start to look like the rest of the nation, when it isn't just a bunch of white men representing us.

In the broadcasting industry and in society, the higher you aspire to go, the more difficult it gets and the more male resistance you will usually encounter.

Joanna Bistany, ABC News senior vice president, concurs with this assessment but speaks with high praise about her boss, the inimitable Roone Arledge, chairman of ABC News:

I think that in some places there is still a male bastion at the very highest levels. But Roone is really gender blind. I do have more access to him than almost any one does and I get away with murder. I mean, Phyllis McGrady and I were talking about this. He takes it from a woman for some reason. He likes women, but he takes it from you. He'll take a disagreement or whatever and listen. But I think it's still pretty much a boy's club in terms of the numbers and less of a girl's club. I think that will change as more and more women enter the ranks of management. It's numbers to some extent. And I think, also, that as you have a new generation of managers coming up, they've come up together. They've worked together. It's a different situation.

The even-handed manner that Roone Arledge deals with the men and women in his news stable is pointed to with pride by Bistany:

Roone believes in diversity. It's why he brought David Burke in from Democratic politics. He basically brought me in from Republican politics. He doesn't care. He likes diversity. He thinks that women add a dimension, and a different voice. Just as a black man has a different voice from a white man, there's just certain things they will see differently or they'll see certain things that the other person won't see. It's just a different life experience perspective. What I found with Roone is that he is an equal opportunity promoter and he is an equal opportunity "I'll take your head off if you screw this up." It makes no difference whether you're in a dress or a three-piece suit and wing tips. You screw up, he hands you your head and he'll do it in front of five other people. And if you do something well, he'll give you the credit and he'll make sure you get rewarded for it. Which is all you can ask for.

Few would have cause to disagree. Fairness and diversity are crucial to the effectiveness and efficiency of any news organization. There is little reason for strong, achieving women to be viewed as a threat to strong, achieving men.

The year 1998 marked the 150th anniversary of the women's rights movement in the United States. A convention by women demanding the right to vote was launched in New York in 1848. It took Congress seventy years to grant women the basic right to vote. That original convention also saw protests concerning men's control and tyranny over their wives. Many women would argue that this fundamental freedom from tyrannical husbands and bosses has yet to be realized. There is intense need to champion a work ethic that has women and men standing shoulder to shoulder with shared goals, commitment, and vision.

3
Looks
and
Longevity

> You gain strength, courage, and
> confidence by every experience which
> you must stop and look fear in the
> face. . . . You must do the thing you
> think you cannot do.
>
> ELEANOR ROOSEVELT (1884–1962)

The emphasis on beauty and youth in our society creates an insecure
and threatening environment for women in television news. The double
standard for appearance and age communicates itself daily in the media
and reinforces the secondary status of the women who are striving to
compete with men on an equal footing. Since beauty is subjective, the
male-dominant culture sets the standards of acceptance. In television, a
visual medium, the bar is set higher for women. The show-business aspect of the television medium creates a superficial set of values that often
conflict and take precedence over critical journalistic capabilities.

Andrea Mitchell, NBC News, candidly comments:

> These are old boys networks in many ways. The people making the
> decisions are all male. The people executing the decisions are male.
> They tend to drift toward people with whom they are comfortable

and when they choose women, they often choose women who represent their own fantasy lives, not necessarily the best journalists. Or they choose women they think will be attractive to their audience rather than what many of us in the business feel, which is that viewers want to rely on broadcasters of both sexes who know what they are talking about, whom they can trust.

Heather Allan is the Los Angeles bureau chief for NBC and the first woman to hold that post. Originally from South Africa, she is the first non-American the network ever brought to the United States as a senior management person. She is a major fan of Andrea Mitchell and compares her with Margaret Thatcher:

If you're in a man's world you've got to be bigger and better and stronger, and I think she is. I think she's just astounding and I just don't think they can put her down. And, I know a lot of women who work here that feel the same way about her. We root for her daily, every time we see her on air, because she is what it should be, substance over form.

Judy Muller, ABC News, freely admits not being hired because of her looks. She tells the story about Charles Gibson who interviewed Liz Trotta, a pioneering network news correspondent, who stated her belief that you could not get hired as a woman today unless you were a Barbie doll, unless you were pretty. Trotta told Muller that Charlie Gibson went on the air and said: "Well, I beg to differ with you. We have a number of women who clearly weren't hired for their looks." He mentioned Jackie Judd and Judy Muller. Muller told me that she called him up and said, "Thanks, but no thanks. Next time you want to compliment me, don't do it that way."

Judy Muller was just back from a medical leave when I interviewed her. She admitted to having had facial plastic surgery:

Men can still get bald and portly. Women cannot turn grey and wrinkled. I've been very up front about it with everybody I work with and people who know me that I had some plastic surgery done this year. I really wrestled with that a long time, because my kids said, "Oh, no, that would go against all the values you've taught us about aging and being happy with who you are." But I'm in this business of a visual medium. If I were still in radio, I don't think I would have had it done. But I got sick of people saying, "Gee, I don't think they're lighting you well." Well, they were lighting me well. I was just getting older. I'm going to be 50 soon and I had a half job done on my neck and stuff. And, I've got to tell you, when I go on camera now, I feel better about it. So, I don't know what that says. I mean, I finally just gave up and said, "Okay, I'm going to do this and feel good about it." I told the guy, "Leave lots of wrinkles so I don't look weird," and he did. Nobody really knows. If I hadn't told them, they wouldn't know. Now I'm wondering if I got my money's worth.

Basic standards of appearance and grooming apply to all women and men who broadcast news. They must never allow their looks to distract from what they are attempting to communicate. But women find the standard they are held to more difficult to accept and maintain.

Ann Compton had been covering the White House for ABC for over twenty-two years when we met. She speaks frankly about on-air appearance:

> There is a certain standard of good grooming that every correspondent on television has to adhere to whether you are bald and wear a bow tie and report on economics for a network or whether you're a very attractive blonde woman trying to impress your audience that you have credibility on an economic issue. All of us must rise to a certain level of simple good taste and good grooming. We cannot be disheveled. We cannot appear not to have bathed or washed our hair. We cannot wear clothes that are outrageously distracting or no one will listen to what we say.

Compton goes on to comment about the need for both men and women to bear the years with appropriateness and not try to either camouflage flaws or be deceitful about age. She remembers appearing on the *Phil Donahue Show* in 1983 when she was pregnant with her third child, and one of the issues was what will happen when you reach fifty? Will you still have a job? Lesley Stahl and Jessica Savitch were there with her. Compton remembers the "great hand-wringing" among her colleagues sitting there:

> I remember resting my hands on my stomach and I said, "You're all crazy. Of course we're going to be here when I'm 50. If we sit here and say that we'll be thrown off the air when we approach that age, we're just going to make a self-fulfilling prophesy." Well, I'm not 50 yet, but a couple of my female colleagues are and we're still on the air

and none of us have been tossed away because we have grey roots showing or because we have bags under our eyes, other than normal wear and tear from a long assignment. So I think that men and women both wear pretty well on the air.

Compton also comments on the realities of grueling travel and her rules for the road: "No matter how long the trip, never pack more than you can carry. No matter how long the trip, never pack more than you can carry at a dead run. And so that's what I do. That's how I cope with the physical demands of traveling and still having to be presentable on the air or off."

Barbara Walters is indisputably the most successful woman in television news. She is also the most senior. To this writer, she looks better today than when I first interviewed her in April 1973. She told me that she believed that physical appearance is important and that age is important:

I never thought that I would be working this long. But people's idea of age has changed. On the other hand, you have somebody like Mike Wallace who at the age of seventy-seven is still on the air and looks great. I very much doubt that I will be on the air at seventy-seven. I wouldn't want to be, and I think different things are expected of a man. A man can look craggy, a man can have bags under his eyes, and if he's fairly trim he can stay on, as we see with Mike, who just looks terrific. But a woman is different. It's reflective of this society. Certainly, it's much better than it is in Hollywood where after the age of forty you're playing character roles. But this is true in our whole society. It's not just television.

For many of the women working on air today, the question of how many wrinkles they will be allowed to acquire remains a big question mark. Cokie Roberts has found getting older to be an advantage because what she does requires people to have trust and confidence in her. Roberts states that she is part of an entire generation of women who came into television together: "The civil rights law was passed in 1964. It's the year I graduated from college. We came in with the law on our side and we've been working our way through the workplace for the last thirty years. We don't know how long we will be allowed to stay on the air as a whole generation."

Judy Woodruff, CNN anchor and a respected journalist who has been working in television news since 1968, believes that this group of women correspondents working today have a value that is too costly to discard:

> I don't see how the networks could train us, promote us, groom us, cultivate us, push us along all these years, and then suddenly put us out to pasture, because you have a valuable commodity. Someone who has a name identity, well, there's value in that name identity and you just can't shove somebody like that out the door. But that doesn't mean women don't get pushed out all the time. They do.

Connie Chung believes that women have the need to be "prettier than men in television," but that there has been some movement on the double-standard issue of ageism:

> I think that's the one area that women have made some very healthy progress—thanks to Barbara Walters, who will be on the air until she's 202 because she looks terrific and she is the hardest worker and the most successful person, I think, in television news. She is the most successful broadcast journalist in terms of her ability to deliver the story, deliver the news, deliver the interview. And because she has created her niche in the television news industry, I think all of us will be able to stay on the air longer. Those of us who are in the next generation—she's in sort of the first generation of television news women—we're in the next generation. All of us are in our fifties now and we are lasting very nicely, I think. I think Barbara's generation was pushed off the air sooner than they should have been.

When I first interviewed Lynn Sherr in January 1973, she was a reporter working at WCBS-TV in New York. She candidly admits being fired—or as it was then said in television land, "her contract was not renewed." She first learned about it from a column in the *New York Post*. No one spoke to her about it personally. Then, an outrageous item was printed stating that what was wrong with Sherr was that her shoulders were too broad for close-up shots. She declares, today, with unabashed pride, "I think I have very nice shoulders." So do her many admiring viewers who watch her regularly on ABC's *20/20*. Sherr believes that television presents cosmetic problems, whether you are male or female. While in her office, she showed me a framed letter dated October 23, 1980. It was written in response to an interview that she did for *TV Guide*. The letter read:

Dear Lynn,

    I read in the paper that you feel some good looking reporters are seductive and make love to the camera. You also say that we should have some over-weight women chosen to be TV reporters. There is nothing wrong with a cute lady becoming a TV anchorperson, as long as she is talented. For example, I saw you not too long ago and you are reasonably good looking and have some talent.

Sherr says she keeps this as a constant reminder of how important it is to be honest.

The men I spoke to were equally adamant about the need to be able to communicate the news without being a distraction. However, they were also in agreement that women face a more difficult set of circumstances and that society imposes a double standard that affects the world of broadcasting.

Dave Marash admits with refreshing candor:

I'm living proof that the standards are much wider than the standards for women. I am not a handsome guy, I have what's known as a radio face. I don't look like Brad Pitt or Peter Jennings, for that matter, and that hasn't seriously held me back. In fact, I suspect that really hasn't held me back at all. My wayward obnoxious personality has held me back more than my beard or my face. Although one would say that one is an expression of the other—the truth is if I forgot about the beard, if I were an overweight woman, I would find it harder, I think, to get on camera than I did as an overweight man.

Marash believes the advantage of youth and glamour are stronger today than twenty years ago. He sees the portrait of the on-camera woman being more and more narrowly and conventionally defined as well. Marash speaks of the stagnation and retrogression of progress for women in front of the camera. He restates his viewpoint: "The chick quotient seems higher than it was twenty years ago."

Richard Threlkeld, CBS news correspondent, readily acknowledges that women are held to a higher standard than are men working on air:

Well, I think it's much more difficult if you're a woman than for a man. And I think that's always been true. If you're a man, you look distinguished as you get older, and if you're a woman, the perception is you just look older. Although it's interesting that, without naming names, there are a number of fellow correspondents who happen to

Betsy Aaron, CNN

be men who I know have had about as many face jobs as women. That may be beginning to change as well. I think that the prejudice against women is greater, at least in on-air roles, as they get older, and all you have to do is look around to find the evidence of that. David Brinkley is still on television, and Mike Wallace is still on television, and a lot of the women that we knew, like Marlene Sanders and others, aren't.

Betsy Aaron, Richard Threlkeld's wife, explained the pain and discomfort that the advancing years created for her in the work environment and how she was forced to come to grips with it:

I worked at CBS in New York. While I was recuperating from my injuries in a car accident and I moved back to New York, Bill Small introduced me to my now husband, Dick Threlkeld, who was coming back from Rome to anchor the morning news with Lesley Stahl. So I guess you should never say all things are bad because that's probably the most important thing that happened to me. So we stayed in New York and he went from anchoring a morning news to doing a cover story on Sunday mornings and I worked out of the northeast bureau with him. Our offices were next to each other. And I did *48 Hours* and I did hard news. But it was becoming more and more clear to me as my contract was running out in the nineties that this was a network that was trying very hard to get younger people and to set up a star system of much younger reporters. I have to admit that while I don't want to be younger than I am, and I'm really a pretty positive person, it came as quite a shock to me to realize that some of the people I worked with, some of my bosses, were going to reject me because I was that older woman. And that decision was made regardless of work.

I've given it a lot of thought, because maybe when I was their age, I certainly was never rude to anybody, but maybe that was my attitude about people who were my age now. I just don't know. But there definitely is a feeling of discomfort on the part of younger people who are working with older people. And it's a terrible generalization to make because there are plenty of older people who I find very boring, who live in the past, who I would never want to be around. And there are plenty of younger people who are really very exciting and bring a whole new prospective, who are terrific, as well as younger people who don't know anything. That's how I really judge people. But to realize that you do fit into a class, into an age, where you're going to be judged just specifically on your age and not on anything else, is very, very difficult for me to deal with.

I think the way the networks are solving the age issue now is instead of continuing to hire older people, they're just firing older men and women. So the women still may be at the short end of the stick. They certainly are because of looks and the perception that they all have to look twelve. But I think the solution is "Oh, then we'll also fire the men who are loosing their hair and look older." Which is very disturbing and obviously not the solution you want. I think there ought to be a mix. I've never subscribed to the theory that because you're older, it makes you automatically better. I do subscribe to the theory that experience is something to be factored into your qualities as a reporter and it's a big part of it. These judgments are very harsh and these companies get larger and larger, the firings get more impersonal and more impersonal, and people feel less loyalty. So I grew up in an age where naively you believed that you worked for the company, and the company cared about you, and the people who ran the company cared about you. Now you realize that your loyalty certainly has to be to yourself. You do the same good job you would do no matter where your loyalty is, but you take nothing for granted and you certainly don't plan ahead.

So in 1994 I left CBS. My contract was not renewed. I was never able to see the president of CBS News to find out why because he was too busy to see me. Eric Ober was the president. I think they have a perfect right to fire anybody they want to. I was not angry that I was fired. I was terribly hurt that after you put in so many years for a company and you cover stories—I had been in the Persian Gulf for CBS and during the run of that contract, I had gone twice to Baghdad. I had been in harm's way. Again, nobody owes you anything because you do those things. I think it's an honor to cover those stories and I'm very glad that I had the opportunity. But I'm a little old-fashioned and I don't understand when it is time to go, why you suddenly become a pariah and where nobody owes you any explanation. And I think that's all they owe you, a little bit of truth. So if there's any lingering resentment—unlike other people I know who have not been renewed and they're very angry and they can't understand it, I understand it. Time moves on and then you look for other things to do that are more interesting. But there is a meanness factor that's very difficult to get over, and I think that's where the pain lingers.

So I left, there and then. For the past two years I've been freelancing and I've worked for NBC in Rwanda and London and Haiti. I've worked for the USIA in Macedonia and in Jordan. It's been very, very interesting, but I really wanted to be busier and I wanted to cover news. My husband was offered a job in Moscow as the CBS correspondent in Moscow, and I said, "Well, I'm not going unless I can work because I'm not going overseas without a full-time job." Very fortunately, CNN offered me a job in their Moscow bureau, and they've been wonderful. That's an example of a company where most people are very young, but they have been very gracious about wanting someone with some experience and giving me an opportunity to go and report for a network that has a lot of airtime. So I'm very excited about it.

I'm still worried about a lot of my friends at the networks who are afraid. I think the worst thing for a journalist is to be afraid. They are afraid of being let go, afraid of being noticed, and maybe noticed in the wrong way. But nobody knows what the wrong way or the right way is, because you're hot one day and you're cold the next. I think journalists do not operate very well when they're covering their backs, and it really pays to cover your back. Although there is no script, so if you spend your time covering your back, you still may be out. But that, to me, is where the business has changed, and that's very, very sad.

There was genuine progress being made in the early seventies to root out—in public discourse, in the marketplace, and in advertising—the shallow and demeaning attitudes of what was desirable and demanded in a woman. Since then, there has been a backsliding with a vengeance that places more of a focus on women's beauty and glamour rather than on her ability and intelligence. As our economy, society, and social mores permitted greater equality for women, the male-dominated power structure began to feel threatened and the ensuing backlash made women once more vulnerable to superficial values.

The admonition that aging makes a woman less worthy, communicates itself daily in the mass media. NBC's Tom Brokaw, one of the three males currently sitting at the pinnacle of the journalism profession as sole evening news anchor for a network, frankly agrees there is a different standard applied to a woman's looks in society. The fact that he is the father of three daughters causes him to be even more acutely aware of this situation than others. He says, "I think there is more of an ageism bias toward women. But I think that's true in society as well. I think it's true in film, it's true in music, it's true in life. Men are allowed to grow old. A woman was saying to me over the weekend that women find grandfathers sexy. I don't think that a man would say to a woman who is about to become a grandmother that young men find grandmothers sexy. I think that's a reality."

As a senior correspondent at ABC, Sam Donaldson has watched the changing development and progress of women in television news. He believes the gap between men and women is closing: "The man who could get away with just being dumpy and sort of disheveled because that was the correspondent's image, can't do that today. Although I still believe today that a woman is held to a different aging standard. I think women are still under greater scrutiny because I am told that we still glorify youth in this country."

Robin Sproul is the first woman to be appointed Washington bureau chief for ABC. Sproul says viewers do form opinions about what is being said based on how the person looks and how it is being presented and appearance is crucial on television. She remarks, "Sometimes people who start looking one way, if they're heading for an unattractive weight gain, we do talk about it. We talk about hair, we talk about makeup, we talk about shadows under the eyes, we talk about what colors look good on people. There is clearly a show-business aspect to what we do."

Betty Rollin, NBC News correspondent, was emphatic about the "pretty quotient" that affects decision making in the executive suite. She declares, "You'll see women who are not at all pretty and who are successful and are doing great. It's because they're so strong and so great that even though they're not pretty, they're still going to be out there. But I think it's an in-spite-of situation."

Consultants are routinely brought in to work with on-air correspondents about their image. Hair is the most frequently discussed and notoriously changed aspect of a woman's appearance. Any retrospective of a news woman's career bears testimony to the number of hairstyles that have been worn and shorn through the years. Viewers are more likely to comment on hairstyle than on story content, a sad but true reality about the television business and about American society. As a result, more time is spent worrying about physical appearance by women than ever before. Women who work in this medium, those who desire to have a long and successful career, must consciously deal with the quest for physical acceptability and attractiveness every single day of their lives. It extracts a heavy toll.

Nina Totenberg, National Public Radio legal correspondent, speaks of the lesson she learned about appearance and what is viewed as appropriate attire for on-air acceptance:

> If you were the hunchback of Notre Dame you'd have a hard time anchoring the evening news, but Charles Kuralt was no pretty boy and he was pretty successful in some ways. Even Walter Cronkite was no pretty boy, he got prettier as he got older. And you don't want to be so alluring. This is a great story about television. I did this half-hour piece for *Nightline* about a woman who had successfully sued

the CIA for sex discrimination. It was quite an arduous investigative piece in which we got a number of top spooks to talk to us. I wore my most beautiful and expensive blue, cloudlike blouse, with this sort of scarf that was the same material at the neck. It's just a gorgeous blouse and it was an obscene amount of money that I paid for it. When I came out of the studio I got a lot of ribbing about how beautiful the blouse was. The piece got put together, and Ted [Koppel] saw it. He took me to his office and really in the gentlest way, more gentlemanly than he had to be with me, he said, "You're going to hate me for what I'm going to say." And I thought, "Oh shit, he hates this piece that I've worked on for months and months." He said, "The blouse has to go. It's so beautiful that we're thinking about the blouse and not what you're saying." And I said, "Fine, I'll wear something else." And he was right. He was absolutely right. I looked at it and he was right.

Some women refused to conform or place the necessary emphasis on their image. Their career paths were blocked as a consequence. Gloria Rojas, former WNBC-TV news reporter, reflects on the decisions she made during her on-air reporting years:

I'm a very bad one to talk about image. I never cared. I cared that my hair was done when I was going out with a man I was in love with. I never cared about my image on the screen and I'm sorry about it now because I look at old tapes and I could have been a lot more glamorous. But I didn't have ambition in that respect, you know, to be a star. I had this kind of almost reverse thing. I probably did care, but it was my pose, my defense, to say I don't care. That's how I lived and it's sad that I did that. It's part of the job. When you are visible people are looking. I used to get letters that would say things like, "As a Puerto Rican woman, you should be more aware of how you represent all of us." I mean, I had nice clothing and stuff, but I really did not get my hair done. I just didn't put a heck of a lot of importance into that.

Melba Tolliver, former correspondent and anchor for WNBC-TV and News 12, in Long Island, New York, has been the recipient of much viewer outcry when she chose to let her hair grow back into its natural Afro. She has fought long and hard to be accepted as an individual without the prejudice associated with being a minority. She explains: "I think racism is an over-used word. I think I'm held to a standard by ignorant people who don't know anything about hair, who are afraid of anything that's different than what they're used to. I think we're just held to a different standard because of ignorance and fear." She relates an experience that concerned the late New York City anchorwoman Pat Harper:

> Pat Harper had cut her hair, and they sent the letter to her and a carbon copy to me. "Dear Pat, The only person who has a worse hairdo than you is Melba Tolliver on News 12, Long Island." The people don't want women to come in two days in a row with the same dress or even the same color. I mean, if I were to just wear black everyday or wear something like men do, you know, blue suit, red tie, every day—a woman couldn't get away with it. The audience wouldn't stand for it."

Gloria Rojas remembers when a woman reporter was only allowed to wear a skirt on assignments. She remembers being told that it was okay to crawl around a subway tunnel in a skirt. She recounts how that finally changed:

> It took Pia Lindstrom to break that stupid rule about our wearing skirts. She came in with pants and that was that. The barrier was broken. But we had always worked in skirts. Can you imagine climbing up to some of the places that we climbed up to wearing skirts? Well, all of a sudden it was Pia who did it at WCBS. She came in with pants. She was Ingrid Bergman's daughter and she was beautiful and she looked great in pants and the rest of us had that barrier broken. It sounds so silly. It sounds like such a nothing, but it took courage. The right to dress comfortably and be yourself was a wonderful, wonderful thing. And it happened in the early seventies and it was just great.

Gwen Ifill is NBC's Capitol Hill correspondent. She crossed over from print to television and accepts the fact that the physical is now much more important: "Part of the deal you sign with the devil to do TV is that the physical aspects of who you are often override your professional abilities and you just have to find a way to balance that out."

Female foreign correspondents face a unique set of circumstances in their assignments. For them, it is more desirable to have rubber-soled shoes and a pocket knife than a lipstick. Christiane Amanpour admitted that she has never had anyone attempt to change her appearance. She simply would never allow it:

If you start changing your appearance, you start changing yourself. If you start changing what you look like to match what you think somebody thinks you should look like, it's a slippery slope. The whole credibility issue starts. You can't mess around. This is the way I am. Clearly, I brush my hair. I put on some lipstick sometimes and I try to look decent. But I'm not going to go to the hair-dressing salon or to the makeup salon every time I go on the air. First of all, I can't. It doesn't match my professional environment. It would look ridiculous if I turned up on a war front with some blown-dry hair and acres of makeup. It would just look ridiculous.

The women in these difficult and dangerous arenas are constantly being tested and need to prove themselves on a daily basis. Some of the women who do this work are better at it than some of the men simply because they have to be so much tougher to prove themselves worthy.

Maria Shriver works as a correspondent for NBC News. She believes that she always had to work twice as hard as anyone else in order to dispel any residual feeling that she received advantages because of who she was and the family she came from:

> When I went back to anchor the *Today* show this year, one of the crew guys came up to me at the end and said, "You know, I just wanted to say that I had always seen you. I've known you worked on television and I always felt that maybe you got the job because of who you were or because you were a pretty girl. But now having worked with you this week, I realize that I was totally wrong." So I said to myself, after that, thank you very much. Nineteen years later and there's still the feeling that maybe I got to do the *Today* show because I was a Kennedy or because I was a pretty girl."

Bob Zelnick is a correspondent for ABC News in the Washington Bureau. He is concerned that the search for good looks has taken its toll on the quality of the journalist being selected for today's jobs.

> The danger that I see is too many pretty people on TV these days. Too many people are popping up as anchors who have never covered a story in their lives and in a couple of cases have covered stories so badly that they were quickly taken out of the editorial mix. But as far as I'm concerned, I'm not worried about women or men being kept off TV because they're ugly. I'm worried about too many getting on because they're pretty.

But Zelnick is pleased to reflect that he gave one of the early women pioneers an opportunity to continue to use her talents when age forced her retirement from television:

> In those days I remember Pauline Frederick as being one of the giants reporting mostly out of the UN for NBC News. And I looked upon Pauline the same way I would have looked upon Edward R. Murrow or Eric Severeid, some of the early giants of radio and television because that's clearly what she was. She told me that she had been required to retire at NBC because of age. But she enjoyed the work and still felt she could do it. Could we talk? And I said fine. I visited with her on a trip to New York. I just felt having someone with Pauline's stature and experience associated with National Public Radio would be very beneficial to the organization. Well, Pauline was by that time probably in her early seventies, maybe mid-seventies, but the thing I remember about Pauline was her incredible professionalism. There were days when she used to call me every single day from the United Nations. She would call me when there was a story. She would call me when there wasn't a story. If there wasn't a story, she'd tell me what was going on behind the scenes. If there was a day when she thought she wouldn't be on the air, she would try to fill me in so I'd be current about what was happening there anyway. Pauline Frederick's reporting out of the UN for us was everything that I remembered it being when she was with NBC radio. We were pleased that she was selected in 1976 to be on the panel that questioned presidents during the candidates' debates. I think it turned out to be one of the useful steps in the maturation of public radio. I think we were good in those days, but we didn't have the national recognition that NPR has in this day and age. I think Pauline was one of the early contributing factors.

It is not unusual to see a younger woman anchor with a man who is much older. At almost every local station in the country the image is that of a powerful male paired with a pretty young face, a female. To some in the profession we seem to have developed an "anchor doll." This tendency must be continually challenged and countered by serious, smart reporters who refuse to allow people to define them in terms of how they look. It is important to have women respected for their ability, for their journalistic capabilities, and for their integrity.

Rita Braver was chief White House correspondent for CBS News. After viewing the film *Up Close and Personal* starring Michelle Pfeiffer,

Rita Braver, CBS News

who plays an ingenue television reporter, and Robert Redford as a former White House correspondent, Braver became incensed and wrote an
op-ed piece for the *Washington Post*.[1] In the film, Pfeiffer (Tally Atwater)
is hired (even though she has sent a fake résumé tape) because she is so
telegenic she "eats the lens." Braver was on a panel of journalists who
was asked to talk about what it was like to be a TV reporter who also
happened to be a woman:

---

[1] Rita Braver, "Up Close and Misleading," *The Washington Post*, March 14, 1996,
p. A27.

I listened to their stories of taking crummy assignments, working nights and weekends and constantly having to prove themselves. I told a few tales of my own. But mainly I was struck by the fact that what drew all of us to become reporters was that we wanted to understand the world and help explain it. I know that films are make-believe. But too many women TV reporters have paid too many dues to let Tally Atwater stand as their symbol. She succeeds without ever working the phones, developing a source, covering a beat or even a single story for more than a few hours. It's true Redford and Pfeiffer were nice to watch, especially in those steamy love scenes. But their fun is over. I'm going to be sending all the starry-eyed job seekers to them.

At least eight other prominent women journalists voiced their discomfort and dismay to me about a film that perpetuates the myth that women are rewarded for their beauty without regard for their intellectual ability and journalistic skills. The progress of women in society depends on their acceptance and value as competent professionals who are able to compete on an equal footing with the men with whom they work. The truth remains that while there are many attractive people on television, their enduring success is the result of talent and hard work.

4
Aptitude
and
Attitude

Supposing you have tried and failed
again and again. You may have a fresh
start any moment you choose, for this
thing we call "failure" is not the falling
down, but the staying down.

MARY PICKFORD (1893–1979)

There is genuine consensus concerning the skills and qualities necessary
for success in the competitive world of television news. Those attributes
most highly valued were good writing, curiosity, well-honed reporting
ability, intelligence and tremendous energy. The need to have a deep
sense and knowledge of history is regarded by many as the basic foundation required for a successful journalist's career.

David Brinkley, retired senior ABC news correspondent, stresses
these basic qualities: "Intelligence and a lifelong interest in news and
public affairs. If you're not interested in it, you can't do it well. A knowledge of history: you can't be a journalist if you don't know some history.
You can't succeed as a journalist if you don't know some history. You
don't have the means of judging the quality or value of a piece of news
unless you know some history." So many of the qualities people stressed

have no base in gender but are viewed as mandatory for any person seeking to achieve success as a journalist.

Susan Zirinsky describes the need to have a passion for knowledge. She says there should be the "desperate desire to know more about ourselves and to understand why things happen. To have an innate curiosity about the world and the love of knowing something first. You have to have unlimited energy and a real drive." Zirinsky describes doing job interviews and knowing within 15 seconds if that person is going to make it. "I think there's a genetic quality that we share, those of us who are sort of possessed share a genetic marker. And I believe it's not male and it's not female. It's asexual and it creates a drive and a push. That is what we all look for." She calls her own thirst for knowledge and curiosity "insatiable." Her remarkable career gives testimony to that.

Kathy O'Hearn, executive producer, *Weekend News* for ABC, talks about the need to "have a fire in your belly and a curiosity for knowing facts about any given story. You have to be someone who loves to devour newspapers, who is fascinated by the world around you, who loves being able to peek into other people's lives."

Judy Woodruff, CNN anchor, emphasizes the necessity for a strong work ethic:

> You've got to be able to work very long hours and put in time that other people would think was just brutal and ridiculous. If you want a 9 to 5 job, forget it. This is a job that will require you to come in weekends and nights. So it's an incredible work ethic and a willingness to work very hard. A very tough determination not just to hang in there with the story, but to get the story and get it first and have the best sources to tell the story better than anyone else. To write it better. To present it better on television, to make sure that it is edited better, and to follow through with all the people you need to deal with in television, the editors, the camera people, the producers, the studio, the make-up people, the hair people. If you work in a big television news organization, you've got to have people skills.

Diane Sawyer admits that the one quality that she did not give sufficient weight to when analyzing the demands of the profession was stamina. She describes on the need for sheer physical stamina: "The ability to take the red-eye back, get up at the crack of dawn, make 16 phone calls and then go on the air. And I should say, go on the air with extra make-up under the eyes. But, still make it. A lot of it is getting there early and staying late."

Christiane Amanpour also emphasized the importance of stamina in achieving a successful broadcasting career. She refuses to define success as inclusive of fame but prefers to embrace the concept of journalistic achievement:

I think the skills that are necessary to achieve a high level of journalistic skills are a commitment, first of all, to know exactly what you want to do, why you want to do it. The willingness to take the risks and do the hard work that simply has to be done. A willingness to understand that there are no shortcuts. I think, also, you have to have a real sense of passion about what you're doing, because I think this is a particularly difficult profession to be in. And I speak only about my profession, which is foreign correspondent. That's what I am. I cover wars and other such things. I think you have to have an enormous amount of physical stamina, mental stamina and simply a willingness, sometimes, to take risks, whether they are physical risks or editorial or moral risks. There are times when you have to put yourself on the line, physically and metaphorically. I think all of those combine to produce a kind of bag or basket, if you like, of necessary attributes.

Sam Donaldson emphasizes the need to work hard in order to "beat the competitor both within and outside of your organization." He advocates the willingness to be inquisitive and aggressive:

Aggressive doesn't necessarily mean shouting and yelling and being full of bombast. But, you can't sit back at the back of the row of the press room waiting to be called on and succeed, in my judgment, in this business. In television, of course, there are, today, certain traits that are in demand. I think some of the friends whose names I will not mention, both women and men, particularly men (because in the early days it was mostly us) who were at least the mid-level, good, great correspondents of the 50's and 60's who couldn't get a job today at the entry level because of their voice, or frankly, because of their appearance. Not that I thought they looked bad, but today the emphasis is on those things. And with all due respect to my close personal friend, Charles Kuralt,[1] just very few Charlies can make it in this particular field. I don't think you have to be Hollywood

---

[1] Charles Kuralt retired from CBS News in 1994 after thirty-six years with the network. He died of lupus on July 4, 1997. He was sixty-two years old.

handsome or beautiful or anything like that. But, whether you're Bill Clinton or someone running for the presidency, or in our business, presentation is very important.

Barbara Walters is outspoken about the critical skills required for lasting success in broadcasting. She has repeatedly stated that it is important to "get in there before anybody else does and work hard all day, learn your craft." She candidly commented:

> I think you have to be able to write. I think if you're going to do a program in which you are on the local or the network news, where what you are doing primarily night after night, is reading from a teleprompter, you don't have to be able to write or know how to produce and edit. But the three male anchors of the network news now can do all of those things superbly. And so when they are in a time of crisis, or at their desk, each of them, Peter Jennings, Tom Brokaw, and Dan Rather, can write and edit their own pieces. They know what they have in mind and what they want to say. If you're doing a program where you don't have to do this, well, then, sometimes all you have to do is look good and have the right voice.

But that's truly not enough. Walters emphasized the need to be able to write and edit your own material. She said:

> We've had people who have come here from anchoring a program where writing skills weren't necessary and have not been able to prepare their own material. Then, it's very hard for them when they have to do magazine pieces. So these are skills you must get. If you are interested in a career in television news, you could gain experience on the local television in your area. I think you must have that basic training. These days you must also have to be able to use a computer. But that is true in almost every field. But you need to pay your dues. You need the years of experience. There are too many women who say, "Oh, I want to do what you do. I want to be in front of the camera." And then you see films like the one with Michelle Pfeiffer in which she was just terribly pretty and had a mentor who said do this and do that. He pushed her and pushed her and eventually she became this beautiful news person. It just doesn't happen that way.

Betty Rollin acknowledged, with a different view, the need for network correspondents to write well and to work effectively with the producer. But she speaks of the practice of propping up a person who does not write that effectively with a producer who will do the main writing. She calls this "the Jessica Savitch[2] syndrome." She explained: "I think of Jessica Savitch as the beginning of this realization on the part of news executives, 'Oh, they don't have to know that much or be that smart, or write that well, as long as they look as if they're smart and know that much and look as if they write that well. And we can prop them up. We can have the producer write.' And that was a big change I would say for women. Now a lot of women *can* write. But, I think since then, it's not as crucial as it used to be."

While Andrea Mitchell agrees that it is mandatory to be a journalist first and a good writer in order to attain success in this field, she notes that, unfortunately, those attributes are not always the ones that are most valued: "This is a visual industry so cosmetic values are often very important. I think people do get hired, men and women, who are not always the best journalists."

Walter Cronkite places journalistic capabilities as the highest priority for success in television news:

> I dislike the readers on television who pose as newspeople. I do not object at all and think that we should make greater use of news readers. But, they should be labeled as such. If they are posing as journalists, then they should have journalistic qualifications. That is, they should understand the necessity for honesty, accuracy, fairness in the presentation of the news. Integrity should be the first order of business. In television there is, unfortunately, and I say that advisedly, unfortunately, the necessity of a comely appearance. This does not mean that people have to be movie perfect in their appearance. But, they can not be so sloppy as to distract attention from what they're trying to broadcast.

Patience and perseverance are qualities often mentioned and urged more diligently by women who are today working effectively in broadcasting. There is still the need expressed for women to work harder and longer to be accepted. Kathy McManus admits the necessity for women to possess "a little more survival skills." She states: "Although I am fortunate because I am the next generation, and the way was paved for me, I think that maybe we are required, as women, to have a little more

---

[2] Jessica Savitch was an NBC anchorwoman who joined the network in 1977. *Newsweek* dubbed her "NBC's Golden Girl" after she anchored the 1980 presidential conventions. When she was thirty-six, her life ended tragically in a car accident.

patience because I don't think the equality thing has quite been equalized yet."

Connie Chung also observes that "women probably have to work harder. They have to be a touch more tenacious and they just have to prove more."

While Dave Marash believes that the skill and qualities needed for success in broadcasting are basically the same for women and men, he is quick to also acknowledge that there are extra burdens women still face in their career climb. He said:

> I think that women are still required to have more patience because there's just more petty crap and misjudgments that they're going to put up with than men are going to be called upon to put up with. The basic qualities of journalism are, you know, marvelously few. Curiosity is the quintessential quality. You've got to instinctively want to know. Dr. Johnson, my great hero, said, "There's nothing so minute or inconsiderable that I would not rather know it than not." Well, that boy was the first and greatest journalist of us all and that's the quality. The second quality is closely related to it. It's what Walter Cronkite called the "Iron Butt," and that is endurance. A lot of feats in journalism are the product of nothing more than outlasting everyone else. Just hanging out until something happens in front of your face and you knew the itchier types have packed up and gone. They're writing their stories but you're willing to plant your ass there and keep watching. Curiosity and endurance. Just about everything else is secondary to that. That's as true for women as it is for men. Although, as I say, I suspect women's endurance qualities are called upon more frequently.

Many broadcasters continue to acknowledge that you still must just work harder if you are a woman just to prove that you are as good and as qualified. There is also the continuing need to aggressively challenge assumptions about what you are able and willing to do.

Linda Ellerbee remains an outspoken critic of the standards and skills that have become an integral part of the world of television news. She feels that rather than being rewarded for being good at what they're doing, many television anchors and reporters around the country are rewarded for looking the part: "You don't have to be a blond anymore, but you do have to have a certain look, and a certain way of speaking. It's like we developed an anchor doll in this country. You have to look that part. Beyond that, you have to be obedient to your employers and aggressive, or seemingly aggressive toward the outside world. You don't necessarily have to write, but you have to read a teleprompter as though you did write it."

Since 1975 Virginia Sherwood has been serving as a coach to help on air television reporters and anchors throughout the country.[3] One of only two women at ABC News in 1973 when my original interview with her took place, Virginia was responsible for some ground-breaking work at the network. She learned on the front lines the skills necessary for advancement. When I mentioned her name to veteran correspondent Bob Clark, he said of Sherwood, "This is a treasure. This is a pioneer who made it possible for so many to follow in her footsteps." Virginia Sherwood says her number one priority is to care. There is the need to care enough to tell a story in the best way possible. She believes the emphasis must be on the story:

> It bothers me today when I see anchors or reporters who seem to be playing a "role," and I put that in quotation marks, rather than concentrating on the story, and reaching out and sharing that story with us. Your job is to inform, to explain, to talk to us, to educate us, if necessary. The best thing you can do is forget yourself because you think so much of that story and then the real self will come through. What you do is explain. You talk to us. The camera is not a camera, it's people. It's your conduit to people. Forget about the phony head movements and the vocal acrobatics or the vocal games which say, "Look at me. Listen to me." Rather than, "Listen to this story. It's something you need to know, you ought to know, you want to know."

Katie Couric, co-anchor of the *Today* Show on NBC, believes in addition to the hard work, the need to be a quick study is crucial for effective on-air performance. The need to be able to absorb and disseminate information immediately is important. But the key to Katie's success in her own estimation is that, "I am comfortable in my own skin. You know, I am what I am and I don't try to be something I'm not. And I

---

[3] Virginia Sherwood's long client list includes Elizabeth Vargas, Wendy Takuda, Colleen Williams, and Lisa McRee, who left her anchor position at KABC-TV to replace Joan Lunden as host of ABC's *Good Morning, America* on September 8, 1997.

think viewers appreciate that. You know, if I'm not a sports fan, I don't pretend that I know what happened in the last play of the game. Or if I do, I do it in a kidding way to be a goof because it is so clear that I'm completely inept when it comes to sports. But, I think, that's why I've been embraced by people. They know that I'm not perfect and I think they feel they know me as I really am."

The ability to tell a story with a beautiful writing style is a highly desirable quality and one that is not easily found. Judy Muller has been credited with this talent. Muller states that at the network level, it is important to write successfully, colorfully, fast, and have an ability to synthesize complicated news, in order to get at its essence:

> I can go out and do research for 3 days on a complicated issue and I have to boil it down to less than 2 minutes. Even though that is in many ways simplistic, it is also very difficult to do well. And I don't think many people do it well. I know not many people do it well in a short amount of time. If you're given very little time to do something, you've got to think fast, understand fast. So the skills are having the background and being well read, being up on things so that you have all of that knowledge sitting there ready to be used.

Muller finds working in television frustrating because it is done by committee. She admits candidly that as a result of her controlling personality she does not do well with this aspect of the business:

> If you're going into television news, you really have to have an attitude that a lot of people are going to screw around with your work. And you'd better save your fights for the big ones because you can't fight every day like that or you will get worn out, worn down, and fed up. And I've come close because, quite frankly, I think I know more about a story that I've covered than somebody sitting in New York who has no idea. That's the chronic complaint of network correspondents that back in New York, they sit there and they have nothing else to do but look at your script every day and try to figure out how to justify their jobs and so, therefore, they must change it. And it makes you crazy if you're a person who's a very tight writer, who segues from one thing to the next and is proud of that. It's real hard. So one of the things, if you're going into television news, is you really have to have an attitude that not every piece is life and death. Save your fights for the big moments."

Judy Muller, ABC News

The atmosphere in a television newsroom calls on women and men to hone their survival skills. The ability to have a thick skin is a prime requirement necessary in order to endure the criticism that is a normal part of the work scene. Carol Jenkins survived more than 23 years at WNBC-TV in New York until she left for Fox news. She advocates that you cannot be sensitive and you cannot take the criticism personally:

> I think that it is a profession that's extremely competitive. You have to work very, very hard and you cannot let the criticism affect you.

You have to learn from your mistakes and just hang in there. I know a lot of people who have quit or given up or retired or left a position because they felt uncomfortable. I've known lots of brilliant people who had all the smarts. They were nine times better than anybody who had the reporting job. But, they couldn't take the criticism, the competitiveness or the back stabbing, all the things that go on in a newsroom. So I think you've got to be amazingly thick skinned in order to succeed in this business. In addition to being smart, inquisitive and all of that stuff.

There is genuine consensus that the most outstanding and admired people in television news have an innate sense of curiosity and seem to be truly curious about everything that occurs in the world. They have a passion for the story and seem to live and breathe the news. Although television can be a very tough world to inhabit, the truly accomplished journalist and communicator is capable of passing along that curiosity and enthusiasm through their writing and through their presentation. It is the ability to work extremely hard and to live a lifestyle that is not predictable or stable. As Amy Entelis describes it, "You never quite know where you're going to be from one day to the next. And there is a certain kind of person that does well in that way and there are other people who would rather sleep in their own bed at night."

There is also the ability to communicate and convey credibility to the viewers. The capacity to tell a story in a way that allows the viewer to experience the importance and compelling interest of the event. The sense of discovery becomes crucial to an effective presentation. Viewers need to hear things that surprise them, that inform them. It is crucial to bring meaning and perspective to the news so that the viewing public understands the context of the story.

A checklist of assets must include: a skeptical approach to the world, not to merely accept everything as a given; the determination and courage to go against the current of conventional media thinking. The ideal is an amalgam of these things combined with a commitment and determination to ferret out the truth. For good or ill, television remains a critical tool in the democratic process and the dominant force in American society.

5
Sex
and
Sensibility

> The world has never yet seen a truly
> great and virtuous nation, because in
> the degradation of woman the very
> fountains of life are poisoned at their
> source. LUCRETIA MOTT (1793–1880)

The issue of sexual harassment is a factor for women in the workplace
everywhere. Television news is a field where this issue has created horrific problems for some, and mere discomfort for others. The problems
were more acute in the early years of a career climb when women in
broadcasting were few in number and when there was little protection,
support, or recourse from blatant acts of sexual harassment.

Linda Ellerbee recalled her own experiences:

We were sort of trained from birth, women my age, to ignore it because if you weren't going to ignore it, you were going to spend all
your time in court. In fact, nobody ever talked about spending time
in court. Just being sexually harassed wasn't a crime. We had bigger
problems. We had problems getting in the door. My Lord, the last
thing on our mind was the fact that once you got there they were

going to treat you like a piece of meat. Of course they were going to treat you like a piece of meat. That was a given.

When Ellerbee was a general assignment reporter for WCBS-TV, she was sent out to cover the settlement of the *New York Times* Newspaper Guild strike. It was a windy, cold November day in 1975 and her long brown hair was being blown as she stood in the street before the camera doing her story on the settlement for the nightly news. Then WCBS city editor Marvin Friedman called Ellerbee into his office not long after the broadcast; in front of several others gathered there, including assistant news director Eric Ober, he said, referring to Ellerbee's windblown hair, "You looked like a two-bit hooker standing in that doorway." Ellerbee told him that he could not tell the difference between indoor film and outdoor film and that, in fact, she was standing outdoors in the wind. Friedman retorted, "Then you looked like a three-bit hooker." Enraged, Ellerbee went to Dave Marash, then co-anchor of the eleven o'clock news and shop steward for the American Federation of Television and Radio Artists at the station. Marash advised her to get an apology. She did. She soon left the station for NBC, which turned out to be a very positive career move for her. "Sweet are the uses of adversity" is an adage that comes to mind here.

Maureen Bunyan, former anchor at WUSA in Washington, D.C., acknowledges that the work environment has fundamentally changed over the last twenty-five years:

> In the seventies there were no laws. People forget that before sexual harassment laws were put into effect, there really was nothing to protect women in business and certainly in the newsrooms. And I could tell you, and many women that I worked with can tell you, lots of stories about being groped and propositioned and threatened. All we could do about it was swallow our pride and keep going, or slap the guy and threaten him, or get our boyfriends to come in and beat them up. Whereas today, you get the manual. They teach you. They say, "You sit down for two hours and you learn these are the parameters and if you don't do this, you are going to be sued or you lose your job." This is new. So the women today are protected. They can come to work in an environment in which they feel, I hope, comfortable that they can do their job and not have to deal with all that other stuff on top of it.

Cokie Roberts believes the changes are enormous concerning male conduct in the newsroom:

In the old days there was not even a question about men coming on to you, men putting their hands on your knee, men trying to make it clear that if you had a relationship with them that things might be better for you. And, you know, you did a lot of just laughing it off. I was always married. I mean, I've been married since I was twenty-two years old so that for me it was easier than for a lot of people. But the shocking thing for me as a naive twenty-four-year old when I was job hunting in New York was how inconsequential my shining new wedding ring seemed to them. I mean, I even had a guy who was a boss coming on to me when I was quite pregnant. I thought he was a little peculiar. But all of that is fast changing. In some ways, almost too much so, to the point where people don't feel the comfort of joking with each other in the workplace the way they used to feel.

Rita Braver calls herself "lucky." The things that happened to her were always "very mild" and she always felt she could handle them. She never felt threatened or scared: "I never felt if I didn't succumb to someone's charms that anything bad would happen to me." Braver believes that since she was always married during her career at CBS and that everyone knew her husband, a respected lawyer who represents many leading broadcasters in the industry, there were fewer problems that she was forced to deal with. She admits, however, to experiencing occasions when people were more physical than she felt comfortable with: "I think now I would probably be more clear with them about the need to stop this as opposed to just shrugging it off."

Braver also faced problems with certain people when she needed to get information: "It was in another country where I was trying to get an interview with someone and his lawyer said to me, 'I will give you an interview if you sleep with me.' And I said, 'You've got to be kidding.' He said, 'I'm not kidding at all.' And I said, 'I guess this is one interview I'm not going to get.' And I didn't."

During her career climb Katie Couric remembers attending an executive meeting in the early seventies that was all male. The only other woman was someone in charge of promotion. It was an editorial meeting and Couric was substituting for a vacationing producer. As she walked into the room where twelve to fifteen people were sitting, a major executive was saying: "That's not the reason for Katie's success. She's successful because of her hard work, her intelligence, her industriousness, and her breast size."

Couric was so insulted she wrote him a memo saying that she found it humiliating and completely inappropriate for someone in his position to make that kind of sexist remark. She also wrote that she was not going to take this any further and that it was to remain between them. Although Couric received an immediate telephone call replete with fervent comments concerning how much he thought of her, she was later demoted and finally left the company.

During the same period of years, Jennifer Siebens recalls an episode involving an executive producer, who no longer works for CBS:

> I was going down a long, narrow hall. I passed the newsroom and a bunch of side offices and I was at one end of the hall and he was entering from the opposite end. And he yelled at me. He said, "Siebens, did anybody ever tell you that you have ugly legs?" He yelled it at the top of his lungs. And I usually wore jeans and I thought to myself, another reason not to wear dresses, because I happened to have a dress on that day. And I turned around and I was so embarrassed, so humiliated I wanted to die. And I wanted to yell at him, but I was too scared. I was twenty-nine or thirty and this was a lion of CBS. I wanted to yell, "Well, did anybody tell you that you had a small prick?" But I didn't. . . . And it was so public and I barely worked for this guy. I didn't know him. Never to this day—this was a smart, literate, cultured man. What the hell was he thinking? And these stories go on and on. It's just nuts what goes on.

Siebens believes that today there is much less sexual tension in the newsroom since men are now more used to working side by side with women. Instead of dealing with someone who pinches you, there are just the small indignities that a woman must put up with: "When you come in wearing a dress they say, 'God, you look good today,' and you want to just slap them because the implicit thing is you look like shit every other day. They don't know. It's just the way they are."

Kathy McManus, Jerusalem bureau chief for ABC, admits to experiencing sexual harassment over the years but she credits her four older brothers with giving her a different view of the issue. While she was growing up McManus states that her four brothers were very mean to her so that she developed a razor-sharp tongue, which was the only way she could fight back: "When any man ever said anything to me in the workplace that I thought was inappropriate I would turn and just try to verbally rip his lungs out and move on. I have learned as a manager that the definition of sexual harassment is repeated and unwanted advances. After the lungs had been removed, it was never repeated again. But I've seen other people go through just horrible, horrible incidences."

Kathy O'Hearn acknowledges being harassed from time to time but, because she was the kind of woman who was able to just throw it right back, she never found it to be a factor in her career:

> It never seemed threatening to me because I'm tough. I have a hot temper so I think I was able to fight back. What I think part of the problem of sexual harassment is there are lovely and softer people, be they male or female, who don't have the instinct to fight back and who feel the hold over them. I mean, it has to be somebody with power over you and it may simply be your peer. I was in the technical line. It was simply my peers, other technicals, but they had more power by their length of time there, by their reputation. I was new. It was just a different time. Those men, some of them did things—they were just going to give me a hard time no matter what. But it did not get in my way. I feel for people who have been more damaged or affected by it. I think it's a very frightening and severe problem. It has diminished a great deal and the magnifying glass is too intense now.

Wendy Takuda, anchor at KRON in San Francisco, relates the story when she was looking for her very first job in the early seventies. She went for an interview at a local television station in Seattle. It was close to lunch time when the interview ended. There were no jobs available but they talked about some positions that would open and she was invited to get some lunch:

> I was young and naive and I really needed a job. So we went to lunch and he has a drink and then he has two drinks. He's kind of loosening up and he says, "You know, I'm going to tell you something and if you ever tell anyone I told you, I'll tell them you lied. They wouldn't hire another minority in that newsroom if they were paid to right now. But there is this mailroom job. That might be good for you because you get into the general manager's office every day just to deliver the mail and he sees you." He went on to say: "I do know one other job. I need a housekeeper. Maybe you have a friend who might

be interested in this job. Actually it's more of a house sitter. Somebody who can watch my house because I have to travel a lot. I'm gone a lot. I'm gone all the time. Somebody to feed the cats and stuff." And then the premise changed from "maybe you have a friend" to "you would have your own living quarters. It has its separate entrance and you wouldn't have to do that much. Just feed the cats, keep an eye on the house. It's not a housekeeper. It's a house sitter and I'd never bother you."

Takuda declares that given her youth and inexperience, the man was confident that she would never do anything about what he said to her.

The worst case of sexual harassment that Linda Shen confronted was at WETA in Washington, D.C., in 1979. It lasted for nine months and Linda describes it as the most miserable experience she ever had in the news business:

> I knew that the executive producer was after me. I wanted the job. I figured that was all right. I could fend him off. He would show up at my doorstep at one in the morning. I did manage to fend him off. But I just became the victim of this incredible campaign to undermine the work I was doing there. It was an ill-fated show to begin with. But it was a very miserable year. I hated Washington, D.C. I hated WETA. I hated having to face this man every day. I really didn't ever recognize this in any articulate way, until oddly enough the Clarence Thomas confirmation hearings, which made me weep. It's really very liberating to have somebody else lay it on the line on behalf of the rest of us. Anyway, I wasn't able to recognize what was going on at the time. I was fired after nine months for what was described as gross incompetence. Which I believed, of course. Though a friend of mine persuaded me that there are any number of valid reasons for which I could have been fired, but gross incompetence was certainly not one of them.

The humiliation, the indignities, the self-doubt, the emotional drain and severe emotional duress and the ability to impact adversely on the future of an individual gets tied up in the disingenuousness and pervasiveness of the package labeled sexual harassment.

The woman responsible for breaking the Anita Hill story, Nina Totenberg, tells of her own discomfort at being the first woman at the *National Observer* to work in the print shop with the printers one or two

CAPITAL CITIES/ABC

Nina Totenberg, National Public Radio

days a week. It was part of her job as a news reporter there and it made her "most uncomfortable." She believed that it "just went with the territory, but it wasn't any fun to walk down the hall and have everybody sort of dissecting your body." As a result of the Anita Hill story this kind of conduct that was tolerated (but so uncomfortable) is no longer acceptable. Totenberg reflects on the difference it has made:

> I think it's changed the entire working environment. First of all, until certain Supreme Court decisions in the eighties, there really was no recourse for women in the workplace. And secondly, it's changed in terms of what's just socially acceptable. When I was a bit reporter in Washington, and I would walk through what's called the "Speakers

Lobby" on the House side, there would be a lot of old geezers sitting there on the benches who would literally catcall me and ask me if I wanted to come sit on their laps and just ridiculous fraternity-row kind of stuff. No politician in his right mind would do that today.

The most defining story of Totenberg's career created moments of extreme discomfort in her life. She describes an incident she wishes, with hindsight, she had handled differently:

> I would not have lost my temper at Alan Simpson after the *Nightline* broadcast.[1] I mean, it took me three weeks to figure out what to do. I should have called the police, with him ranting and raving at me and not letting me leave, instead of getting mad at him. After the *Nightline* broadcast, I was very angry. He impugned my integrity. He said I didn't have an unbiased bone in my body and I was essentially part of a hatchet job on Clarence Thomas. And while I socked it back to him on the broadcast, saying that there would have been no story for me if the judiciary committee had done its job and I think, I know I got the better of him on the broadcast; I've had conservative Republicans as well as Democrats tell me that, but I've got a temper. I could feel the blood rushing into my ears when he was attacking me on the air and it was a true experience in will power that I smiled and answered him appropriately. But afterwards, I didn't want to see him. I went out to the car that was waiting for me and got in the car, and he came chasing after me waving papers at me and screaming at me. I didn't say anything at first, but he wouldn't let me leave. He had the door open to the car and he wouldn't let me leave. Finally I blew. I think I called him a fucking bully. And that other people maybe had to take this shit from him, but I didn't. He continued and just wouldn't let me leave. I realized that he was completely out of control and that I'd better shut up. I may have lost my temper for thirty seconds, but that was not equivalent to whatever was going on with him. I just didn't say a word. Whatever he said to me, I just looked at him. I realized weeks later that I should not have lost my temper, because he immediately leaked the fact that I had yelled at him "the F word." I should have said to him, "If you don't stop it, Senator, I'm going to call the police." As it turned out, he apologized. I took him

---

[1] On October 7, 1991, ABC's *Nightline* aired a segment, "Sexual Harassment by Clarence Thomas Alleged."

to the White House correspondent's dinner with me. He was very gracious. We've been really very good friends since then. And I think he apparently has had some serious emotional problems over the years and he was just out of control. But if I had a single thing to do over again, it was the only time I didn't act like a lady and I regret it.

Totenberg describes the postscript to this story as "really kind of sweet." She recalls:

I was on a panel in New Orleans at some broadcasting convention and somebody asked me what we didn't like about our job. I said the only thing I really didn't like about my job was that some people hated me, and that I'm just like everybody else, I like to be popular. I like to be well liked. But because of what I do, some people get very angry at me and really hate my guts. At the end of the panel discussion this very lovely young woman came up to me and said, "Miss Totenberg, I don't hate you and I'm Alan Simpson's daughter."

Anita Hill's testimony at the Clarence Thomas confirmation hearings held working women around the country mesmerized. It released an avalanche of feelings and experiences that became a topic in the public forum ranging from intellectual discussion to heated debate. This shared singular event led to a catharsis of emotions that had long been hidden and held as secrets of shame and personal failures. Women in the workforce stood taller and planted their feet more solidly on the steps of a foundation that would elevate ability and intelligence over gender and sexual favors. Most important, women everywhere knew they no longer stood alone. Sexual harassment was given form, face, and substance.

There is little doubt that harassment has been a greater problem for some women than for others, and the way it is handled depends on the personality, and the strength, of the individual.

Phyllis Haynes, a former ABC news correspondent, tells of enduring shocking sexual harassment in her early career:

We didn't have a term for it when it happened to me. How I handled it was to be diplomatic, don't burn bridges, and try to avoid that person. I remember my first day at WOR-TV. A cameraman walked into the dressing room and smacked me on the rear end and wished me a good time at WOR. I looked at him and I said if you want to keep that hand, you won't do that again, and he never bothered me again. But you know, today I would react differently and put that person on report. There was no vehicle for reporting that. You'd be laughed at.

Law suits are expensive for companies and sensitivity training is now a regular feature of the practices of stations and networks.

Al Primo heads a company called Primo Management Service. Formerly vice president of news for all ABC television stations, Primo is credited with the development of the "eyewitness news" format. As a news consultant to television stations, he is heavily involved in trying to make stations aware of the rules, the regulations, and the reality of what sexual harassment is all about. Primo states that people must be made aware of the fact that attitudes and comments that may have been thought of as harmless, are serious topics to be discussed and avoided. He gives the illustrative case of a man who would never go to another man and say, "Gee, you really look great today. I love your outfit." So there should be no reason to make such a statement to a woman. Even if no harm was intended.

Tom Brokaw acknowledges that he is conscious of sexual harassment issues and the sensitivity of language in the workplace. He states, "You know, there are people in this organization, for example, who are homosexual, and there is language that is used that can be offensive to them. So we have to be conscious of that as well, and that's a form of sexual harassment."

For some newswomen, the complexity of male-female relationships in our society creates ambiguity and even contradictions. Pia Lindstrom believes that many women have lost their sense of humor. She began her reflections on the issue by stating that she had never been subject to sexual harassment:

> Any sex I had, I wanted to have. . . . Nobody's ever said, "Go to bed with me or you're going to lose your job." But now, of course, people think "harassment" if somebody says, "You've got great tits." I mean, I'm not going to sue somebody. I'll say, "Well, really?" I don't know, but people are awfully serious now that political correctness has taken over. When I first started [at KGO-TV] they used to show dirty movies in the back room, Roger Grimsby and all his guys. I started as a general assignment reporter in San Francisco and I was the only woman reporter there and I was the first woman reporter at the station. They liked to show dirty movies after the broadcast. They would all go in the back room and show these behind the green door.

They liked their little world there and it was annoying and they were embarrassed that I'd be in there hanging out. I didn't report them for this. I mean, to me that would be laughable.

Today, Lindstrom admits that everyone has become "super sensitive" and careful of what is said. After serving twenty-three years at WNBC-TV in New York, many as the arts editor and theater critic, she reflects:

If I call someone who's Oriental . . . no, it's called Asian. You mention Arabs, you're in trouble no matter what you say. You don't even want to review a movie with Arabs in it. You're going to get somebody saying either you're for 'em or you're again' 'em. We've become very sensitive. Maybe it's a good thing because maybe my children will be more sensitive to this as they grow up. I understand you grieve over things when somebody says, "You go to bed with me, or have sex on this desk or you lose your job." Of course, if that had ever happened I would have done something about it. But all the other things that people are doing now—it's a very confusing thing. I hear people saying about some of our executives, "Oh he does this and he comes on to women and we're going to get him. One of these days he'll get caught." I mean, I'd be terrified if I were a man.

The fear factor is one that Sally Quinn thinks created an atmosphere for change:

Men are scared and they know better. We had a situation during the Anita Hill hearings, a lot of things came up. There were two or three things at the *Washington Post,* and people were talked to and reprimanded. I haven't heard anything like that happening again. So I do think this Anita Hill thing was a great, great thing for women. It's putting the fear of God in men about what would happen, the consequences. Even if they didn't get fired or go to jail, the humiliation would be so great and the embarrassment—it just wasn't worth it. And I do think people are a lot more careful.

Quinn does not believe that situations involving harassment are as ominous as they used to be. Mostly it is "just kind of gauche and bad taste and stupidity rather than real malice."

Each of the networks continue to monitor the issue of sexual harassment through seminars, sensitivity training, and individual counseling sessions. Andrea Mitchell credits NBC with doing a very good job of alerting people at every level of the organization what will not be tolerated. She is quick to differentiate between the camaraderie and appropriate joking and kidding that occurs between men and women in any working environment and the more serious examples of sexual harassment:

> I've been in plenty of situations where I was the only woman and where a level of rudeness was imposed on me, either because I was in a small broadcast booth and the only television set was turned to something that was pornographic, which was the choice of the three men with whom I shared this little office space, or because of the constant joking and teasing that took place. The really egregious behavior that I recall from the sixties and the early seventies has probably disappeared.

Mitchell says this is a direct result of everyone being made aware of what our rights are and what our obligations are to ourselves and to other women: "I think everyone has grown up a lot—including the women."

Ann Medina remembers that when she was working as a network correspondent in the United States, sexual harassment was rampant. But her solution was just to tell them "screw off." She remembers two bosses who deftly made advances and she has difficulty pinpointing the exact number of senior correspondents who made advances. She says that women didn't say "screw off" enough. When she moved to Canada she said she was notorious and known for not playing around in the workplace:

> When you're in the field 80 percent of your time, I slept with (a joke) more male producers than anybody on earth probably. Of course, all of those sleeping situations were done on a hill, where you have to roll down. So, I had to put my foot against a tree. And, of course, we were surrounded by seventy Nicaraguan Sandinistas. Or in a little hotel where I discovered how two people can sleep on a very small double bed and not touch one another. There was only one bed. But once there was the rule laid down, if you will, without it ever having to be said, I had no problems in Canada.

Susan Zirinsky describes the work relationships that are an integral part of the news business: "We are in an industry, as in Hollywood, where there's a lot of intimacy because of the situations you're in. But it's a tough business, because the line is very fine, because you're in situations when you go to a war, when you're sleeping on the floor with fifty people. It's tough."

Heather Allen, NBC's Los Angeles bureau chief, is from South Africa and the first woman at NBC to serve as head of a major bureau. Allen describes the newsroom as a very tough environment where strong interpersonal skills are demanded to effectively survive. She does not think that there is any room for "cry babies" in the newsroom:

> I think you've got to decide where the bullshit ends, where real harassment starts. I think that the people are more aware of it. I think that in this country women are so much better protected than anywhere else I've ever worked, certainly better than in the third world where I came from, where it's just chalk and cheese. I think it's a very good thing. I think it just puts everybody on notice. I take it very seriously.
>
> Having said that, I have a lot of young news associates that start with me every year. I tell them this is a rough and tumble world out there. In this newsroom people have worked together anywhere from twenty to twenty-five years. That breeds a certain familiarity. I say, "You know you're going to hear stuff out there. It's going to be our cue to decide. It's one thing if somebody directs something to you, but remember these are people who go back a long time with one another. You should decide before you come in here telling them you're going to take offense with it. If it's truly offensive, I'll be out there like a flash. But what I expect you to do is grow another skin. I expect you to give as good as you get. And get tough because you're going to have to do that. This is a controlled environment and everybody knows the boundaries. But you are going to go out in the world and the public can be very rude to you. You're going to have some really ugly things said to you. You're going to have people slam their doors in your face and make racial and sexual remarks." So I said, "I'm not saying this is right. I'm just saying it's going to happen and you're going to have to toughen up."

The candor with which women as well as the men in broadcasting acknowledge and discuss the problems of sexual harassment and its impact on their daily personal interactions in the workplace testifies to its continuous presence.

Elizabeth Vargas, ABC News, said she would be surprised if there was a woman who had not experienced sexual harassment at some point in her career. While she admits that she was "never a victim of these extreme horror stories," the sexual harassment she did experience was a very uncomfortable situation. But she choose not to pursue it:

> I was very careful to keep records and to inform enough people so that I would have witnesses should this turn ugly. But you find yourself having to handle it. I think when you have men and women working together, unfortunately sometimes things like that happen. Where it becomes uncomfortable is when whoever is making these kinds of advances also happens to be in a position of great power over you. That is sexual harassment and that is where it is extremely uncomfortable. . . . It's happened to me several times. I never had to go to a superior to lodge a formal complaint. I have managed to handle it on my own. And in all cases, I was the victim of somebody who could very easily, without having to explain to anybody, hurt my career. They could have said, "You know what, let's not have her be the weekend anchor anymore," or, "Let's not have her fill in on this anchor's show anymore," or, "Let's not have her do this anymore,"—with impunity. So, I was very aware of the fact that I needed to be extremely diplomatic. And it worked out just fine.

The way people react to interpersonal relationships and the factors that combine to produce insensitive and blatantly overt advances are as unique as their individual personalities and positions. Diane Sawyer knows that sexual harassment is a factor in television news broadcasting. She states: "I recognize that it has been for a lot of women and that I'm not dismissive or smug about those women who have had to go through some very rough times. It's not happened to me. Have some sort of very highly questionable things been done? Yes! But my reaction has always been, 'Are you kidding?' And it's always worked, so that I never felt that my job was on the line one way or the other."

At ABC Lynn Sherr is the person that women or men go to talk to if they do not want to go to the official person at the network. Her responsibility is to get to know and understand the story. Usually, the individual is frightened and Sherr believes that she is viewed as more approachable and available to talk with. She knows sexual harassment remains a workplace concern:

> It's still going on. In subtle and not so subtle ways. I think it's greatly reduced. I think we have an extraordinarily enlightened man-

agement. I hope it maintains. The Cap City [Capital City] management—Dan Burke and Tom Murphy—was foursquare on this issue and was terrific about it. I don't know what the Disney approach will be. I have no reason to believe they're any different. I just know that Cap City was wonderful. So yes, I've heard of situations, some of which went further, some of which never went further than my office. Except, I would discuss them blindly, anonymously, with the powers that be and we were trying to work things out. It's still there. It's there in subtle ways and, occasionally, not so subtle ways. But I think we're making progress, some progress anyway.

Joanna Bistany was the first woman promoted to vice president at ABC News. Her senior position in management makes her analysis important. She thinks that sexual harassment is a factor in every workplace: "It is something that I think is better under control today than it was five years ago because of the absolute clamping down that we've done as a company, on offenders. We've taken very drastic measures. In fact, we release people as a result of instances of sexual harassment."

A similar attitude is expressed by Cheryl Gould, the highest ranking woman in management at NBC News. She admits that while sexual harassment was never a factor in her own career, there have been problems in her world created by this issue: "I would be a total ostrich to think that just because I've not experienced it, that it doesn't exist. Of course it has existed. But I think that post–Anita Hill, there's much more of an awareness and much less tolerance of it. Any time it is brought to management's attention, it is taken very seriously. I know of specific instances where people have lost their jobs because of it."

The highest-placed woman in management at CBS News is Linda Mason. She is now vice president of public affairs and executive producer of *CBS Reports*. Mason was first hired as a desk assistant in radio in January 1966 and says she was the first woman in every job she ever had at CBS. At the beginning there were instances that in retrospect would be thought of as sexual harassment. There were a number of offers but none ever escalated and she just single-mindedly went on with her work: "I was on the road with male crews and I guess they felt macho. They had to make some kind of advance. I never felt I had to do anything. They never got obnoxious." Today, Mason believes there is much less evidence of harassment issues because there are so many more women working in the news field. But issues and examples of these issues persist. "For instance," she says, "there was an editor who had suggestive pictures in his cutting room. This was considered offensive to some people and so he was asked to remove them. When you have this many people in these kinds of situations, I'm sure there is some sexual harassment that goes on. But I don't think it's any more or less than any other institution."

The changing work relationships in newsrooms affect men as well as women. Newer situations require insight, introspection, and often enlightenment among professional colleagues. Phyllis McGrady, executive producer of ABC's *PrimeTime Live,* reflects on a long conversation she once had with a male senior producer who did not understand that when he received his promotion, his ability to date co-workers took on a different dimension. McGrady tried to explain that when he was a colleague and someone said, "I'd like to go out" and he said no, it was in her words, "basically no big deal." But "In a senior position it can be interpreted differently. And I think that there are times when males don't quite necessarily understand that. Interestingly enough, I have now been in the business long enough so that I have also had it on the flip side. I have a young production assistant, male, who felt uncomfortable in a situation with a woman, who was senior to him. So interestingly, we've reached a point now where I've seen it on both sides."

Bob Zelnick describes personal experiences at the times he was hiring for new positions or promoting, when women "either offered themselves or made their availability known." Zelnick acknowledges the depth and complexity of the problem for both sexes. He states that he thinks "there are men in large numbers who were sexual harassers." He also declared that "there are women who played the game and to this day play the game from their end." He believes the cure is an evolution that will occur over time. When women become managers and vice presidents and become "integrated at all levels of the broadcast hierarchy, then you don't have a situation that rears itself with one class playing each role. You may have individual situations where people use their sex to gain opportunity or use it to exploit the power that they have. But it's not a hierarchical situation at the point where all the contestants are female and all the decision makers are male." The integration of women and men at every stage in the organizational structure may prove to be the most positive way to diminish the effect of sexual harassment on the careers and lives of people striving to achieve success based on competence, perseverance, and professionalism. Yet, Bob Zelnick also reminds us of the unsavory characteristics of certain people, "You know, it's a cruel world out there and people exploit other people in a variety of ways, for a variety of motives, in a variety of circumstances."

The instances of inconsequential sexual harassment are down, according to Dave Marash. He dubs Anita Hill "homecoming queen" of the era that has made issues involving sexual harassment change. Anita Hill, he believes, epitomized the determination and strength of will that gave women a heightened sense of dignity. They were given, through her example, a stronger will to act out what so many had been experiencing and were fearful to speak out about. However, Marash has grave concern about the ingrained sexism in our society that leads to the need for dominance and subservience in our cultural role playing—"the more dangerous and subtle sort of subcutaneous action, the paradox of judgment that eyeballs the male just a little bit differently than the female, is just as strongly rooted as ever, is my guess. It is more strongly and positively sanctioned by the public transactions of American culture in the last ten years. I mean, look at the advertising, print, and television that one sees and you will see female flesh being marketed as brutally as in 1955, more brutally. . . ."

Despite accelerated change and a growing number of women working throughout the television news industry, despite the strong policy stands taken in many networks and stations, despite the open acknowledgment that sexual harassment will not be tolerated and must not be ignored, the fact remains that many women continue to be harassed on the job and most remain fearful to come forward because of potentially unpleasant professional repercussions in their future career climb. This is particularly true of women who are working in positions that are at the lower levels of the power scale.

If there is no longer the "firehouse mentality" that existed in the newsrooms in the late sixties and early seventies, described by Rose Ann Scamardella as "one big bundle of sexual harassment," the climate of the country still reflects the deep-rooted ideas about sexual role behavior that continues to be reinforced on a daily basis by the mass media. Powerful systems of belief are slow to change. Perhaps sexism is best defined by cultural expectations about women and men that are shared by both and have become an emotional habit.

Elinor Guggenheimer, currently president and executive director of the New York Women's Agenda categorically states that sexual harassment is not just physical but that the worst harassment is the feeling that

73

women simply don't measure up or have the capacity to do the work that men do in leadership positions:

> I think one of the things we are seeing is case after case where women get their heads above water a little But they get their heads lopped off. Men are not enamored of highly successful women. We evolved from a whole preceding history of life. After we all evolved, the patterns of life demanded strength. You couldn't survive unless the man could go out and kill a mammoth. Women weren't good at that. I think in today's world, it's hard now to adjust to the fact that women really can be not just equal, but different, with different perspectives that are enormously important to the continuation of life.

There is still so much prejudice and discrimination to conquer before the workplace can truly become an equal playing field for women and men alike. Theresa Brown, former reporter for WPIX-TV in New York, describes herself as one of the first brown-skinned women to be on the air. She talks emotionally about the effects of sexism:

> I feel sexism is insurmountable. Racism you can rise above. Women all over the world are meat. They're chattel in most of the world, still. We're in such a privileged situation in America. We don't see ourselves against the world view. And in my mind, dealing with men in business, is one of the most difficult, draining, and thankless tasks one can have. We still see these poor women going out for men's jobs and being raped and beaten up and called names. You know, the first in whatever it is, the first lady firefighter. . . . It just leaves me speechless. The last thing I expected was to have sexist problems. I thought my problems would be racial problems. But my problems have been sexist problems. The conclusion I came to was that what difference does it make what color you are, you're still a woman!

The harsh reality is that we still live in a sexist society. There are major prejudices and discriminations out there to be conquered. A majority of men, even now, truly do not believe that women have the intellectual and emotional capacity to take on the extremely difficult and complex jobs of leadership. It is still out there. The women I spoke to feel it constantly. There is continuing need to overcome this history of sexist conditioning that creates regressive policy and oppressive prejudice against women in the workplace. The promised land of equality is still the ideal, not the reality.

74

6
Anchors
Away

The thing women must do to rise to
power is redefine their femininity. Once
power was considered a masculine
attribute. In fact, power has no sex.
K A T H A R I N E   G R A H A M

The power, prestige, and symbolism of the network evening news anchor makes this on-air job the most coveted and important in television
broadcasting. So while women may have cracked through some of the
biggest barriers in the broadcasting business, it is crucial to evaluate the
progress women have made toward gaining access to this most powerful
position. The nightly network news chair historically has been the prov-
ince of men—with two exceptions.

On October 4, 1976, Barbara Walters officially became television's
first network anchorwoman when she made her debut as co-anchor of
the "*ABC Evening News* with Harry Reasoner and Barbara Walters."
This pairing and ascendancy created a tremendous upheaval in the nation's news media. Her decision to leave her position as co-host of
NBC's *Today* show where she was acknowledged to be the most popular personality in American morning television created such an explo-
sive furor that Walters felt for a while that she had committed a crime.
With her break into the males-only anchor club came an outpouring of
doubt, speculation, recrimination, and anger. In a *Newsweek* magazine
cover story headed "The New Look of TV News," then CBS news anchor

Walter Cronkite was quoted as recalling that when he first heard about the Walters-Reasoner pairing, he experienced "the sickening sensation that we were all going under, that all of our efforts to hold network television news aloof from show business had failed." [1] John Chancellor, NBC's anchorman at this time, expressed relief that Barbara Walters was not acquiring half of his anchor.

Chancellor's partner David Brinkley remarked that he suspected that Walters would find her new job more difficult than expected, "Being an anchor is not just a matter of sitting in front of a camera and looking pretty." [2] While Harry Reasoner admitted he did not know what to expect, he stated that while he was with Barbara Walters during President Richard Nixon's trip to China, he never actually witnessed her work, "All I know about her from that trip is that she rides a bus very well." [3] This was an on-air relationship Reasoner never wanted and never accepted. He never wanted to be forced to work with a partner and he never wanted to work with a woman. His public displeasure was obvious from the outset. Harry Reasoner was an old-school news broadcaster, trained in print journalism and honed in the classic, formal anchor mold that honors the voice of restrained authority. Barbara Walters's journalistic skills were learned in the television medium itself and her incomparable interviewing talent included a fundamental break with the traditional anchor personality. Instead of an Olympian commentator, Walters offered a more human and personal side of the news. This was a time when the ABC network was battling its perennial problem of news credibility. The youngest of three networks, ABC News had major ratings problems. The ABC network gambled on Barbara Walters to bring in a larger news-watching audience. The television anchor person represents a newscast's most recognizable style and personality. The impact of this person on the viewer creates the program's most significant ratings draw. The face of the network news anchor is known to be the single most important representation of the entire network in the minds of the American viewing public. The Reasoner-Walters team was an ill-fated match which created such discomfort and conflict that Av Westin was called back to ABC to try to solve some of the frictions. He spoke to me of how there were two hostile camps with two factions

---

[1] "The New Look of TV News," *Newsweek*, October 11, 1976, p. 68.

[2] Ibid.

[3] Ibid.

Connie Chung

operating in the newsroom. When Westin came in, he was told by the "Reasoner camp" that they were owed four and a half minutes since Walters was said to have been on air that many minutes more than Reasoner. This was not a working atmosphere where one of the most important sources of information in our society could flourish and fulfill its responsibilities.

On June 1, 1993, when Connie Chung took her seat next to Dan Rather as co-anchor of the *CBS Evening News,* she became the second woman to be named the full-time anchor of a weekly evening newscast at ABC, NBC, or CBS. Once again the move to elevate a woman into what is acknowledged to be one of the last bastions of male dominance in the news profession created controversy, criticism, and intense scrutiny. The pairing was described by some as a cosmetic change needed to bolster the demographics and ratings of the CBS newscast. The choice was also said to be less a result of journalistic accomplishment than due to Connie's high Q rating, a television industry measurement of a person's likability and recognizability among viewers.

Twelve days shy of her second-year anniversary as co-anchor of the *CBS Evening News,* Connie Chung was dropped from this position. The failure of this on-air dual-anchor team became one of the biggest media stories in 1995 and raised heatedly debated issues relating both to gender and to journalistic integrity and ability.

In my interview with Chung, she offered some reasons why the pairing failed:

> Not a great deal of thought was given to exactly what would happen after I arrived at the anchor desk. I think that if it had been thought out more clearly as to what one person would be doing, what the other person would be doing, and how it would work and how the program would be produced, it could have been successful. We were actually doing quite well in terms of just pure ratings. During those two years that I was doing it, we moved into a number-two position. But then we went back down to number three. But I believe that it could have worked had there been sort of a clear plan. I also think that it probably would have worked had the two individuals arrived at the same time. If a new team was formed and put in place, as opposed to one person being there, asked to move over a few inches to welcome the arrival of a new individual, that's difficult.

Chung believes that there is validity to a comparison to her co-anchoring experience with Dan Rather and that of Barbara Walters working with Harry Reasoner. She says, "There were similarities in that both men who had been in the job were asked to accept a woman to share the responsibility and the load. My sense is that both men didn't find that to be an appetizing prospect. But what was different was that Barbara worked for Roone Arledge who, as president of ABC news, decided to find something special for Barbara to do that became her special interviews, her 'specials.' She always told me that just when she thought everything was really difficult—she was at one of the worst times of her life—she worked very hard, then, to create a new niche for herself. And we have seen the fruits of that over the years. Another difference is that the viewers actually are ready to have a woman and I think twenty years later they're probably more ready and in the next few years, they'll be even more ready."

When asked if she would make the same decision again if she were given the opportunity Chung answered without hesitation, "Yes. Absolutely. That job was certainly the job that I had always dreamed about. I never thought I would be asked to take that job. Nor did I think any woman would be asked to take that job in my lifetime. So it came as a very delightful surprise and I would never have turned it down and I would not turn it down today."[4]

Barbara Walters talked to me about her perception of the co-anchoring situation she experienced as compared with Connie Chung's:

There were some similarities, but great differences. Harry Reasoner resisted me. He did not want to have a partner, male or female. It was obvious on the air. We had to be separated because the program wasn't doing any good and because neither one of us was coming out looking good. When Connie came on the program, Dan did accept her. The similarities are that Harry and I were miscast and were not a true partnership and didn't support each other. Although, Dan and Connie supported each other and Dan was very gracious with Connie in his acceptance. After all, he was doing the show alone and it couldn't have been that easy for him. But they were mismatched. And the program simply wasn't successful. I don't think it had to do with sexism. I think that they had to decide that since the ratings were down, they had to do something. It was very painful for Connie. But I don't think it was an act of sexism. I don't think it was "get rid of the woman." I think that it just wasn't working.

---

[4] Connie Chung joined ABC News as a special correspondent in 1997.

Dan Rather has been in the anchor chair at CBS since 1981 when he succeeded the icon of anchormen, Walter Cronkite. He was not reluctant to discuss his views on what his former co-anchoring relationship had meant to him personally and to his future:

> Connie herself said that she did not get the job because she was a woman, and that was true. It was a business decision to try something new and a business decision to end it. This I do know, that after careful thought went into it I was enthusiastic and determined not to just give it a good try, but I went in determined to make it work, saying to myself, "Don't go into this Dan unless you are really committed to it." Despite everybody's best efforts, it didn't work. It was a business decision to do it, to try it, to experiment with it.

From the time it became apparent that the double anchor relationship was not working until the minute he heard Connie was leaving, Dan Rather believed—assumed—that CBS management would ask *him* to leave and let her remain as sole anchor of the *Evening News*. He went on to explain: "I've been living on borrowed time for a long time as an anchor person. Stop and think about it. Where else in America is there an anchor person at any level who is sixty-three years old. That's what I was when that decision was made." He went on to give more reasons, including the fact that the news business is even more intensely motivated by demographics and the ideal demographic for advertisers is the younger viewer. He also revealed: "I hope I have a reputation to be a good reporter. But I don't have a reputation of being the easiest person for management to handle. I've crossed swords with people and management any number of times over what I and they consider to be principle. I'm a little reluctant to say that because, while I have scars, I like to think that all of them are from the front and honorably earned. But I do have scars."

When I repeated Rather's comment that he worried that he would be the one asked to step down from the anchor position in favor of Connie Chung, Reuven Frank, the man responsible for the legendary pairing of Chet Huntley and David Brinkley on NBC in 1956, replied tersely: "If you believe that, I have a bridge to sell you."

Connie Chung was the subject of a barrage of criticism from many national critics and reporters for her coverage of sensational news figures and her interview with House Speaker Newt Gingrich's mother in which Kathleen Gingrich said her son had called First Lady Hillary

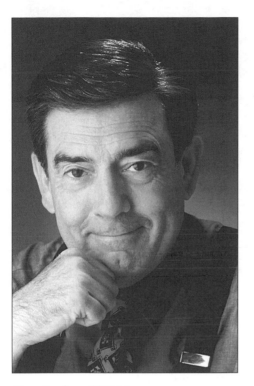

Dan Rather, CBS News

Clinton "a bitch." This comment was whispered after Chung told her the remark would be "just between you and me." CBS management, many believe, was not publicly supportive and Chung was personally blamed for a lack of ethics and professionalism. Her credibility as a journalist suffered also as a result of the decision made for her to cover such tabloid news figures as Tonya Harding, Faye Resnick, and Heidi Fleiss. These interviews were done for her CBS prime-time news magazine *Eye to Eye with Connie Chung*, which premiered on June 17, 1993, a few weeks after she began her duties as co-anchor of the *Evening News*. Her professional reputation was heavily damaged as was her public image.

Ann Compton was quoted as saying that she thought Connie Chung got a "black eye" from the whole fuss about Newt Gingrich's mother. During our interview, Compton told me that Chung, who has been a

friend for many years, sent her a little handwritten note and a tape of
the interview. In it, Chung said, "Oh please, Ann, look at the story. It's
Newt-spin. There was nothing wrong with the interview or the way it
was edited." Compton wrote her back and candidly said,

> Connie, you missed the point. I saw the interview. There was nothing
> wrong with the interview or the way it was edited. What's wrong is
> that you have reached the highest position of any woman in broad-
> casting. You have a chair, an anchor chair, on a major network eve-
> ning news show. Yet you will always be remembered for a cutesy in-
> terview, a personality interview done for a news magazine that got
> blown up into a big story. I want you remembered for being the first
> woman, for an extended period of time, to sit and anchor the evening
> news. And that's going to be lost in all this. . . . I wrote that back to
> her and I really feel strongly that Connie will not be remembered as
> co-anchor of the *CBS Evening News.* She will be remembered as the
> one who did a personality interview with Newt Gingrich's mother
> and coaxed the woman into saying a five-letter word about the first
> lady of the United States.

When I asked Compton to compare the situation that confronted
Connie Chung at CBS with the earlier experience of Barbara Walters at
ABC, she put it into historical perspective:

> When Barbara Walters and Harry Reasoner co-anchored a broad-
> cast, it was a dual-anchor chair that had been held down for many
> years by Howard K. Smith. The new anchor combination paled by
> comparison with the old anchor combination which had a tremen-
> dous amount of chemistry. The American people were used to tun-
> ing into Reasoner and Smith, just as they were used to tuning into
> Huntley and Brinkley. The idea of a combination anchor was some-
> thing well-rooted in America's acceptance. Americans seemed to like
> it and the chemistry between the two anchors was very strong. It's
> not something that you can explain and quantify. But it was truly
> there. To replace a news team that had very strong and well-accepted
> chemistry with a woman who came, not from the ranks of correspon-
> dents or hard-news journalists, but out of the ranks of very aggressive
> news interviewers, and who, herself, was something of a person-
> ality—add to that the fact that there was a very different, a very de-
> structive chemistry, or at least we were allowed to believe that there
> was this very poor chemistry between the two anchors. It was a mat-

ing that was doomed from the beginning. ABC really did want to be the first to make a combination like this work.

With these two failed experiences, what did Compton believe was the prognosis for a woman to anchor the network evening news? She absolutely believes it will happen, but she does not expect to be the one to sit in that chair herself. She describes the pyramid shape of the news business:

> Just take the three networks and CNN. Let's say there are 150 on-air correspondent positions. Ranging up from that, there are a kind of senior favorite star-rank reporters (and I'm talking about the news broadcasts and the news magazines, not the specialty shows like *Nightline*). So you get down to maybe ten or fifteen correspondents at all the networks who are really considered the stars of those broadcasts. When you get down to the number of anchor chairs, its musical chairs. There are not nearly as many chairs as there are pretenders to the throne. I have never felt that I was on that track. Of course, I have done anchoring. I have done it on virtually every broadcast that ABC has had—with the exception of the evening news Monday through Friday. I've done it on weekends. I've done it on holidays. I've done it on late-night news. But I have never felt that ABC saw me on a career track to the evening news, which is fine. I have no problem with that. I'm in good company with a lot of other people who aren't on that track either. So I don't see myself in the endgame at all. However, the question's always, "Would you like to be an anchor some day?" Any correspondent who says, "No, I would really like to be out in the field close to the story," is lying. Where is the money? Where is the prestige? Where is the visibility? Where are all the benchmarks that count for something in our business? They're all in the anchor chair. . . . Will there someday be a woman anchor? I think there certainly will be and whether it's a woman with the glamour of a Diane Sawyer, whether management decides on someone with the stability and authority of a Judy Woodruff, I don't know. Management's going to have to answer that question for you. But I certainly think that day will come and I would love to be the correspondent with the lead story on the first night she's anchoring.

The power of the sole anchor is coveted and not easily given up or shared. Many broadcasters were able to acknowledge that whether you liked or disliked Dan Rather as an on-air personality, he works alone, he does a "single." Therefore, it was viewed as being irrelevant who was brought on board, it could not have been a workable situation. Jennifer Siebens, who has worked for both Walter Cronkite and Dan Rather, gave a forthright analysis of problems the Rather-Chung partnership faced: "I don't care what Dan told you in that hour. It's a humiliation in front of Tom [Brokaw] and Peter [Jennings]. This is a very competitive group of guys. There's just the basic dynamic of sharing only twenty-two minutes a night. The high visibility and Dan feeling 'I don't notice Tom and Peter having to share so why do I have to share?'"

Siebens also commented on the way the newscast was set up:

> Dan kept the title of managing editor. Connie never had it and Dan was told, "You're still number one." Connie was told, "But you're equal." They came in with different expectations. So we've got two high-powered conscientious people, with only twenty-two minutes, coming in and it's already off kilter. Ultimately, Dan has his difficulties as an anchor. Connie has her difficulties as an anchor. Between the two of them, Dan is definitely the more qualified to be the anchor. Connie got beat around the head and shoulders enough. She had done magazine work. But she hadn't been in that daily grind. Dan had been in that daily grind. To be an anchorman at that level, you've got to be in that daily grind for longer than you can think. Connie hadn't. Clearly, her anchor skills are superior in some ways to Dan's, but not her reporting skills and not her ability to rock and roll. And I love her. She is close to a perfect anchor in terms of personality. Easy to work with, very open. Dan is very focused, very taunt. Their chemistry was bullshit. They were not made for each other.

When Connie Chung was named to co-anchor the *CBS Evening News* she was only the second woman but the first Asian-American to hold the title. Chung spoke of how in the Chinese culture boys are prized more than girls and boys are the ones to carry on the family name. With her work and success as a journalist, Chung thought of herself as her father's son. Chung's visibility as an Asian-American woman, according to former newswoman Linda Shen was a factor contributing to her initial acceptance. But it brings with it an indictment of the broadcasting world's ability to accept diversity. Shen stated that she could personally understand and relate to Chung's career rise:

> The fact that she is an Asian-American woman played into a lot of white men's fantasies. And I think it made it very easy for them to

elevate her to that position. She clearly had a long track record in the business, so she could be defended on a professional basis. But at the same time, she was this exotic Asian flower who would look really good next to Dan. I also happen to think, especially looking at this interesting new trend in television soaps, television series, and advertising, that little stabs are being made at mixed-race coupling and the easiest one for people to accept, or at least the easiest one for people in power, decision-making power, to put out there, is the white man and Asian woman. I think that we've seen it historically for a lot longer than we've seen any other interracial couple. It's somewhat complex and at the same time, it's a very simple issue.

In a quest for ratings and market share, what the American public is perceived to find acceptable and palatable is usually the focus of management decisions. When one of the networks attempts to change the face of the evening news, inevitably that changes public reality and perceptions. Walter Cronkite sat in the anchor chair at CBS between 1962 until his retirement in 1981. The power, loyalty, and trust invested in this broadcasting giant by the American public remains unequaled. His authoritative style is sometimes referred to with affection and reverence by those in television news as "the iron-bottom school of journalism." He spoke to me about his own views about the dual-anchor role:

The two-person anchor is a very poor idea in my mind. There's a whole waste of time in assignment of stories to one or the other, the rivalries that the individual staffs might involve, the complications of preparing a script for two people. I think it's a ridiculous idea myself. It's purely a show-business gimmick, an attempt to lure more people to enter the tent, if you will, by having one or the other person appeal to them. I'm afraid that women have been misused in this category as beauty spots for the broadcast rather than for their reportorial and broadcast abilities. That doesn't mean and should not indicate at all that I don't think that those who have appeared are in most parts capable. Most of them are. And they're certainly showing their ability in every other aspect in the news. There's no reason at all that a single woman should not be a news anchor. But in all show business aspects of dual or triple anchors, even, as some stations do today, with a weather person thrown in, a sports person thrown in, it's a vaudeville show. And that's not what you're trying to do. You're trying to communicate information.

Walter Cronkite believes that the quest for ratings has created broadcasts that are no longer "news" but rather "features material" or what is called "back-of-the-book stuff." He says he feels sorry for those who are faced with this need to attract a bigger slice of a smaller pie as network evening news programs continue to erode in viewership. But this "tragedy" that he sees is truly one, he believes, we all must share and suffer with.

Tom Brokaw had been with NBC News since 1966 and the sole anchor of the *NBC Evening News* for thirteen years at the time of our interview. He contends that with the changes he sees reflected in the news business, he and Dan Rather and Peter Jennings are the last three white males that will be anchoring the evening newscasts. Brokaw acknowledges that gender bias may have played a role when he and the other two network anchors assumed their roles. But they all were well trained and positioned at the networks to step into this top post. But, even if they have paid their individual dues, there seems little doubt that when they retire, three white males will not be their replacements.

Tom Brokaw, also, does not believe that a dual anchor is workable. He pointed out that when he did the newscast together with Roger Mudd, it did not work. He went on to declare:

> It doesn't have anything to do with gender. It has to do with the fact that there's just not enough time for two people. And what people tend to forget about Huntley and Brinkley is that David did only the Washington stories and he was on very briefly in the course of half an hour. But when he was on it was memorable, obviously, because he was almost more commentator than he was anchorman. And Chet did the rest of the news from up here [New York]. Now its harder to divide up that twenty-two minutes of news between two energetic, intellectually alive people.

Brokaw admitted that when he first got into the business thirty years ago

> we had women who were mere tokens and they were primarily tokens on the air. Now if you go into our 3:30 meeting or 2:30 meeting for nightly news in the afternoon, I look at one whole side of the office. It's all women. Producers and editors and technicians and senior people on the broadcast are women. So I think women have found their way into all of the different parts of the organization. Now, they still haven't percolated to the job of primary anchor on the evening broadcast, obviously. There's not an executive producer

Tom Brokaw, NBC News

within nightly news or within any of the programs who is a woman. But that will happen.

Sam Donaldson spoke out about his personal experience as a senior male correspondent who has enjoyed a distinguished and sometimes controversial tenure at ABC News and his emerging consciousness of the role and influence of women:

It is true, when I got in the business, there weren't any or many women at all. It was a man's world. And I climbed the ladder competing against men, measuring my success or lack of it against the success of other men, feeling when I lost, a certain upset. But it was the upset of having lost the competition against an equal. I've never thought of myself as a sexist in the extreme. But I guess being sixty-two years old, obviously, I had a lot of the same social feelings as to gender. . . . Being teamed up with Diane [Sawyer] on *PrimeTime Live,* I've had to understand that in this competition, now I'm competing with women on an equal level who can and do beat me—for a job, for a plum interview, for recognition. Now you go back to the fifties, when you read the clips about who were the great recognized reporters, they're all men. Edward R. Murrow, Howard K. Smith, down the line, in the sixties, in the seventies. Today, women are the recognized reporters as well as men. I'm on a broadcast where there's a co-anchor situation. I've had to read for years how Diane Sawyer's the major anchor and I'm the minor anchor. I've had to read for years clips of Diane's successes, every one of which she's deserved, in my opinion. And I read some clips about mine. But you see what I'm trying to say to you. And I'm trying to be very honest with you. I've had to accept that and I've discovered not only can I accept it, but I see nothing wrong with it. If I was in New York, and Diane was in Washington, the shoe would probably be on the other foot. But I'm not, and the program makes use of her talents brilliantly, I think, and my talents very well, too. And it all works. I suppose what I'm saying in a nutshell, men have to understand that in this business now, people are going to give lip service to the idea that women are equal. And it's an equal shot, back and forth. Then we have to give emotional service to it also. So it's one thing to say, well, "Peter Jennings is the senior anchor at ABC and I'm not, and that's fine." Maybe I would have liked to have been; it doesn't matter. But it's also the same thing to say that "this woman," whether it's Diane Sawyer or someone else, "is also senior to me at ABC" and that's all right, too. I said I wouldn't generalize, but in my observation of some other men in this business, I find that with some it's a tough thing to recognize that.

Diane Sawyer observes that a news division that wants to remain on top will promote and encourage the strong and creative women that are doing such formidable and superior work at the networks. When asked about the single-anchor role, she replied, "These are jobs held by very accomplished and very experienced and very good men. I don't think that the fact that no woman has that job at this point is about sexism as much as it is about the fact that there are just three of them on the main networks. At CNN they have joint anchorships. It is the fact that there are just the three of them at these three networks and they're still doing the job wonderfully."

Diane Sawyer's name is the one most frequently suggested as a possible successor to the position of evening news anchor. At ABC, Joanna Bistany had no qualms in stating that the female anchor is here right now: "I think if Diane wanted *World News Tonight*, it would be hers in a heartbeat if Peter [Jennings] were to get hit by a bus tomorrow."

There is little doubt that ratings and economics become the catalyst for change. The continuing erosion of the networks' audience share may prove to be the stimulus for the emergence at a different level of a single woman anchor. But you must have the opportunity, the space. It could never happen until one of the men currently occupying the anchor chair decided or were persuaded to give it up or move over. It would be a bold step for the networks, but one that will be driven by demographics if and when it happens.

Sheila McManus does not believe that a single woman anchor would mean the full integration of women into the broadcasting profession. She comments, "I think the world is still a boy's club and I think as long as the world is a boy's club, television will be a boy's club."

Maureen Bunyan sees a tie in the relationship between the political life and the public life and the public image in mass media. She believes that if we elect a woman president or vice president of the United States, then we will get a woman anchoring the evening news. She says, "When women achieve high political office in this country, it will be because the American public has said we accept top leadership from a woman." This would mean that this elected woman won with the support of all people and not just because she happened to be a woman, or only women voted for her. Bunyan indicated that this would be a breakthrough in the consciousness of the American people. When other countries and cultures are examined and when you see that women have been accepted into the top political roles, you then find that it has become easier for women to transcend into other positions of authority in their mass media. She declares, "It's sad to say that in our American culture, women have to keep fighting so hard to be accepted."

The sex-role strategies and the strong double standard that exists for women remains a discomforting reality to those who strive to reach the top echelon of their professional and political world. Elinor Guggenheimer has spent much of her long productive life working both in the media and as a political activist. She has witnessed the intense intolerance our society has shown for strong women. She pointed to the continuing attacks on First Lady Hillary Clinton. Elinor feels that women are going to continue to suffer from feeling that they must be sweet and more accommodating than men:

> I know Hillary Clinton. I know her as a brilliant woman and one who has a lot of softness and a lot of feminine characteristics. I also watched Eleanor Roosevelt being demolished when she was in the White House. She only became First Lady of the Universe after she didn't have any power anymore. When she had power, believe me, she was demolished. And Hillary has certainly been demolished. They've got her boxed into doing nothing now.

As a society we remain terribly divided and ambivalent about women aggressively pursuing a career and what the acceptable roles are for these women to play. In their heart of hearts, a large number of people resent powerful women. There are still major sexual stereotypes impeding the integration and acceptance of women in the professional world.

Since the start of the broadcasting industry, women were considered unqualified for big positions because of their voices. The qualities that make a woman's speaking voice pleasant, including its pitch and inflections, have always been held against her. As Judy Muller asserts, the male voice still dominates on the air:

> People still see men as authoritative. That's why you don't hear many women on the radio. It's our own prejudice. It's our own bias. We want to tune in to see Daddy, whether it's Peter Jennings who's kind of an attractive Daddy, or Charlie Osgood on Sundays who's Granddaddy. We feel more comfortable with a male presence for some reason. I think that's the culture. With more and more women moving into positions of authority everywhere, we're going to be more comfortable with the idea that this woman knows what she's talking about. But it's still funny to me that I'm regularly told I have an authoritative voice. And that's probably because I'm a tenor. It has nothing to do with the fact I'm more knowledgeable than other people. It's that I sound more knowledgeable because I have a very deep voice. And it's silly.

The American culture is reflected and reinforced daily by decisions made by corporate America. But there are many network executives who acknowledge that the viewing public may indeed have a strong preference for a father figure in times of national crisis, and the male-anchor tradition continues to fill that seat.

The fear expressed by several female correspondents deals with the changes that are often reflected in a profession when key positions are finally given to women. When men no longer do the job, will the profession became downgraded? Will the status and power and pay become lowered? When women are allowed full integration in all levels of the broadcasting hierarchy, will there be a disintegration of news as we know it?

Richard Threlkeld thinks it is irrelevant to worry about a woman assuming the role of network evening news anchor. He is confident that the nature of television news is going to change. He told me, "I think that the TV network newscasts really are dinosaurs and we're not going to have conversations like this in five or six years. I mean, we're not going to have conversations about whether there should be more women doing this, or that, or the other thing. I don't think, bless their hearts, I don't think Dan Rather and Tom Brokaw and Peter Jennings, those chairs are going to be that important in five or six years. The business is exploding. Cable is doing lots of things and people are getting out of the habit of watching an evening newscast."

With the loss of network power and status, with the loss of advertising revenue that will inevitably be the outcome of a reduction of viewership, there will usually be a decrease in salary and benefits. Historically, as women enter a profession, the salary scale lowers. This phenomenon is noted by Sheilah Kast, ABC news correspondent: "I think as television gets to be less lucrative for a lot of people in it, these jobs will suddenly be available to women. Surprise! And so you'll have the culture changing, becoming more of a pink-collar culture. And women will have more influence on the way the news is presented, both in front of the camera and behind it. But that will be because men will have other fish to fry that pay them more."

Marlene Sanders emphatically agrees. She believes only when it becomes really inconsequential will we see women as the leaders of the news profession. She states, "Only when the networks have diminished in influence and are no longer very important will that happen. I think it is so far down the road that we will be long dead before it happens, if it ever happens. But I really think that women ascend as the organization looses its clout."

Cheryl Gould adamantly believes that in the management ranks "when the right woman comes along and is qualified and has the qualities that are needed, I think the parent companies care about the bottom line more than they care about anything else. If it's a Martian who has two heads and is green and is going to do the job, they'll hire that person." But she also wonders if the nightly news will remain the defining icon of the network. The women who are successfully anchoring magazine programs have taken on significant roles. So, the nightly news may not remain an adequate measure of the advancement of women in broadcasting. There is some agreement that in the future the anchor position is not where the power will remain.

David Brinkley believes there is a total acceptance of women in network news. For him, it is a nonissue. He indicated in our interview that he has worked with numerous women over his long and distinguished career, and that he regards them as professionals:

> They do what they're hired to do, what we expect them to do, and do it very well. I can't even remember all of the women I've worked with and I've never given it a thought. It doesn't matter. In fact, there is one women I do remember but I can't think of her name. I didn't know which gender she was until she appeared on air. Her name did not tell it. It was some name that could have been male or female. And I didn't know or give a damn. Turned out she was a woman. I didn't know it until she came up on the screen. So it didn't matter. It doesn't matter now. We have numerous women here in this building. We have numerous women on our program and nobody gives it a thought anymore. I don't mean to belittle them by saying this, but they've become part of the wall paper like all the rest of us.

Barbara Walters does not believe it matters anymore whether or not a woman is the network evening news anchor. She told me and has said repeatedly that the glory that is attached to being the first, or second, or even third women news anchor is just a myth. She sees little difference to anchoring the news on the weeknights or on Sundays as Carole Simpson does for ABC. Both require the same skills, have the same format, and use the same teleprompter. She went on to indicate that there are women both in front and behind the camera who play the predominant role. On 20/20 she often finds herself the one who's doing the harder news stories. The news magazines, in particular, are hosted individually, or co-hosted, by women playing a very dominant role.

Walters admits that the network evening news is one of the last bastions, the lone holdout for women. But she believes you will see a woman in that role as well. However, she no longer feels it is an important issue or a cause for concern.

Connie Chung, in retrospect, is glad she actually did make it to the top job at the network: "I was only the second. Barbara was the first. And there will be a third. I am confident that what Barbara and I were unable to do and by that I mean stay there longer than two years, the third will be able to do. I would be so thrilled if she were not in a co-anchor situation and she would be the only one, be the single anchor."

It is the words of Dave Marash that echo the sentiments of many of the women working in television news who know the need to keep fighting and proving their worth: "I think if women hang in there and utilize patience, be like that bulldog. Grab the throat and don't let go. Just hang in there and bleed them. The logic of the situation is inescapable. Women are as capable as men. They are as authoritative as men. They're a larger part of the audience than men. So hang in there, baby. You will get there."

An appropriate response came from Deborah Potter, "Boy, I hope it doesn't take too long. But I'm not holding my breath."

7
Minorities
and
Mandates

"We the people." It is very eloquent. But when that document was completed on the seventeenth of September in 1787, I was not included in that "We the people." I felt somehow for many years that George Washington and Alexander Hamilton just left me out by mistake. But through the process of amendment, interpretation, and court decision, I have finally been included in "We, the people." BARBARA C. JORDAN, JULY 25, 1974

The factors of race and ethnicity are crucial considerations in all aspects of American society. The need to include members of all population groups to broaden the cultural diversity, to provide new attitudes and perceptions, is critical to adequately reflect and serve the public. In the mass media in general and in television news more specifically, the gap between what is and what should be remains a wide abyss.

Minorities endure a much more difficult struggle than do women in breaking through the broadcast barriers. Clearly, gender, race, and ethnicity have had a dramatic effect on the face of television news. Yet, Caucasian males continue to dominate the work force in television. A survey among all 1,196 operating nonsatellite television stations conducted in the last quarter of 1995 by the Radio and Television News Directors Foundation and Ball State University found the minority work force comprise only 19 percent.[1] Women now make up 37 percent of the full-time work force in television news. A breakdown of positions by race shows 91% of News Directors are Caucasian, 1% African American, 4% Latino/Hispanic, 2% Asian American, and 2% Native American. At the Executive Producer rank, 93% are Caucasian, 3% African American, 2% Latino/Hispanic and 2% Asian American. A more careful analysis reveals that minority news directors were disproportionately working in news departments at ethnically oriented stations.

The survey also indicates that the job of news anchor is held by 81% Caucasians, 11% African Americans, 4% Latino/Hispanics, and 3% Asian Americans. News reporters similarly breakdown to reveal 76% Caucasian, 13% African American, 7% Latino/Hispanic, and 4% Asian Americans. The statistics further show that women make up 41 percent of middle management (assistant news director, executive producer, managing editor) and almost two-thirds (64%) of the producers. Women already comprise the majority of news anchors at 51%. But, the traditional role of sports anchor remains 97% male.

The Directors Guild of America figures for 1995 documented that of the 10,624 members (including director, unit production manager, assistant director, and production assistant positions), 345 or slightly over 3% were African American. The Writers Guild of America reported that of its 7,768 members, 235 or 3% are African Americans.

A 1997 media study of the network evening news programs indicated that minority reporters comprise 18% of the network news corps and reported 15% of the total stories. This represents a 50% increase in

---

[1] Bob Papper, Michael Gerhand, and Andrew Sharma, "More Women and Minorities in Broadcast News," *Communication*, August 1996, pp. 8–15.

visibility over 1993.[2] It is noteworthy that when each of the networks changed White House correspondents in 1997, white males were selected to fill each of these prestigious positions. According to Professor Joe S. Foote, the author of this study, "when Sam Donaldson returned to the White House beat this month, he rejoined the same kind of white male bastion he left in the late '80s."[3] So while there has been some progress, the road remains arduous, tedious, and troublesome. Hard work, determination, proven ability, and a willingness to fight ingrained discrimination remain the basic prerequisites for minority achievement in the media, but by no means do these qualities ensure success.

The woman most admired for her fighting determination, accomplishments and concern for the role of women and minorities in television news is Carole Simpson. Simpson is the only African American woman to regularly anchor a network news program. She flies down from the ABC Washington bureau every Sunday morning to anchor the *Sunday World News Tonight* in New York. Her story is singular and inspiring. In 1962 she was the only black woman to graduate from the department of journalism at the University of Michigan. She was the only one of the 60 graduates who was not offered a job. The head of the journalism department finally arranged an internship for her at the Tuskeegee Institute in Alabama. Simpson explains what it was like for a girl who grew up in Chicago to go south to a rural town of 5,000 people at the height of the Civil Rights movement: "I had to go to segregated things. I had to shop in Montgomery, Alabama. You could not try on clothes. You had to guess at things because black people were not allowed to try on clothes. You couldn't try on hats. I refused to use the water fountains in the bathrooms. I would just hold it rather than go to a colored washroom. But it was an amazing experience."

After receiving her Masters degree at the University of Iowa, she became the first woman to broadcast news in Chicago over WCFL radio. In 1970, after five years of doing hard news reporting, Simpson began her television career as a reporter at WMAQ in Chicago where she wanted to anchor. She was told that women did not want to hear other women on the air:

---

[2] Joe S. Foote, "Women Shut Out of Top Ten Network News Slots," press release, University News Service, Southern Illinois University, Carbondale, January 21, 1998.
[3] Ibid.

Carole Simpson, ABC News

I was told that white people didn't want to hear news from a black person. Now here comes the obstacles of what you can't do and what nobody likes. It was patently absurd because I'd always been told I had a good delivery. I had an authoritative delivery. I had the credentials. I had the education. I had the experience. How could somebody say that I would not be able to anchor? And then they said my enunciation was too perfect, that it was too clear and too precise. And I'm going, "Excuse me. Isn't this what this is all about?" Yet other black reporters in Chicago were told they sounded too ethnic. So, it was all the discriminatory efforts to keep us from the higher paying jobs, the top jobs, the jobs with more visibility. We were kind of window dressing. It became quite clear that we'd been hired so they could say they had one. But that was it. You can come this far but no further. We'll let you report but you can't anchor. So at WMAQ, I fought and fought and fought to be able to anchor and I finally got a chance to anchor on the weekends. It was okay, white people could hear somebody black give news on the weekend. It was 1972, the beginning of the women's movement. Now everybody's got to try to put a woman up there. Then I was a "two-for." I was black and a woman so I became a double token. But my emphasis was always to show, "Look, you're not hiring me because of what color I am or what my gender is. It's because I'm good. I'm a good anchor. . . ."

So the struggle began when I started with television in 1970 and has continued to this day. We are sitting here in 1996 and I tell you to this day, I am still battling. I thought it would end at some point, but it has not ended. I was sure it would have ended at this point, at my age and with my depth of experience, and it has not. I'm still fighting. As vigorously as I fought race and sex discrimination through the years, I will fight age discrimination.

In 1982 Carole Simpson was hired by ABC News and after 16 years in the business she found herself fighting roadblocks and the stigma of being an affirmative action hire: "So again it's this battle, battle, battle, battle to get on the air, to get the assignments, to get the opportunities. I knew that the squeaky wheel gets it. I knew early on that nobody was going to help me but me. I've never had mentors. Everything I had to do myself. I had to scratch and claw and beg and plead and cajole, everything short of compromising my principles and lying."

Kathy O'Hearn is the executive producer of the weekend news for ABC. While serving as Bureau chief in Los Angeles, she spoke about the events surrounding the video taped beating of Rodney King. When she first saw the tape she was horrified. The male producer who came in to do the piece looked at the tape and said, this is what happens out there. He said it was police work and it was not a story. O'Hearn relates how a Latino technical manager and a black cameraman who were in the newsroom at the time turned on their heels and said to the producer quite pointedly, "You just don't get it. You have no idea how different it is for us."

The cameraman Charles Pinkney told how he was frequently stopped by police on his drive home to Malibu where he lived because, what is a black man doing in Malibu? The technical manager, Burt Tapia, had also been stopped by the police because he was a dark-skinned Latino male. O'Hearn recalls:

> They were furious. They had never said anything like this in the newsroom, because it was always sort of a patina of getting along. But this case brought up the exact opportunity to hear all these different voices. I, as a white woman, certainly had never been discriminated against by police. So it was a fascinating exercise in seeing how important it was to hear from all these different voices in putting a piece together. To understand and put into perspective what happened to this man and what was right and wrong about it.

Racism is an undeniable part of American society. The need to have more ethnically diverse representation in the broadcasting profession was almost universally acknowledged by the women and men who were interviewed for this study. The difficulty remains in the outreach and the recruiting. Andrea Mitchell admits, "The most appalling situation of all involves race because we have been running back away from any kind of real diversity in this profession. Where I think there was a perceived sense of pressure in earlier decades, I don't think that anyone is trying hard enough to bring minorities into this profession. We all have our special programs of outreach. But it just seems absurd that as we sit here in 1996 that networks are still saying they can't find qualified people. I've been hearing the same thing for thirty years in this profession."

Amy Entelis is one of four vice-presidents at ABC news. She is in charge of recruitment and development of on-air talent. She considers herself the "talent scout" for the news division. She looks for talent for all of the ABC news broadcasts and bureaus around the world. Amy states that ten years ago, the lack of diversity in the news personnel was recognized and a recruiting strategy was started. But, the balance has not changed dramatically over the last 10 years. She states:

> We have a correspondent development program which I run which takes young correspondents usually from local stations or from newspapers or anywhere we find them in our own producer ranks and we develop them specifically for correspondent positions. We either put them in local stations or we train them under our own roof. This is a minority oriented program built from the recognition that we had to do more even on our own to develop people and that we couldn't necessarily just wait for people to pop out fully formed and ready for us.

This program was started in 1993 at ABC and in 3 years two people have risen to the rank of correspondent and three other people are moving forward in the pipeline. One of them is at the network and 2 are presently at local stations. The first person to go through this program at ABC was Michelle Norris who is a correspondent in the Washington Bureau covering education for the network. Norris came to television from a print background. She spent two years in a training program at the *Los Angeles Times* before going to work at the *Chicago Tribune*. She was then hired by the *Washington Post* where she covered education. One of her first assignments was a piece about a child growing up in a crack house. It was called "A Child of Crack" and it was published as a two-part series and it won several awards including the Livingston award. But, the residue from the scandal of Janet Cooke who received a Pulitzer Prize in 1981 for a story about an 8-year-old heroin addict that was proven to be a hoax, still walks the halls of the newspaper. The *Washington Post* returned the Pulitzer amidst extensive public humiliation. But, the memory of Janet Cooke still makes it very difficult for a number of African American women who followed in her path.

Norris admits to enduring all kinds of ribbing from people because she is African American. She also suffered certain indignities from the paper. She spent weeks with her 6-year-old crack child:

> I had a notebook full of interviews. I had pulled every possible piece of paper that you could pull on this child, his school records, a copy of his birth certificate. I mean, I had everything because I understood that the ghost of Janet Cooke was still very much alive in that newsroom. I made sure I documented everything. And we had also shot at least 70 rolls of film. . . . At one point the paper decided to send my

Michelle Norris, ABC News

editor out to physically view the child. As a reporter that's offensive.
But, at the same time, I understood why they were doing that—but
it hurt nonetheless."

Norris understands institutional racism and the need to deal with it.
At the *Washington Post* she talks about

a long line of very talented African American women who have left
the Post because they felt it was not a nourishing environment for
them. And in many cases they felt they were held to a double standard. . . . If Janet Cooke had been a white woman, I'm not sure that
they would have made the same kind of comparisons to white female
reporters who followed in her path. Unfortunately, it's all too easy

for people to make those kinds of comparisons. And that's one of the burdens that we, as African Americans, bear. I know when I come to work everyday, I can either open a door for someone who will follow behind me, or I can slam it shut if I don't do the best job I can possibly do. It's a burden. I don't mind carrying that burden because I think it's just a fact of life.

Norris speaks about the need in television to help identify people with potential and then provide the opportunity to allow them to develop television skills. The development programs at ABC attempt to attract talent from other media and provide them with the tools they need to work in television. "The good thing is that I was able to work with a voice coach, I was able to work with a single producer for a long period of time who really taught me television. I was able to learn television in a protected and controlled environment. So I wasn't out there making mistakes on World News. . . . The bad thing is, there's a certain stigma when you happen to be an African American woman who comes to the network through what many people would perceive as a side door."

Michelle Norris keeps a quote from Booker T. Washington in her desk that says, "Demonstrating success in a demanding field is the best challenge to prejudice." She says she has to look at it every so often to remind herself that you cannot change what people think but you can force them to challenge their assumption by doing the best job that you can do.

Michel McQueen is a 1980 graduate from Harvard College who also began her career in print journalism at the *Washington Post*. She is now a correspondent for ABC News. When she first went to look for an apartment after having been out of college for nine months, the landlord asked, "Where were you before you were at work?" She answered that she was in college. He said, "Where were you at college?" When she answered that she went to Harvard he demanded to see her diploma. McQueen says you have to handle the racism. "If you grow up with this, you either deal with it or you go crazy. And I'm not going to let these people make me crazy. So that's how I deal with it. I just basically say, this does not reflect on me, it reflects on them. It's just a reminder to me of how far we have to go in this country. Not just among people who are avowed bigots but among people who think of themselves as progressive but who clearly don't take the time to look in my face and see what I look like."

McQueen was surprised to learn how important it is for people of color to see others like themselves on television. She became aware of it only after her arrival at ABC News. She explains her experience:

One of the things that was surprising to me, was how important it is for people of color to see themselves on TV. I was not at all aware of this until I got here. I must tell you, it is very humbling some days. I was leaving a restaurant and a kid comes running after me. I don't know how old this kid was. He could have been nineteen, twenty. He comes over to me and says, "Can I take your picture? I want to be a journalist. Can I take my picture with you? This is the highlight of my week." Sometimes I wish it weren't that way, just because I feel like it's a measure of how far we have to go that it still means so much. It shouldn't mean that much. It doesn't mean that much to a white boy to see Chris Wallace on TV. He doesn't say to himself, "Maybe that means I can do that, too." He may, but it isn't quite so powerful. On the other hand, it's a tremendous source of strength like when you're going through issues with people and people are acting in an ignorant fashion. You say to yourself, "Wait a minute, I'm here because I have to be here so that somebody else won't have to go and do this." It's just my philosophy that every coin has two sides and every negative has a positive side to it. It's very important for people of color to see other people of color presenting themselves in an honorable fashion on television because there are so many images of us which are negative and degrading. So it is very important.

McQueen says she is constantly being confused with Gwen Ifill, Capitol Hill correspondent for NBC news. They look nothing alike. McQueen's attitude is that they are only looking at her skin color. It's an indignity that she must suffer. "We have such a legacy of racial tension in this country. Race plays a role in everything."

Gwen Ifill believes that it is imperative to learn early not to take everything personally. She acknowledges that in the visual world of television people take into account that she is a black woman. It is just a fact of life:

Sometimes that helps you and sometimes that hurts you. If it hurts me, I don't want to know about it. You can always suspect. In 1996 no one's going to say we're not giving you that job because you're black. I do know that at other networks and in other settings, they do treat us as interchangeable. "Oh, they have a black person, well we don't need another black person." As long as they have me, they don't really feel the need to more than one. They feel they've done their diversity job by making sure there's one visible face. I hate that because it underestimates not only me, but the people around me. You travel the country and you watch the little anchor teams in every city in America. There's one man, one woman, one black, one white. That's just the way it happens.

Some of those things are offensive and some are a way of life and you just decide whether you can deal with it or not. I have a few close friends who have made this move from print to television in the last several years. We compare different networks and we compare notes a lot about what we call our "TV days." You know, "I'm having a TV day," that kind of thing. We know that means that something has happened which would only happen in television, that is unique to this very strange kind of medium and if you talk about it, it makes you feel better.

Ifill shares her candid views of racism in America and the role it plays on those women and men who work in the media:

America is not at the point yet where race is an irrelevant factor, either for the good or the ill. And, as long as people are still struggling with what their attitudes are toward people of color, what their attitudes are toward gender, it's going to play itself out in the workplace. That's not a terrible, horrible thing. It's just that we're still in the process in television, and in every other industry, coming to grips with how to do that. I think that we're moving slowly, and every now and then I'm shocked by how slowly actually it is. But, I was raised in a family which believed very much in the possibility of positive change and uplift. So if I ever abandon my optimism about the ability of America to make itself a better place, I wouldn't be who I am.

Essentially, we are all constrained by the kind of society we are in. One of the things is that we are in a society where it is very, very difficult to be a black male. There's just no question there are disadvantages all along the way. People in hiring positions still remain intimidated by the black male. Even men who have succeeded, who play by all of the rules. So there is no question that it's a tougher row to hoe a lot of the time. It's hard enough as a black female sometimes, to prove yourself and not to be a threatening factor. So, it's difficult for me on occasion; it's got to be difficult for black men all of the

Gwen Ifill, NBC News

time. And there's always got to be tempering that goes on in the way a black man carries himself, the way he functions, his aspirations. Because people will just as quickly say that a smart black man is uppity as they will say that a woman is arrogant instead of assertive. If you decide it's important for you to achieve in that milieu, then you adjust to that. If you decide it's not important, then you do something else.

The local stereotypes that are woven throughout American society often place the African American male under even more pressures and misunderstandings than women. The contemporary image of black American men is usually that of a street thug or an athlete. The portrayal of the black American man is rarely positive. He is almost never seen using his intellect. This makes it very difficult for an African American man with intelligence and ambition to break into television. He must work to overcome ingrained preconceptions and prejudices. He must also fight to overcome the fears he engenders. Black American males have been attributed a power that is viewed as fearsome by many of the white majority. This affects the hiring and firing of black men in the media. The roles of African Americans in our society are conscriptive and those who attempt to create a role outside what is accepted and prescribed require fierce determination and patience. One must fight the prejudice, one must fight the preconceptions, one usually suffers and one does not necessarily succeed.

Bryant Gumbel is considered to be the most prominent African American male in television news. After 15 years as anchor of the *Today* show on NBC, Bryant stepped down and moved to CBS where he developed his own news magazine. He has always been outspoken on the role race plays in society: "The facts of race in America are desultory. We're building a permanent underclass. I see an absence of willingness of people to accept others, and I see an increase in hostility among people who certainly couldn't be classified as racists."[4] His evaluation of the state of television news and its employment of African Americans is summed up with the statement "Anytime you can say it hasn't gotten better, you can say it's gotten worse."[5]

Bryant Gumbel answers his critics who accuse him of being arrogant by declaring that "in this society, unfortunately, there are people who have problems with black men who are intelligent and proud and ambitious and aggressive and who don't stand around grinning and shucking and jiving all the time. It means you must be angry or upset about something. Well, I don't smile all the time. But I'm happy."[6]

The most fundamental issues of racism affect not only those who get hired but the assignments they are given and how frequently they appear on the premier news broadcasts. There is little disagreement that white males predominate on the network evening news programs. However, the 1995 study of ABC, NBC, and CBS evening newscasts conducted by Professor Joe S. Foote at Southern Illinois University, showed a minority on the list of the top ten news reporters for the first time ever. Bill Whitaker, an African-American reporting for CBS television, ranked second in the number of stories reported on-air. Most of

---

[4] Cary Verne, "Beyond Today," *Los Angeles Times Magazine,* January 2, 1997, p. 2.
[5] Ibid.
[6] Alan Carter, "Black by Popular Demand," *Emmy,* February 1997, p. 29.

the 140 stories focused on the O. J. Simpson murder trial. The person to finish in first place, David Bloom, a correspondent for NBC also reported on the events of the Simpson trial. The top woman was Rita Braver who then covered the White House for CBS. She commanded the third spot in the rankings.

The dominant media attention to the O. J. Simpson trial did make 1995 an aberrant year. Nonetheless, five minorities finished in the top 50 while fourteen made it into the top 100. It is interesting to note that according to Professor Foote who has been charting news trends since 1983, as recently as in 1991, minorities were conspicuously absent from the top 50. An analysis of Professor Foote's 1997 tracking reveals that NBC's Jim Avila, who is Hispanic, ranked fifth among the top 100 correspondents. CBS's Bill Whitaker took twenty-ninth place. A closer look at this study reveals the NBC network had nine minority reporters (17%) who contributed stories to the evening news; ABC had 11 minority reporters (16%); CBS had 10 minority correspondents (21%). Overall, there were 21 African Americans; 5 Asians, and 5 Hispanic reporters that comprised the network evening news corps.[7]

So while the visibility of minority broadcasters is improving, the fundamental struggles toward equality remain. The need to consciously make the faces of reporters and anchors reflect the diversity of America is critical. The positions of responsibility behind the camera also demand quality people of different ethnic and racial backgrounds. The continuing dominance of the white American male must be challenged and changed.

Dave Marash sees women beginning to advance to positions of real responsibility and power behind the camera but not minorities: "I see the old pattern still holding true that the opportunities for on camera highly visible jobs is greater than the opportunity that I see behind the camera. I have not seen a generation of black, Latino, Asian producers becoming seniors and becoming executive producers and moving up the management ranks. I know that is true at ABC and I'm pretty sure it is true at the other four networks including Fox and CNN."

Gloria Rojas was a street reporter for WABC-TV and an early graduate of the Columbia University School of Journalism's Minority Program. She left the news profession in 1991 after 23 years. Rojas believes racism is an integral part of American society that has not changed very

---

[7] Foote, "Women Shut Out."

much over the years: "We still have our tokens. Nobody has made it big who's an Hispanic. Yes there are some blacks who have made it big, but not in the numbers they should have. I mean, I can name the African Americans and the minute you start being able to name somebody, then you know that you don't have enough people." But Rojas acknowledges that improvements have taken place: "I used to be assigned strictly Hispanic stories when I first started and that changed. I remember thinking that if they hire another Hispanic, they'll have to let me go, since who needs two. That's changed. Sure it's better. I'm not patting myself on the back, but it's better because a little girl named Mina Morales could turn on a TV and see me and know that it's possible for her."

The number of Hispanics that appear with any regularity remains woefully low. It is an acute point of contention among those who number themselves among the few. Elizabeth Vargas states:

> There are very, very, very few Hispanics at the network level, much less Hispanic women. There is no excuse for it. The networks have been slower than local stations to, I think, have their on-air talent be representative of the population. Although, you still will turn on some local stations in some markets and see three men anchoring a newscast, all three of them white. The networks need to do a better job to make the people that you see delivering the news more representative of the audiences watching them.

It can prove to be beneficial out in the field if you are both a woman and a minority. Phyllis Haynes comments: "Yes, I think there were stories that I covered because I was a short, brown female, that I got to walk into some buildings because they thought I was a secretary and I could get behind the scenes because no one thought I could possibly be a reporter. I got close to Geraldine Ferraro that way a few times because no one else could walk into the buildings. But I could walk in. There have been some advantages in terms of covering stories. I'm nonthreatening. Women are nonthreatening most of the time."

Wendy Takuda was an anchor and reporter for NBC4 in Los Angeles at the time of our interview. She now anchors for KRON in San Francisco. She remembers seeing an Asian American woman on television in Seattle. When she would appear on-air, Wendy's Dad would call the family into the front room to watch her:

> It was such an amazing thing to see an Asian American on the news—and a female. It was not until I saw her that I realized a career

like that might be a possibility. Had I not seen that first wave of people of color and women showing up, I don't know that I would have thought of it. For me, given my background, to come up with a career choice like that is something akin to telling your parents you're going to the moon. . . . At the time I became a reporter, which at this point is 20 years ago, there were still only a hand full of Asians in the whole country doing what we do. So, for my family, it was extraordinary. Remember, my parents met in prison camp. You don't come from that kind of background and easily work your way into the fabric of America.

Takuda discusses the dichotomy between the atmosphere of the newsroom and her own cultural training: "As a Japanese American female I was raised to be polite. I was raised to respect authority. I was raised not to bring attention to myself or to my family, not to ask a lot of obnoxious questions, not to be pushy. Well, put that in the newsroom and think about how long you'd last."

The discrepancy between the number of Asian American men working in the television news business and the number of women exposes the depth of cultural stereotypes affecting both sexes. The Asian male is portrayed much more negatively in the media. The stereotype of the Asian man is usually a gang member or a "geek." Both are negative kinds of images and fail to provide a positive role model. The Asian woman is stereotypically subservient, exotic, obedient, beautiful, and nonthreatening. The images are powerful and play a major role in institutional racism.

The hope for more effective representation is the knowledge that if the newsroom does not reflect and represent the interests and needs of the population it serves, the population may not choose to view that newscast. It is important for minorities and women to know that viewers generally want to look at people who look as they do. Thus, the market has the power to dictate to television executives that the newscast must have people on air who represent the people watching their screens or risk declining viewership. The pressure of regulatory laws is less formidable and dependable than the bottom line. Broadcast management will work harder to achieve diversity if it will be good for the pocketbook. This will not be a decision made out of the goodness of their hearts.

8
Datelines and Deadlines

Inherent differences between men and women, we have come to appreciate, remain cause for celebration, but not for denigration of the members of either sex or for artificial constraints on an individual's opportunity.

RUTH BADER GINSBURG,
SUPREME COURT JUSTICE, 1996

The role of the broadcast journalist to bear witness to history as it is happening brings with it a tremendous opportunity as well as an intense burden. The special motivations of a journalist must give them opportunity to gather and communicate information which affects people's lives and the decisions they make. The heart and breath of a functioning democracy demands an informed citizenry. Without adequate access to complete and unbiased information, the future of all peoples and their fundamental freedoms are at risk.

The journalists I spoke with understand and appreciate the burdens of the responsibilities inherent in their profession. Many have spent their entire career attempting to bring home to audiences in the United States the defining moments of the world we live in. With professional lives that often span two and three decades, it is both significant and revealing to learn what kinds of stories or assignments provided the greatest sense of satisfaction.

Heather Allan, NBC's Los Angeles bureau chief went back to her South African homeland for the release of Nelson Mandela and again for the presidential election that followed soon after. Allan views the coverage of the election of Nelson Mandela as the highlight of her career:

> I want to shake Americans and say, "You don't know how precious your vote is." When I went home there was such a vibe. In a country where there had been so much animosity and bitterness, there was such a feeling of hope. To see people queuing up to vote for hours, black and white, women who had been their maids and who brought up their children, waiters, miners, everybody just queuing up to vote. Then when they raised the new flag, there was no bitterness. I covered the Philippines when the Marcos were deposed and when Corazon Aquino got in. I covered the elections in Israel. Yet I would say this was the most thoroughly satisfying story. It was a good news story. There was nothing bad about it.

This same news event was singled out by Carol Jenkins who was sent over to South Africa by WNBC-TV in New York. Jenkins describes arriving into the country just as Nelson Mandela was released from prison and the impact it made on her: "I just don't think I could ever do anything that would top that because as far as I was concerned, that was the story of three decades."

Bob Clark has been a journalist for forty-eight years and with ABC for thirty-five years. By what he calls "some sort of tragic coincidence in my life," he was present at both the assassination of John Fitzgerald Kennedy and of Robert Kennedy: "I was the ABC man in Dallas covering John Kennedy and was the network pool man that day and for some years have been the only surviving member of the network pool. I was in the pool car and that meant we went speeding on to the hospital with Kennedy." He remembers being about the sixth car in the procession: "That position put us almost directly under the window, so we heard the shots very clearly from where we were and also the pool car was the only press car that went on to the hospital. I still find people that are astonished to hear this because the photographers jumped out at Dealey

Heather Allan, NBC News, with President Nelson Mandela

Plaza and so there were no photographers. But the four reporters in the pool car were permitted to go up and stand right over Kennedy and stare down at him."

"In 1968," he continues, "I was ABC's Bobby Kennedy correspondent during the campaign and was with Bobby when he was assassinated and went through the same experience. Later I had to stand over Bobby and decide whether he was still alive or not."

Bob Clark still feels he has a serious obligation to go through the myriad of documents that have been released by the government with the hope that he will uncover things that will shed a little more light on the truth of the JFK assassination and help eliminate what he views as the ridiculous conspiracy theories that have emerged over the years. Basically, Clark strongly believes the findings of the Warren Commission were correct. The Commission "did some dumb things in the way it conducted the investigation," he acknowledges. "But in the end, its findings have withstood the test of thirty-three years quite well. And yet, we continue to get polls that show something like 65 percent or so of the American people feel there was a conspiracy behind the assassination."

Of Oliver Stone's film on JFK, Bob Clark made these candid comments: "The two words I apply to the movie and to Oliver Stone are *absurd* and *contemptible*. Absurd because it picks up the wildest of the conspiracy theories and contemptible because it slanders many American leaders. He just flails about at Lyndon Johnson and the Warren Commission and the military and everybody that supported the Vietnam War in any way. And it's a contemptible thing to so grossly distort history."

David Brinkley looks back on a long and distinguished career in broadcasting but selects the televised coverage of President Kennedy's funeral as his finest contribution: "Spending three days and nights with the Kennedy funeral, I think we really saved the country from some kind of crisis. I think we calmed them down. Kept them informed minute by minute by minute. I'm very proud of that."

Walter Cronkite does not limit himself to a single story but rather talks of a category of things over his illustrious career:

> There's great satisfaction in discerning the need for a particular story, developing it and having it prove to be influential. An example of that was our two Watergate stories at the time when the Watergate scandals were almost passing out of people's consciousness. They were almost forgetting about it and we helped bring it back by the dedication of the evening newscast primarily to recounting the real horror of that scandal. The attempt to steal our democratic rights from us by a sitting president and his cohorts. There was the breaking story that you handle well. The assassination of President Kennedy would come under that case. There's the story that goes on to have major influence, and that was our story in which we interviewed Sadat and Begin and in effect brought them together. There's the story that you prepare for which has great immense historical interest and you and your team handle well, and that sort of thing was the landing of a man on the moon.

Many journalists are forced to face issues and situations that are difficult to live with and create lasting scars. Sheila MacVicar speaks candidly about the burdens of those women and men who work overseas:

> I think the reason why I became a journalist and why I remain a journalist is that there is the vague hope that you can make a difference. And on those stories where you think that you have seen movement of policy or recognition of a problem or seen some kind of change, I think those are the things that you walk away from feeling

better. But there is also, sometimes, an obligation to bear witness and to just go over it and over it and over it again and sometimes you feel a real obligation. To a certain extent, I feel that about Bosnia. It may sound insanely silly, but I feel real guilt that for two years of the Bosnian war I was doing a magazine show that had no interest in Bosnia while there were horrific atrocities taking place. And occasionally, that really bothers me.

The story that gives Susan Zirinsky enormous satisfaction as a human being is her coverage of the democratic uprising in China:

I think covering Tiananmen Square and the evolution of the student movement from marches and demonstrations to a revolution and the effort of gaining control of your life. Because democracy was a different phase for them than anything we understand. It was an amazingly fulfilling experience. The reason China and the students were so important was because it was being on the ground floor of this revolution. To this day I have remained friends with several of the student leaders of the Tiananmen Square event, whatever you want to call it—massacre. Several are in this country. I see them quite regularly and it was an amazing story to be a part of.

The awesome power of television is demonstrated by the story done by Kathy McManus on Sarajevo for the ABC program *Turning Point*. It involves a girl named Delila who was then seventeen years old and living in Sarajevo with her parents. She had been standing in a water line during the war and the Serbs shot a few grenades into the water line as people waited. Delila's parents ended up essentially being decapitated in front of her. She threw herself over her little brother and saved his life. As a journalist, McManus was allowed to go in and out of the war zone, but none of the residents could leave. McManus describes how she began to feel an attachment toward Delila:

I would bring her things, sneak in stuff because we weren't allowed to bring things in. I would sneak in makeup, lacy underwear, magazines, coffee—all the stuff that a seventeen-year-old girl any place else on the planet would have. Every time I came back she would be waiting in the snow, or she would be lugging wood up the hill or something like that to see what I brought her. Fast forward, the program airs and a lot of people want to help and a U.S. senator got special permission to get the Pentagon plane in and rush her to the airport. She now lives in the United States. She's totally fluent in English. She's got a job. She's engaged to be married to a guy who saw her on *Turning Point* and found her and they fell in love.

McManus admits that she does not believe there would have been such a strong bond if Delila was not a woman. She declares, "There was this horrible unfairness that I, a woman, could come in and out of this war zone and go back to my nice house in New York and not have anybody shooting me, but she could do nothing." McManus found television an amazingly powerful tool and a force for helpful change.

Carole Simpson is confident that she has made a difference through the stories she has done on family and social issues:

> I've done stories on families that were in destitute conditions and people respond and send them money and send them help. I did a piece on a man who couldn't get a job, fifty-four years old. He'd been in middle management and got caught in corporate downsizing. He was out of work for a year and a half. He walked streets in the rain going to the employment office and cut out ads in the paper. He got a job. The public can fixate on one person and respond. It's hard for them to see all of the people out there. But you're making a difference.

For Simpson, nothing is more rewarding than doing stories that touch people, that make them think and make them feel and make them respond.

Richard Threlkeld believes the most significant story of his career was the war in Vietnam:

> I think for all of us, the journalists of my age, the Vietnam War was a seminal event as it was for a couple of million American GIs. We were all, most of us, very young. We'd come from fairly sheltered existences and all of a sudden you got shot at and, in my case, spent three years there and it just completely changed your life, your outlook. You got shot at a lot and watched people die and saw this crazy war. All you have to do is see the Francis Ford Coppola movie [*Apocalypse Now*] and you know what we're talking about. I think that changed us all in so many ways. Marriages broke up, people went off in different directions. Some people never quite got over it. So, I think for those of us who started in journalism in the sixties, that was probably the major event in our lives.

Sam Donaldson believes the best work he has ever done in his expansive broadcasting career involved a man few people ever heard of:

His name was Eric Priebke. I found him in Barilache, Argentina, eighty years old then. Just a kindly looking old grandfather who I interviewed on the street for about fifteen minutes because in World War II he was Captain Priebke in the SS, the number-two Gestapo chief in Rome. He helped organize the massacre of 335 Italian civilians and he tortured many people in Gestapo headquarters in the last year of the war. The documentary evidence is overwhelming that he helped deport six to seven thousand Jews to their death in the death camps. Now, today as we speak, he's on trial in Rome having been extradited after a year and a half. There's no death penalty in Italy so he's on trial for life imprisonment. And they're going to convict him in my judgment—because we found him and because we brought him to American television and he discussed openly his crimes, which he did not see as a crime. Now, the younger generations think I should fall back on Gorbachev or Sadat or Reagan. But to my generation, World War II is still one of the seminal events in our lives and in history. Even though I was too young to fight in it and even though I lost no family to World War II. But all my life, in the movies I've been watching him just following orders and here he's telling me, "Well, I was just following orders, those were our orders." We argued about it and debated it. So, at the moment, always waiting for tomorrow to come, that's the work I'm proudest of.

When I spoke with Diane Sawyer she described a recent story on day care centers that brought her significant satisfaction: "It was the first one that has been done in which we showed you what it was like for children in day care centers where there are too few adults, which is roughly half the day care centers in this country. And how terrifying it is, and how the children have nothing to do, and a child lighting a match by a stove. Really heartbreaking treatment of children, which you never would have known if we hadn't been able to get cameras in and show you."

Connie Chung looks back to her interview with the captain of the *Exxon Valdez:* "I got the one and only interview for television with Captain Hazelwood who ran the *Exxon Valdez* aground in Alaska. He didn't do any interviews before or after. I did the only one and it was of great interest, obviously, because no one had ever heard from him and no one knew what he would say."

An exclusive interview gives Chung great satisfaction:

The one that we are all trying to get away from is Barbara Walters, because she's probably already nailed it, because she is the best. So that would be one great accomplishment, not only to get the interview, but to somehow have gotten it away from Barbara. Pure luck. Serendipity if you get it because Barbara will always get the exclusive interview of the person of the day or the person of the year. The person that everyone wants to get, Barbara will get it because she is the most tenacious, the most dedicated, the most persuasive, the most attentive to the interviewee. She knows exactly how many times to call, how many times to write without overdoing it. She is extraordinary.

Katie Couric is also ready to acknowledge the pleasure of getting the first available interview, particularly "if you beat out people like Barbara Walters. That doesn't happen very often, but when you do, it's wonderful." Couric speaks of the interview she did with George Bush, off the cuff, as a defining moment in her career: "I was pleased that it went so well and I was able to pull it off because, believe me, I saw my career flash before my eyes. I was so afraid I was going to say, 'So, let's talk about Ranger. What's your favorite room at the White House? What's your favorite food?' You know when you get in that situation and you have to keep doing rapid-fire questions, you envision yourself drawing a complete blank. So, I think that was a very important moment for me professionally."

Katie Couric is an example of a woman who appears to be very feminine and full of spark but who is also a serious journalist capable of being tough and direct. Her interview with presidential candidate Bob Dole on the *Today* show is a case in point. She pointedly asked him about his belief that tobacco was not necessarily addictive. Dole's testy response and flare-up in response to Couric made front-page headlines and underscored the reality that strength can be covered in lace gloves.

Judy Woodruff proudly speaks of her coverage of the International Women's Conference held in Beijing in 1995. She requested that CNN send her there: "We did a half-hour report out of there for eleven days that was seen four times a day internationally and once a day in the

Judy Woodruff, CNN, at China's Great Wall

United States. I can't think of anything I've done in my recent career that's made me more proud, because we were the only American television news organization there, covering those issues of importance not just to women but to men in the United States and all over the world. We treated it seriously. We covered the issues and I feel very, very proud of it. There was nobody else there doing it.

Judy Woodruff is gratified to be one of the cofounders of the International Women's Media Foundation:

> We had an idea that is an enduring one and that is women in journalism around the world have something in common with one another. You cannot have a free press unless women are part of it. We are trying to share that message with women journalists in other parts of the world who, believe me, do not have it as well as we women in the United States do. We think we have it tough. We have it so good compared to what women in the developing world, Latin America, Asia, even Europe have to put up with. Sisters of the world unite, if you will. It's a wonderful organization and I think it has made a difference and it will continue to make a difference.

This outstanding organization continues to focus the spotlight on the valor and crucial work of women journalists around the globe.

The most satisfying story Lynn Sherr selects from her long career is one that she did for 20/20 about a woman in British Columbia who runs a clinic that treats anorexics:

> We went out there to do a segment for 20/20 and wound up doing the whole hour. Then we did a follow-up. The response was unbelievable. She says we saved lives because of doing the piece, getting people help, telling people what to do. I'm very proud to say that we won a Peabody for it—and I'm very cynical about most awards in this business. I think most awards are given to get a free speaker and to get someone to show up and buy a table. The Peabody is the one that counts and I was just thrilled that we were recognized. This was a story that I had almost no interest in. I figured we'd all done anorexia to death, pardon the pun. I didn't think I had anything new to contribute. Then I met this woman who was almost like a saint, who treats anorexics and treats them with extraordinary care. And the public responded. So that story just had amazing impact.

In 1988, while Pat Harvey, anchor of KCAL news in Los Angeles, was working in Chicago at WGN, one of her investigative reports caused a change in legislation. For Harvey this was more meaningful than any award she could receive because it facilitated a change that benefited people's lives. The story involved pap smears:

> Lab technicians were misreading slides and women were dying of cancer because their slides were being misdiagnosed. They were misreading them because they read too many. They were getting paid per slide and their managers were telling them the more slides you read, the more money you can make. This was a tremendous detriment to women and to families everywhere. As it turned out, enough people were dying so that the hospitals were looking into this. The more we checked different cities, examined law suits, and talked to people, it became obvious that it should change. As a result, I went to Capitol Hill and testified. The governor came in and signed legislation on the set. We opened their eyes to what was going on.

The continuous coverage of tragic stories often takes a toll on a reporter's life. Gloria Rojas says, "I can't tell you how many coffins and how many weeping mothers and how many airline accidents and explosions I saw over twenty-three years. There's a lot of horror and I was part of it and it took a tremendous toll on me and my family."

But the one story that remains her favorite is about a little boy with muscular dystrophy who lived on the fourteenth floor of a building in the New York City projects:

> His mother wrote me a letter that said she was trying to get off that high apartment so that her boy could go to school. The elevators in the project were always broken and she was at her wits end because she had tried everything she could. She'd even had the firemen come when the elevator was broken to take him down. They were happy to do it once or twice but they said, "You know we just can't continue to do this kind of stuff."
>
> So we went with our cameras, climbed up to see this boy. I said to him, "What's your problem. Lots of kids don't want to go to school and would be happy." And he said, "No, school is so important to me." He said, "I don't have a lot of friends but when I go to school I have a wonderful time. My friends are there, my teachers love me. I need to go to school." And I said, "Well, how would you solve this?"

He said, "They should give us an apartment on the first floor." We put that on the air at six o'clock. This woman had been trying to get a first-floor apartment for years. In two days' time, three days to complete all the paperwork, they had an apartment on the first floor. And I realized how powerful a tool this was, to take the plight of a little boy whose name was Juan Potero. I will never forget, to take his plight in front of the City of New York and embarrass somebody who wasn't doing their job. That gave me the greatest satisfaction.

Often opportunity knocks at very inopportune moments. Norma Quarles, CNN news correspondent, tells a most unique story that occurred when she transferred back to the New York bureau of NBC as a network correspondent. She went into the hospital for elective surgery:

I was in my hospital room when I got a call. It was on a Tuesday night. I was supposed to be operated on at seven o'clock in the morning. I got a call from the League of Women Voters in Washington. I had been selected as one of the panelists for the vice-presidential debate between George Bush and Geraldine Ferraro. It was taking place the next night. What to do? So I said, "I'm in the hospital." They said, "Have you been medicated?" I said, "No, I haven't been medicated." And they said, "Well, will you come to Philadelphia for the debate?"

Well, one of the reasons I needed surgery was that I had something pressing on my bladder so I couldn't last much longer than an hour without having to go to the bathroom. So the first thing I want to know is how long is the debate? It's live TV in front of one hundred million people and it's an hour and a half. It's ninety minutes. It's thirty minutes longer than I've been accustomed to going without going to the bathroom. That's one of the first things. The other things are all the usual things you have to think about among, "What am I going to wear? What do I do about my hair? What do I do about makeup?" So immediately I called NBC and I said, "Can you get me somebody to do these things? I've been selected."

And they indeed sent people down. They sent people to Philadelphia. I had a friend drive me from the hospital in Englewood, New Jersey, to my home to pick up some clothes and then we drove to Philadelphia and got there at one o'clock in the morning. I stayed up in the hotel room until about five o'clock in the morning. I also had

NBC give me research materials. Going over research material so that I could formulate questions for the debate which was going on live the next morning. The meetings were starting at seven o'clock in the morning so I had about two hours sleep. But I kept having this thought in the back of my head. A hundred million people are going to be watching. . . . It was daunting to say the least. We were given a glass of water and I was told don't drink, just wet my tongue, which is what I did. I went to the bathroom right before we went on stage and I never drank any water. I made it through the ninety minutes and it was okay. It was scary as hell, but it was okay.

The broadcast journalist regularly confronts the absolute best and the absolute worst of the human condition. Rose Ann Scamardella remembers the first inauguration she covered. The president was Jimmy Carter. Scamardella recalls her emotions: "I cried through the whole thing. The granddaughter of immigrants was in the first row of the inauguration and talked to presidents. Just think of it. What an incredibly exciting job!"

Judy Muller is particularly pleased with her work during the O. J. Simpson trial:

I think that I really did a hell of a job condensing and distilling large amounts of material and making them understandable and giving them context in terms of more than just a gossipy trial. I think I framed it in sociological issues of race. I think I helped the public understand better some real issues that came out of that trial. I'm proud of the earthquake coverage that I did. This was more of an internal pride because I've always worried that when it came to the crunch of real disaster, that I would panic and crumble. This place was a mess. I had to get a neighbor to help me get out of the door, there was so much debris. All these walls were separated from the ceiling by about an inch. It was pretty scary. But I got dressed. I managed to find two earrings scattered on the floor that matched. I found my computer somewhere. I got out the door, got in my car and was on the air by six in the morning that day.

Judy Muller was satisfied to prove that even in a disaster situation she was capable of responding as a total professional. She went for days without sleep reporting on the aftermath of the disastrous Northridge earthquake, an event that so many southern Californians will always remember with such horror.[1]

For Tom Brokaw, who has a brilliant career that spans more than thirty years of broadcasting history, it is events from 1989 that will remain with him the longest:

> The collapse of communism. The interview with Mikhael Gorbachev standing there the night the Berlin Wall came down. The Tiananmen Square aftermath. That whole period of time when the shape of the world changed fundamentally. Now prior to that, I covered Watergate and the resignation of Richard Nixon and that is right there with those events. But I suppose, in terms of how the world will be remembered in the closing days of the twentieth century, the death of communism and the freedom of Eastern Europe and the brief but shining democracy movement in China will probably linger longer than the others.

As society has changed, so has the way we look at the world. As women have gained a stronger voice in our culture, we have begun to see the emergence of issues of parenting, schooling, gender, affirmative action, and health care. When women's voices raised these kinds of questions, American television values responded. The political and social issues that are critically significant to an understanding and appreciation of the world we live in, these were carried to the forefront by the exceptional women who fought to be seen and heard on the airwaves. Women compose more than half of the national population. Not only must they participate in the events of the world, they must also have the opportunity to help define public discourse.

---

[1] The Northridge earthquake struck at 4:31 A.M. on January 17, 1994. The damage exceeded $350 million.

9

Sisterhood and Support

> I myself have never been able to find out precisely what feminism is: I only know that people call me a feminist whenever I express sentiments that differentiate me from a doormat.
>
> REBECCA WEST (1892–1983)

The television news business is difficult and intensely competitive, but there is a very strong bond that exists today among the women who have shared experiences and who have struggled to climb the ladder of success. Women who have gained prominence in broadcasting can understand and relate to each other's experiences and conflicts. These advances are a result of hard-fought battles and the courage of those women who waged the war for advancement and greater equality on the playing field.

Sylvia Chase, ABC news correspondent, was in the first wave of women in television news who helped open the doors for those who followed. It was a formidable task. Chase was deeply involved in organizing the women at CBS in the early seventies when she was working there in the network news division. She recalls how the women who worked for the executives in the television network came to the news-women and asked for their help in organizing their struggles over the menial duties they were being given, like making coffee. In the beginning these were the issues to be dealt with. Chase was asked to head the group. She says, "I did do that even though I felt it would be in great peril to my own career." She remembers chairing the group that went to Arthur Taylor's office, then president of CBS. She did it because she was asked: "It was troublesome to me, but I carried out my duty because I realized that if opportunities for women were not opened up in the tele-vision industry, that eventually my goose would be cooked. I would have preferred that somebody else would have been willing to stand up and say, 'Yes, I will help organize.' I was the only on-air correspondent who was willing to do it and was willing to be public about it. But I've never regretted that I did that."

Sylvia Chase has remained an outstanding journalist who fights for her story and strives to bring out the real facts of important issues. But the obstacles remain and the task is still not easy to face.

Chase went on to speak about the need for continuing solidarity and support among women in broadcasting:

I got an award from the National Women's Political Caucus at Radcliffe. And I stood up and I said, "You know, all through the years the awards that have always meant the most are the ones from women. I wanted to go to Radcliffe, but my father didn't want me to go because he was afraid that I would get the idea that I should have a career. Well, too bad, 'Dad! Look at this,'" I said, holding this award up. And I just feel these institutions still need to be shaken by women. And I think women are stronger today than they were back then. We've had more experience with the men in these halls and in these conference rooms. I think we're more confident of our own strength. We are more confident of our own abilities and less likely to think, "Well, I'm a woman and therefore they won't consider me." I think the young women today don't have that feeling. So I think that solidarity is just essential and I hope we don't loose it.

With the growing influx of women into news broadcasting, it was becoming obvious to those women who had entered the field that they were frozen at a certain level. They were let in the door, but they were unable to rise up the ranks or win the most visible assignments.

Carole Simpson was one of five women correspondents working at

Sylvia Chase, ABC News

the ABC Washington Bureau in the mid-eighties. She noticed that the women did not get along. There was no camaraderie. In fact, says Simpson, "What I was beginning to see at ABC was an effort to pit us against each other." So Simpson began talking to Sheilah Kast and Susan King who were working there as well. Simpson remembers saying: "This is a bad situation here. We're not going anywhere. We don't have the top beats. If you look at *World News Tonight,* it's all white males who have the Congress, who have the White House, who have the State Department, Pentagon, and Supreme Court. We're all General Assignment. This is wrong. It's now 1984."

They decided to meet at Susan King's house to have dinner and talk. Simpson recalls, "I'll never forget she had a chicken walnut casserole that was delicious. We had salad and we had white wine. There were about 12 of us and we sat around the table and it was really intended as a kind of social thing. Let's get to know each other better. It turned into, I have to use this word, it was a bitch session. We all had stories of things that had happened to us that we didn't even realize."

Simpson stated that after spending between six and seven hours talking, the realization came that they shared a common problem: "Our common problem was the men. And it's not the men because they were men, but it was the old boys' network that was operating."

This was the time when Ronald Reagan had been elected President and there was a climate in the country in which the equal rights amendment was at a dead standstill and affirmative action was no longer an effective tool for meaningful change. So without national leadership and new legislation, Simpson and the other women decided that if any change was to occur, they would have to confront management. They began to meet monthly and recognized they shared a common plight, a common goal and that they had to work together on this to effect change.

They decided to compile statistical evidence. Simpson explains how they chose to do a complete content analysis of every broadcast at ABC News in order to learn how many women were appearing on each broadcast:

> Now you have to remember at this time there were no women foreign correspondents, no women in top management, no women vice presidents, no women bureau chiefs, no women who were senior producers of any of our broadcasts. This is 1984, so you've got a good ten years when women started coming into the business in larger numbers and they are not anywhere in terms of making decisions. I found this horrendous because with more than half the population female, you would have to assume that probably half our audience is female, and what they're getting is a totally male, totally white, totally upper-middle-class view of America.

Simpson reminded me that one of the reasons she entered the field of journalism was her desire "to change the world." To present news with no female or minority input was not acting in the public interest and not fulfilling the industry's professional responsibility. So as the evidence mounted, she and the other women became angrier over the wrongs that faced them.

The opportunity to confront management arrived when all the women correspondents were invited by Roone Arledge, then president of ABC News, to come to New York to have lunch at corporate headquarters in celebration of Barbara Walters' winning the Silver Satellite

Award from American Women in Radio and Television. Leonard Gol-
denson, the founder of ABC, was to be present. It provided the perfect
opportunity to have all management together. Carole Simpson was chosen to be the spokesperson for the group. Simpson's husband, a vice
president of a computer software company in Washington, D.C., col-
lated the data and printed a packet of graphs. There in black and white
was the compelling evidence: numbers of women in top management,
zero; bureau chiefs, zero; senior producers in broadcast, zero.

Simpson describes the experience:

> I'm a nervous wreck. We are at the Westbury Hotel and I had pre-
> pared about a ten-minute presentation. I had written it and then
> memorized it so that I could gesture and walk and move. I started
> getting a panic attack. It was ten-thirty in the morning. Sheilah Kast
> and Rita Flynn were in my room. I'm saying, "I'm not going to be
> able to do this. I'm a nervous wreck." And they ordered me a glass of
> wine at ten-thirty in the morning to calm me down. It's like you've
> got to do this. We're all counting on you.

Barbara Walters did not know anything about this effort. In retrospect, Simpson feels this was a mistake and that she should have been
told. But she had to leave the luncheon early because 20/20 was on that
night. Simpson by now had gotten over her fear and was waiting for an
appropriate moment to speak. Roone Arledge stood up and gave Barbara Walters a toast. Simpson continues her description of this pivotal
meeting:

> We were all dressed up. We looked so pretty. We wore lovely suits
> and coats. It was May 9, 1985, I'll never forget the date. He toasted
> her, "How wonderful you are, what an institution, and we wanted
> the other women to be here to celebrate you, and we'll see you at
> dinner tonight." Then Barbara got up and responded to the toast,
> "This is such a wonderful thing. I never expected that all of you
> would come. This is so nice and I love being at ABC. This is the best
> company to work for. I'm just so happy and I really have to go now.
> I'm so sorry, but I'll see all of you tonight at the dinner." And she got
> up and she walked out of the room. I immediately stood up and I
> said, "Roone, even though Barbara has gone, we're so delighted to
> be here to support her and to be with her because she is the best."
> But then I launched into my "We think we have a problem here. We
> have a problem of institutional sex discrimination."

Simpson remembers how she passed out the documents to the ten vice presidents and to the executive producers of the news shows and asked them to "take a look." In Simpson's words, "Their mouths fell open. We really blew them away." She then told the gathering: "We don't think it's any conspiracy to keep us off the air. You're not bad people that are trying to discriminate against us. It just probably hasn't crossed your mind."

The other women present were invited to join in. They were there for three hours as woman after woman spoke. Simpson continues: "It was incredible. Roone Arledge, and I give him credit for that, listened. He stayed there all that time. And he said, 'You know, I just really never had thought about it before. You're absolutely right. It isn't by design. We hired you all because we think you're talented and we want you as part of this news division.'"

Simpson feels he was expressing his honest opinion. He indicated that he had never thought about it and he was grateful that it had been brought to his attention. He promised to appoint a management committee to work with the women there to improve the opportunities for women at ABC News. In Carole Simpson's mind this proved to be the beginning of what has been an amazing turnabout. She speaks of the changes that have occurred since that fateful luncheon:

> When I look at where we are today, we have four women vice presidents, we had none back then. We have the executive producer of *World News Tonight,* the executive producer of *Weekend News,* the executive producer of *PrimeTime Live,* the executive producer of *Turning Point*—all are women. We've got Cokie Roberts, now part of the roundtable on Brinkley, which had just been [David] Brinkley, Sam Donaldson, and George Will. We have *Nightline* making a much greater effort to bring in women guests as experts on all kinds of topics. Our assignment desk is run by a woman. We have three women war correspondents. I'm anchoring the *Weekend News* now. And we've got Barbara [Walters] and Diane [Sawyer]. We have a good presence. I think we do better now than any other network in terms of the presence of women and women in decision-making capacities.

The courage, commitment, and caring of women like Carole Simpson help to create the atmosphere where change and the correction of past equities become a reality. To maintain the momentum, however, requires diligence and dogged determination.

This fighting spirit is exemplified by Judy Woodruff who knows first-hand the difficulties women faced as they struggled to make advances in broadcasting during the early seventies and eighties: "I know that my generation is fighting, has fought, and will fight as long as there is breath in us. I have to believe that the younger women, if they don't fight today will fight in a few years. Because I think the minute you let down your guard and take it for granted, then I think that you loose ground. So, I hope they don't make that mistake."

Woodruff considers her women friends as soul mates:

> We have the same experiences, the same struggles, the same joys. I'm good friends with people like Andrea [Mitchell] and Ann Compton and Carole [Simpson]. But you just get so busy. I mean, I'm so busy with work and I'm so busy with my kids and my husband. It's hard to make time for friends. I think that's the thing that's really suffered in my life. I hope that other women have not had the same experience. I hope that other women have had more time to reach out and get that sort of nourishment from other women. I think that is so important, I really do. I feel I get it in bits and pieces. But I don't give or get enough and I'd like to do that more. But you just can't do everything.

Judy Woodruff readily credits the women's rights movement for allowing the atmosphere for most of the gains that women have achieved in recent years:

> Women's advancement in television news broadcasting today is a natural outgrowth of the women's rights movement that began in the late sixties and early seventies. I think the sorts of things that the women championed who were activists then have pretty much filtered through society. Much of it we take for granted. Of course, many young women today say, "I don't know anything about women's rights, it didn't do anything for me." Well, the fact is, that it did have a huge impact. Even a conservative like President Richard Nixon was arguing that women needed to be brought into the government at all levels. The Federal Communications Commission under Richard Nixon was arguing that women should be hired in important positions at TV stations across the country. So we owe a great deal to the women's rights movement. And it has taken time, but I'm absolutely convinced that everything good that's happened for women in broadcasting is an outgrowth of that.

It's also an outgrowth of better marketing. I mean, all the marketing research that's been done shows that people want to see women. They don't just want to see white men on the air. The audience wants to see women. Women want to see women. Men want to see women. They believe women. It's a reflection of reality. We are a part of society; therefore we ought to be on the air. The reasons there are more of us behind the scenes is because we've had to push and push and push. More women are getting an education. Some of it's the economy. It's a complicated answer. The economy has drained the two-earner family of income. You have more women needing to work, wanting to work, so more women are working behind the scenes in television.

Achieving women never have sufficient time, but they manage to accomplish more in a limited time frame than almost anyone else. It has been my experience that these same women are available to provide needed help and support while rarely expecting very much of anything in return.

Andrea Mitchell was the subject of a great deal of hazing when she became a "copy boy" on the midnight to eight o'clock shift at Westinghouse Broadcasting in 1967. They did not want to have a woman in the radio newsroom. There was no support system for Mitchell in those days, making the adjustment even more difficult. But things now have changed: "What I discovered in years since is that women provide a tremendous support system for each other, particularly on the White House beat, particularly when you're traveling and working long hours."

Mitchell does not believe that women are hard on other women or are overly competitive among each other:

There was a time when there was only one seat for a woman in each newsroom. When we finally got in, they would have one of us, symbolically. So the thought was that whoever was there would feel threatened if a second woman was hired. When I first came to Washington, I went to Channel 9, the local CBS station owned by the *Washington Post*. There was a very successful woman already there, Susan King, who welcomed me. All the men thought we were going to be great competitors and we weren't. She is still my friend twenty years later, now working for the Department of Labor on lots of issues, including women's issues and family labor. When I was on the White House beat, Judy Woodruff was my mentor and I worked as

Andrea Mitchell, NBC News

her backstop when she was going through pregnancies and taking an occasional week. We became very tightly connected. I saw her last night. I'm the godmother of her seven-year-old daughter. She's now with CNN. She went out of her way to make opportunities for me when I first went to the White House for NBC.

Mitchell especially credits women with helping each other out when they must prepare for a campaign trip or when they are sent overseas and find it necessary to work around the clock because of the time difference. These are hard trips and the sisterhood support is important and appreciated. She also acknowledges that women still face a serious problem: "Women are judged by a different standard and different expectations. We feel very strong among ourselves as a group, those of us at the network level, in government politics. But we had to fight really hard. Sometimes I think that the younger women have no idea what it was like to be in a newsroom where you were just not accepted. Or to be interviewing officials who did not want to deal with a woman reporter." People must be constantly reminded so they will know and appreciate what has been gained by the sweat of others. If not, things may slide back and the role of women could be further reduced and restricted.

It is important to Cokie Roberts that women in broadcasting not lose what is special about them:

> We see the continuum. We know that no matter who's king or who's president or what country wins the war, we're going to be having babies and changing their diapers and burying our dead and taking care of our sick and all of that. And that view of the world is an extremely useful, caring view of the world that we must hold on to. I think I used to worry more about this than I do now, because I see my sisters in the trade who are very caring people.

Roberts numbers among her very best friends Linda Wertheimer, Nina Totenberg, and Lesley Stahl:

> We all are there for each other. If you talked to the women in New York about their response after Nancy Dickerson had her heart attack and stroke, they were around her bedside twenty-four hours a day. Lynn Sherr was a class ahead of me at Wellesley and in my dorm and is one of my dearest friends. Her husband died a few years ago. Everybody was there for her. It absolutely is a sisterhood and I do see people taking care.

Roberts also declares that it is necessary for women to keep their sisterhood strong and not let men put them in competition with each other. Men love to do this, Roberts states with certainty: "It's the whole cat-fight thing, which they find just intriguing, like mud wrestling or something. They find that intriguing and they will set you up one against the other." She warns, "It's very important not to let them say, 'It's you against her,' but for the two of you together to go in and say, 'No, it's us against you. And we're not going to let you set up that kind of competition. It's phony.'"

Connie Chung feels that the men in the industry do not really like to talk to each other and consequently they do not spend time together. The women, however, have limited opportunity for social interaction, but they manage to arrange it whenever possible. She explains:

> We're very supportive of one another. Two examples: [First,] Barbara Walters moms all of us. Whenever she sees us she says, "Are you all right? Are you taking care of yourself? How are you doing? Don't be

bothered by this. Don't be bothered by that." She really does care about all of us. And she will drop us a note if she thinks we did a particularly good interview. Or she'll say, "I wish I had done that. You got a great scoop. I wish I had gotten it." The other example is when I left CBS News, Lesley Stahl gave me a great lunch. It was the most extraordinary gesture on her part, coming from a friend and a colleague. It was terrific.

Chung went on to acknowledge how meaningful the experience was for her:

> The camaraderie that I felt and the sisterhood was beyond my comprehension. I felt as if I was listening to the eulogies at my funeral. The eulogies that you never get to hear. And all of these women that I respect so much. And women outside the television industry. Helen Thomas came as well as Eleanor Cliff of *Newsweek*. All of the key women in television news, Barbara [Walters] and Jane Pauley. Diane Sawyer was on the west coast, so she sent a round of tequila or something lethal like that. And Cokie was there and Katie Couric, and gosh, everyone you can think of.

Chung continued to give concrete examples of how the leading women in television news give each other support and work together to put down fabricated media stories concerning cat fights. She tells of how Diane Sawyer, Jane Pauley, Katie Couric, and Barbara Walters and she were being interviewed about getting guests for magazine programs and special guest interviews. They believed the writer was attempting to create the impression that there were cat fights among the women. Their solution was to talk to each other and then with a united front, they "ganged up on him." They permitted the interview to take place but they each made it clear that they knew his game plan and that it would not work. There is the recognition that a healthy competition can exist between any two people who are trying to get the same story. But the implication of cat fights and feuds have clearly sexist overtones.

Lynn Sherr admits that the network of caring and support among women did not exist in the early days when women were just entering the field of news broadcasting because there were just so few women working then. But now things have changed dramatically. She explains: "We were all clawing and fighting or thought we had to, for the one or two jobs that were available. It's become very clear that we do better united, and that's what's happened. The whole women's movement has taught us all that being together on issues frequently will get us results. We don't have to agree on everything, but being together on some things is very important."

Sherr also talks about the luncheon that was held for Chung when she left CBS. She called it "quite an event." There were many women present with whom Sherr did not agree on many things or about their specific approach to their job in broadcasting. But, says Sherr, "that did not matter because we were all there by way of saying 'Getting fired is awful and we're here to give you a big hug.' And it was very important to have that kind of solidarity." She then referred to her own life experience: "Did my male friends come and hug me twenty years ago at CBS? Absolutely not, and I don't mean to put them down at all. They were very important to me and obviously one doesn't have just female friends in the world. But having other women to talk to about things that happened is quite fabulous."

This issue is one of the reasons that Lynn Sherr wrote the book *Failure's Impossible:*

Susan B. Anthony understood that one hundred years after she was finished, women would not realize there had been a time when they never had the right to vote. It was important to me to resurrect her in order to say to my colleagues and to the next generations coming up, "Hey guys, we didn't do this alone!" Listen, when I first got involved with the woman's movement, I truly believed we had invented this new revolution. I truly believed nobody else had ever done this or thought this before. So discovering Susan B. Anthony and her peers, for me, was a great revelation. What I've tried to do is to pass the word on, which is to say not only were you not born to this job, Miss College Graduate, but, I wasn't either. Someone else a hundred years ago fought even harder than we had to fight to get where they got.

And there is a continuum. I care a lot about history. I care a lot about women's history, and I have made it my mission to remind people about these things. So I think that my generation didn't know we had a debt that we owed to them. And, there's no question but these kids don't really understand what we went through. Part of me thinks that's just great because they're not hung up on it. It's not a problem. They just do what they're doing. Maybe we must get rid of gender distinctions at the workplace. But part of me says they really ought to know because it can slide away very easily.

ROBERT MILAZZO/ABC

Lynn Sherr, ABC News

A vivid illustration concerning the lack of sensibility and awareness of the feminist issues by certain younger women, issues that have been resolved only as a result of courage, sweat, and struggle was told to me by Carol Jenkins when she left WNBC to join Fox news in New York. She describes most of the women working at Fox as in their thirties and not concerned with feminist issues. One of the producers wanted to put on the news program a story about a swimsuit fashion show. Jenkins was, in her words, "horrified they were doing it." She stated that she would like to pass on that story: "Here we went through all this struggle so that we didn't have to do swimsuits. When I started in this business that would be a natural story that a news director might want me to do and now you want to do them again and the producer said, 'Yes, I want to do them.'"

It amazed Jenkins to discover that these young women felt no stigma to putting on a swimsuit contest as a news story:

To wind up in 1996 in a newsroom where the young women were putting the show together and to find that some of them would have no idea that doing the swimsuit story—where in fact the cameraman got down on his knees and shot up at the woman's butt—that somehow there might be something wrong with that. But no. Not a clue. So, there are the older ones of us who have fought to get quality assignments and now we find these younger women who think that it's the most natural thing in the world. Of course they're equal to the men and of course they can do anything they want to do, including bathing suits.

Gloria Rojas emphatically urges the need for women to remain vigilant and protective of their hard-won advancement in the workplace. She warns:

A producer nowadays is not someone who is concerned about feminist issues or has to fight the battle daily and there's a great deal of complacency about women's issues and the coverage of women's issues because people feel the war is over. But it never was won. I mean, I can remember five years ago a cameraman calling me "spick cunt" and not being disciplined for it in any way. In fact, it was I who got the brunt of this confrontation with management. I can remember the cameraman who felt that I didn't know what I was doing despite the fact that I probably knew better than he did what should be done. There were cameramen who resented women in authority, and still do, and they always will, and nobody really addresses those problems. That's out in the field. Inside, I think it's still the male anchor and the female saddle weight. And it may change in some places for a certain amount of time, but I don't think it's changed sufficiently to make me think that this should be a time for complacency.

Linda Ellerbee is no less adamant about the critical need for young women to remain alert and vigilant in order to safeguard the advances that have been fought for with such fervor and pain:

If you are a young woman out there and you're twenty-five years old, you need to know this: The chance you have to get in this door, the chance I had to come in the door, the fact that I'm running a company today, and dealing with heads of networks and that I'm running a multi-million-dollar company, the fact that women are heads of most of the cable networks, the fact that Diane Sawyer is making more money than God, the fact that women have the opportunities, that Cheryl Gould is there, all of these things came about not because networks wanted us or the stations wanted us. It's not even because the federal and state governments said they must have us, though they eventually did. The reason they did, the reason we got in the door, was because of the civil rights movement of the 1960s and the women's movement of the early 1970s, period. It was pressure that got us in the door and these women seem to have forgotten that. Hell, they don't even remember how recent it was that you could be a woman and not inherit property. So why should they be expected to remember how recent it was that they were considered something that would just take all the fun out of broadcasting. They have no idea.

Barbara Walters is named by more women in broadcasting than any other as their source of help and support. Since she stands at the pinnacle of her profession, she is a highly valued and sought-after advisor. Walters talks about her role and interaction with her female colleagues:

We understand each other. I used to be very upset when critics would constantly write about the competition between Diane Sawyer and me because we both do news magazine programs and we're on the same network. I have said there's probably less competition between Diane and me than there is between Ted Koppel and Peter Jennings when they are both offered the same interview. Or, between many of the men. Certainly there's an enormous amount of competition on 60 Minutes. They all talk about it. It was only because we were two women, and there is this old cliché about women being cat fighters and women being jealous of each other. But I think probably women have more of a relationship with each other than the men do. When Connie Chung was taken from her job, Lesley Stahl gave a party for her and we all came. There must have been thirty of us who came to support Connie. We understand each other's lives. We understand the kind of balancing act we have to do. We understand how hard we've all worked. This doesn't mean that we don't compete. But we compete with knowledge and very often with humor.

Diane Sawyer agrees that there is strong sisterhood support. She is credited by many for being an outstanding person who is generous with her help and shows concern for other women who are working in news.

"I think that's what confounds everybody who expected us to be like those old Hollywood movie scripts of women at each other's throats. In fact, we are each others mirrors and shoulders and life rafts and the first call I get when I'm blue and anyone hears about it is from the women I know in this business. And also the first celebrating calls usually come from my female friends."

When Elizabeth Vargas left NBC to join ABC's *Good Morning, America* as their news anchor, she remembers that one of the first people to warmly welcome her was Diane Sawyer:

> I was only here a few days when she organized a luncheon for me. She also called during the months when I was trying to decide which job to take, between NBC and ABC, and she was quick to meet with me and to spend time with me and give me her advice. There was nothing competitive. There was nothing like, well, maybe later on you might be coming to compete with me. She was doing the good thing as a person and as a colleague and that's really great.

The need for society to pit women against each other became an ordeal for Elizabeth Vargas when the tabloid press became eager to invent a feud between her and then *Good Morning, America* co-host Joan Lunden. Vargas told me they both found it first to be "ridiculous, bordering on almost funny because it was so stupid." Later on, however, she found it offensive:

> I think it's incredibly sexist and it's insulting to assume that two women would automatically have to compete with each other. You don't see men doing that. When Matt Lauer went over to the *Today* show as a news anchor and the supposed heir for Bryant Gumble's job, you didn't see people talking about a cat fight between Bryant and Matt. But certainly everybody didn't hesitate to fabricate stories about Joan and myself. Some people are spoiling for that. Some women are not as supportive as they should be. I'm not going to gild the lily here and say that every woman in this industry is completely supportive of the younger women who are on their way up behind them, because some of them are not. But I'm happy to say the vast majority of them are.

Elizabeth Vargas has tried in her own career to be supportive of other women. She acknowledges this is critically important because, in her words, "It's a lonely place out there. It's male dominated." She adds:

It doesn't do any of us any good to shoot each other down. We're still a vast minority and we need to be encouraging more women. It's women like Diane Sawyer and Barbara Walters who are not just great, they're gracious enough to nurture other women who are trying to follow in their footsteps. And, it says something about them as people—that they're secure enough, that they don't have to feel threatened by somebody else coming up in the pipeline. No matter how far away you might be, and how you might not really be that threat. You don't see men doing that to each other, and women need to not only kill the myth, but in those rare instances when it's true, to get over that factor.

Sisterhood and network support are most meaningful to help survive the tough times that are the inevitable part of a high-powered career. Those who have experienced the feeling of a caring and compassionate colleague's concern when their life faced its darker moments are usually committed to reaching out and being there for someone else.

Susan Zirinsky thoughtfully confides:

I take great pride in helping people. I think because I've hit bumps in my career, both while working in the *Evening News* and then when I didn't get the *Evening News* job. I have a much different attitude toward people and treating people. If somebody calls me who's out of a job, who lost a job, I will always take time to talk to that person. When you're younger and you're coming up through the ranks, you have the arrogance that believes that nothing can ever happen to you. Well, let one thing happen and you'll never treat people the same way. This is a very tough, unforgiving business.

These same sentiments were expressed emotionally by Barbara Cochran during our interview. She spoke of how working with the International Women's Media Foundation had provided her with one of her most enjoyable experiences. She mentioned her work with Maureen Bunyan and Carole Simpson and others on the board of this fine organization:

You know, I started out very reluctantly and I found that I really enjoyed being able to build something and to be with women from overseas who do these amazing things. And this sounds corny, but it was almost rediscovering sisterhood. So many people on the board have been through both professional changes and personal things.

People adopted, people remarried after divorces. All this sort of thing and we all saw each other through it. And the same within here; I was going through making a job change last summer, not sure what I was supposed to think about it. One of the nicest things that happened was so many of the mature women and the younger women took the time to come—I think I'm going to cry—took the time to come and see me and to say that they really felt that I had made a special effort on their behalf and they appreciated it. So that was gratifying.

The tears had welled up in Barbara Cochran's eyes as she finished speaking. The pain she felt within came from having been removed from her position as Washington bureau chief for CBS.[1] The feeling was still raw and intense. But those who cared enough to let her know that the work she had done over the years was appreciated and valued provided her with major comfort. It is especially important to have support, acceptance, and acknowledgment to help ease the pain and lighten the burden.

Women in the media must be sensitive to the struggles of those who are attempting to achieve around them. But there must also be an awareness and a support system for the women who struggle to achieve in politics, education, the arts and professions, and the business world. We impact each other. Our individual successes reflect on women everywhere, just as our failures serve to diminish each of us. When an effort is made to reach out to someone who is experiencing a difficult time in life, the opportunities that affect one's own existence are enhanced. The power of sisterhood enables women to make a major difference in the world and to create a better place for all of us to share.

---

[1] On April 28, 1997, Barbara Cochran was appointed president of the Radio-Television News Directors Association.

10
Marriage
and
Motherhood

Nobody objects to a woman being a
good writer or sculptor or a geneticist
if at the same time she manages to be
a good wife, good mother, good looking, good tempered, well groomed,
and unaggressive.

LESLIE M. MCINTYRE

There is no issue that creates greater conflict or introspection than the
duality of career demands and family life. The television news business
is incredibly demanding both in the imposition of time and energy.
News is a twenty-four-hour commitment. Events are continually occur-
ring all over the world and they are assigned and covered on a moment's
notice. There is little or no control over a schedule. This creates havoc,
guilt, and personal sacrifice. The scars are deep and lasting.

There have been subtle and substantive changes in the choices women
are making in their lifestyles. The early class of women who came into
the news business were mostly single. When Linda Ellerbee entered the
profession she was a single mother with two kids. At that time she recalls being told:

If you want us to take you seriously, you must make certain that you are not going to miss a story by going to some stupid school play. You must be available to us every moment we call, because if you are not, we will know that you women, you as a group, are not serious and we were right not to want you. God forgive me, I believed them. So I missed the school plays, and I was there at the conventions. I learned the lesson that although corporations may not keep score, children do. I would do many things differently. I would tell them to go jump in the lake, that I needed to be at the school play, that it was important, more important than your job. We have to find ways in this country so people can be good workers and good family members at the same time. Those few of us that played in this particular field and had children, we suffered and our children suffered. I missed most of my children's childhood. That's a loss that I can never recover.

For many women, their job became their life. Their desire to succeed as a journalist took priority over all else. Andrea Mitchell reflects on how the demands of her career changed her life:

Now I'm left with a very rich life, great experiences, wonderful friendships. But by being willing to work seven days a week for as many years as I did, by being in early in the morning for the *Today* program and then staying through the wee hours of the night to have the latest information for the next broadcast, I was working during crisis periods, eighteen, twenty hours a day, long stretches. Iran Contra comes to mind, and I didn't take vacations that were due me. I didn't take time off. I didn't spend time with my family, with my niece. So has that changed my life? Sure. You don't keep playing an instrument. You don't get season tickets to the opera because you can't plan your life. That's being a journalist. On the way up most women I know felt unable to take as much time off because we always had to be available to try to grab any opportunity that came our way. So I worked weekends for years and years. . . . The hardest choice I guess was I wasn't prepared to be a single parent, so I didn't do what Marjorie Margolies did when she first adopted or do what other women have done. Nor did I feel comfortable becoming pregnant without a spouse. So basically, I've been a single woman blessed for the last ten years with a very serious relationship. But long past the time when I could have children. So I think that's a major sacrifice, not having children during my thirties when I should have.

In retrospect, Andrea Mitchell would probably have preferred to be a little more selfish on the way up. Her engagement to Alan Greenspan, Federal Reserve Chairman was announced in January 1997, and they were married three months later.

Connie Chung admits that her life choices over the years were based on the belief that she could not take the amount of time off that she needed in order to take care of her personal life. So she put things on hold believing she could do them at a later date:

> I had always put off having children, thinking that I could do all of this later down the road. There was always another convention to cover, another election night, another inauguration. I put things off, and that was my own choice. I just didn't realize that I shouldn't have put it off for so long. . . . But at the same time, I feel that the various choices I've made along the way were meant to be, because if my husband and I had not adopted at the time we adopted, we would not have Matthew. And Matthew was meant to be ours, and we were meant to have Matthew. He would not be in our arms. Matthew is the person I wanted to be our son. If we hadn't done it exactly the way we did, and the time hadn't been exactly the way it was, Matthew would not be in our home.

Barbara Walters is considered to be the most famous and honored woman in television news. She is unexcelled in her celebrity interviews and recently aired her twentieth anniversary retrospective for ABC, the network she joined in 1976. She has never stopped working and perfecting her craft. She is competitive and unstoppable in her need to excel. While 1996 has admittedly been acknowledged as the best year in her life, Walters has made major personal sacrifices to achieve her preeminence. She has been married three times. Her first marriage following graduation from Sarah Lawrence College was annulled after less than a year. Two later marriages ended in divorce. She has an adopted daughter, Jacqueline, now twenty-eight, who is a teacher. Walters speaks with pride of her daughter's accomplishments. She acknowledges that few women of her generation in television news chose to have children. The toll the work took made it very difficult to raise a family. Today, however, changes have occurred in the workplace environment, as Walters describes:

> I think that when I had my child there was no accommodation made for a child. I used to say that if I had ever brought my baby into the

office it would be like bringing a dog in that wasn't toilet trained. But today, certainly on the morning shows, you have Joan Lunden who used to bring her children in, Katie Couric who had the baby there, and Kathie Lee Gifford who didn't do a news program, but we heard the baby was in the dressing room. People are a lot more tolerant and they work until their ninth month. We now know that you can appear on the air as Katie Couric has done and Jane [Pauley]. It doesn't matter if the audience sees you pregnant. We didn't treat these matters with the naturalness we do today.

Katie Couric, co-anchor of the *Today* show was married and the mother of two small daughters, a five-year-old and a five-month-old at the time of our interview.[1] She made a very conscious choice not to get married until she was older and more established professionally. She became pregnant earlier than she had planned but believes it to be the "best thing I've ever done and I'm so glad I did it when I did because I'm afraid with the way my career was going, I just might have put it off and put it off and put it off and then had trouble getting pregnant, and waited too long." Couric has always placed high value on being a happy, whole person. She remembers being influenced by the life and death of Catherine "Cassie" Mackin, who in 1972 was the first female network television floor reporter to cover both national conventions. Couric recalls working as a desk assistant at ABC News when Mackin died:

> I used to see her floating around the office and she did float because she was this willowy blond. I used to think, "Gosh, she's so neat, she's smart." She worked for the *Baltimore Sun* and now she's covering Capitol Hill. As a young woman, I was proud of her, proud of her role. When she died of cancer at the age of 44, that was a bit of an epiphany for me because I was one of those young women right smack in the middle of the women's movement who thought, "Oh, I don't ever need to get married. I don't need men." But I remember being so saddened by the fact that she wasn't married and had no children. While her pallbearers were famous people like Teddy Kennedy, I just wondered how truly happy she was and if she died basically a lonely person. You know, I hope not, but I remember thinking, ten years from now people are going to say "Cassie who?"

---

[1] Katie Couric's husband, Jay Monahan, died of cancer on January 24, 1998. He was forty-two years old.

You know she sacrificed an awful lot and for what? I think that if you ask people today, they wouldn't even know who Cassie Mackin was. So the idea of chasing after this sort of illusionary fame made me realize that it was not the most important thing in life.[2]

Susan Zirinsky acknowledges that she adopted those she worked with as her family. Now, she is married, in her mid-forties and trying to truly balance her life and her career. She admits that she is still not very good at it:

I think that I've felt I got so much satisfaction out of what I was doing, that nothing could be as gratifying. And I think I was probably wrong. I think I probably didn't invest enough in life. As Barbara Bush said, "When you're dying, I don't think you're going to say, 'Boy I really wish I had worked more. . . .'" It wasn't until quite recently, and it was really because I did not get a job I thought I was really close to and desired getting and felt very hurt from an organizational standpoint, that I said, "Why am I looking for total emotional, bodily, and intellectual sustenance from a company?" I've gotten to do amazing things at CBS. I called helicopters like most people call taxies. I would say, "I can't believe this is my job." I was just lucky to be alive. Yet, as I get older . . . in your twenties you're so hungry and you are so goal oriented, in your thirties that Holy Grail is still out there, in your forties, you stop. You've reached many of your goals, but you also look for the balance in life. And because I haven't been one of those people that had this great smooth career, that's never fallen down, that's never been punched in the nose, I'm much more conscious of it. . . . I'm not sure I have learned how to make room for life and maybe that's my own insecurity. I waited too long to have a baby, I'm not successful yet, but the game isn't over.

The focus on career to the exclusion of all else is the path taken by women who now reflect and credit the singleness of purpose with allowing them to achieve a greater degree of success than would otherwise have been possible. Betty Rollin did not marry until she was thirty-six years old and she believes this was helpful in her early career:

It was a real blessing that I was a neurotic because, since my personal life was a mess, I couldn't connect with the right, nice man. I always

[2] Catherine Mackin died on November 20, 1982. I interviewed her for my first book, *Women in Television News*, on March 12, 1973, in Washington, D.C.

had boy friends, but they were always, to use my mother's phrase, very inappropriate. I think the fact that I was neurotic was very helpful to my career. I didn't choose to be neurotic, but as long as my personal life was a mess, I was able to focus on my work in a way that I wouldn't otherwise have done. To focus the way I did is really what made me move, because I think early on you needed to do that . . . I certainly wasn't too happy in that period, although professionally I had a lot of satisfaction. But no, it was a trade-off. I think I wound up in a good place. Namely, I wound up now in the eighteenth year of marriage. I wound up also without children. It is kind of a conscious choice and I never was one of those women who just felt that I had to have children. I think there are too many women like me who have them anyway, and I didn't. That, too, was a trade-off. I think it turned out fine, but it's obviously something I've missed in life.

Kathy O'Hearn candidly acknowledges the lifestyle problems faced by news women:

I think it's very hard to have a family and a very fertile personal life. I am still single and forty-three years old. You know, my lover is my work. I have a very full personal life, but I'm not mated with someone. So I wonder about that. I don't know if that isn't just because I love the diversity and thrill of what I do for a living more. I think relationships are work. I think you have to commit to them and really throw yourself into them, and I guess I'm not really a good candidate for that. I don't know. I think women work harder at relationships so that it's easier for men to work and still have the woman come to meet them on the relationship side of things. I don't think men really come to meet women on the relationship side when you're really involved in your work.

Jeanne Meserve got married the week before she started working out of the Washington Bureau for ABC News. Her bosses were not happy with her new lifestyle: "They were shocked when they discovered I had gotten married. I had been told explicitly before I was hired that I would be more attractive to them as a single woman. It was one of the things that would make me appealing. And when I walked in the door with a wedding band on my finger, there was considerable shock."

Meserve continues to analyze their reaction: "I think it had to do with mobility for one thing. If you're single, they can move you wherever they want to put you more readily, and you're not going to object to long assignments. If there are family demands, the equation changes."

After working there for eight years, her contract was not renewed. Meserve believes that ABC was heartless in their treatment of her:

> I knew that I was in jeopardy. I went in to members of management and asked them to please let me know how things stood, that my husband and I had sold one house and were about to buy another. Before I signed another thirty-year mortgage, I'd like to know if my contract was going to be renewed. They would not answer the question. I was laid off the day we went to settle on a new house. I knew I was in jeopardy because I had become a nonperson. There were certain individuals in particular who did not want to take my phone calls, who showed me great disrespect when I attempted to talk to them face to face. Clearly, they were trying to build a personnel file against me, and totally trivial items were being written up and put in my file. Nothing comparable had happened in my previous seven and one-half years. I was targeted for death.

In 1993, Jeanne was hired as an anchor correspondent for CNN.

It is never easy to combine work with family. Every day women feel enormous pressures and tensions from both ends of the spectrum. The strain is intensified by societal expectations. Women feel the age-old responsibility to provide most of the nurturing and to keep the family cemented together. This is the ingrained conditioned sex role women have been fulfilling for centuries.

Jennifer Siebens is married with two daughters, five and ten years old. She is constantly faced with the dilemma of whether she is giving enough to her children. "Women are the mothering influence. In the sixties, when I was a raging feminist, I thought I was equal. But now, having given birth twice, I had to deal with this. Women are the mothers. Women are the wellspring of life. Mothers are the ones whom children turn to instinctively. It doesn't matter how nurturing the father is. The mother is paramount, at least in the early years."

Judy Woodruff, CNN anchor, also believes it is more difficult for women than men to raise a family. Woodruff is married with three children—two boys, fourteen and nine, and a daughter, seven. She stated how hard it is for her not to be able to spend time with her children when she is working. Judy would not take a job that required constant travel because she feels it would be unfair to her children: "What's the point of having children if you're going to be gone all the time. It's hard enough being away from them many evenings. But to be gone most days, most weekends, is just unthinkable for me."

Woodruff has often discussed the duality that she faces with her husband, Al Hunt, Washington editor for the *Wall Street Journal:*

> He loves the children. He's a great father. But he doesn't feel the guilt that I feel. He doesn't feel the acute sense of missing them. We talk a lot about why that is. There's just something about being a mother. Two of our children are biological. Our daughter happens to be adopted from South Korea. So it's not that they came out of the womb. I feel that way about my adopted daughter. I just feel it much more acutely and much more sensitively when I'm away from them, when I'm working.

The one woman who everyone else in the business marvels at is Ann Compton. She has successfully juggled four children and a thriving career. She calls them the achievement she is most proud of: "Unlike many of the women you're interviewing, I have no Emmy on my mantle piece at home. But I do have an award that not many of them have from the national Mother's Day Committee, the outstanding mother of the year in 1987. I'm as proud of that as I could be of anything else."

Compton was thirty-one when she married. She had her first child, a boy, in January 1980. She was covering the Bush campaign:

> I had a baby between the Iowa caucus and the New Hampshire primary. I stayed out of work twenty-eight days. Came back to work. Did a lot of anchoring, especially *Good Morning, America,* when I could be home, not traveling out of town. ABC was wonderful. When the baby was nine weeks old, they called me at home on a Friday night and said, "John Anderson is going to run as an independent. Would you be willing to travel full-time as the lead correspondent on the campaign?" I immediately said yes. I went upstairs, sat in the rocking chair in the baby's room, rocked the baby to sleep and cried, asking myself, "What have I just done?" The whole year, little Bill's first year, I was gone as much as I was home. Luckily, the Anderson campaign didn't have enough money to campaign seven days a week. I was often home on weekends. By election night 1980, I was in maternity clothes with number two. Teddy was born right after the Reagan inaugural, at which point I went back into the White House

Ann Compton, ABC News

as a White House correspondent and traveled full-time with a one-year-old and a newborn.

That was when I realized, first of all, with the second child, the guilt went away. They had each other at home. I realized my wisdom in marrying a doctor. Doctors are always at home, and so while his schedule is worse than mine, Daddy was always in town even when Mommy was away. When I was thirty-six, I gave birth to Annie, my only daughter, in 1983. It happened to come at a time when we were invading Grenada and the American Embassy in Beirut blew up. I remember I had to stop nursing because the president had a trip to Georgia, and it happened at the same time as the invasion of Grenada, and I didn't make it home for twenty-four hours and nursing stopped like that. So I had these three wonderful children and ABC broke my heart. They said in the second Reagan term we'd like you to cover Capitol Hill while our Capitol Hill correspondent goes off and covers candidates. Now I don't know why they did that. They never said it's because you have three children and these people don't. Actually the other people were men and all had children, too. But I didn't know what a gift it was. I went to Capitol Hill and found out that the schedule's so much easier. You're in town so much. It was easy. I had another baby in October of 1985. So Michael was born the night the Gramm-Rudman legislation passed the Senate.

So here I am with four children and a busy schedule. My husband Bill Hughes and I never stopped to say, "Now how is this going to work?" We simply did it. I was lucky. I have children with no great hurdles, no great challenges. We've never been tested with any great tragedy or trauma in our family. I've got four normal, healthy, active kids who are in school with normal, healthy, active sports activities. We've been blessed, both with my husband as a doctor and me as a journalist, with just enough of a flexible schedule to make it all work. As it turns out, tomorrow the president is on the road. But I had to stay back because of a meeting here in Washington. So I will make it to my daughter's last lacrosse game of the year and hopefully to my son's little league game at five o'clock where he's the pitcher before I get on a plane tomorrow night at seven to catch up with the president in Milwaukee.

Ann Compton is certainly unique, committed, and accomplished. With the same job for twenty-two years and the same husband for more than seventeen years, she says she was never forced to make any big dramatic decisions in her life. According to Compton, the worst decisions she made are still hanging in her closet.

The toll on family life is most acute for women who are foreign correspondents. Sheila MacVicar is married and has a seven-year-old daughter. She admits that these assignments are hard and disruptive on everyone. Her husband is a journalist, and during the Gulf War they had just moved into a house in London that they were in the middle of renovating. MacVicar explains how she hired the contractors, drew up the plans, and then left to go to war. Her husband was not amused. At one point she called home from Jordan. She excitedly told him that she had just come from the palace where she had dinner with King Hussein. His reply was, "I don't give a flying bleep about King Hussein. I want you to know that the contractors dropped the wrong wall yesterday. There's plaster dust everywhere. The dog is in quarantine. Your daughter is sick and the nanny is quitting." MacVicar said she would call back later.

When her husband began interviewing for a new nanny, MacVicar monitored the progress. After the first interview, he was not enthusiastic. The second interview also was not promising. When she called after the third one, MacVicar noticed a whole change of tone in her husband's voice. He was very bright and bubbly, saying what a wonderful woman he'd found. Her name was Beatrice, she was premed, their

WOMEN IN TELEVISION NEWS REVISITED

daughter just loved her, and she was just fabulous. He also told her that "she looks like a young Anita Eckberg." When MacVicar hung up the telephone, she went to her bureau chief and asked, "Help me out here. What does a young Anita Eckberg look like?" He replied, "Is this the nanny thing?" When MacVicar answered yes, he said, "When would you like to leave to go home?"

MacVicar says there are days when she wishes that she wasn't so driven to do this job. "There are times when I wish I had taken up something slightly more sedentary like law. But this is what I do and this is what I love to do." But she fought for her right to be assigned overseas and to face the dangers associated with war.

MacVicar recalls the 1990 invasion of Kuwait by Iraq as the lead off to what became Desert Storm when she was a new arrival at ABC:

> I was familiar with Baghdad. I had been reporting from Iraq in the Iran-Iraq war and I went in and out from time to time during that early period. So, it was natural for me to ask to go to Baghdad. It was a place that I knew, it was the center of a big story, and it was a place where ABC, at the time, was frankly not being very well served. There was a lot of resistance on the part of ABC management, where people felt that it was inappropriate that they send a female correspondent, first, and a female correspondent with a child, second, to Baghdad, at a time of great uncertainty. My argument was that this was a risk that I was prepared to take. But they certainly weren't making that judgment about male correspondents, many of whom were also married and had families. It took some time, but eventually that argument did win out. And actually that was the last time that that argument ever has been raised, certainly about me, because they have not subsequently shown such a patriarchal concern for my well-being."

Christiane Amanpour is reflective when analyzing the impact of a family on her career:

> It is difficult, and sometimes it's not successful, but with the right attitude, with the right spirit, you can juggle both to an extent. I do, however, think that it's probably true to say, particularly for women, that you probably can't have everything all at once. I love children and I don't dismiss that idea by any stretch of the imagination. I've said before, if I had a child, I would have the responsibility to stay alive because you can't just have children and rush off and put your-

self in the line of fire voluntarily. So I would probably rethink my work habits somewhat.

Many women correspondents do make significant choices that affect their careers based on the responsibilities they carry as a wife and mother. Maria Shriver had had three children in three and a half years, at the time of our interview; the two girls were five and six, and the little boy was three.[3] Since her second child came she gave up two major network anchor jobs that she told me she had worked fourteen years to get. Shriver has never gone back to work full-time. She negotiates her contract that way. She is kept busy with specials, high-profile interviews at the conventions or the inaugurations, as well as anchoring for NBC's *Dateline*. Since television is incredibly competitive and your value is built on your time on the air and your star status, Shriver is well aware that if she fails to be a successful business option, the network will end the arrangement. She is struggling to remain in the incredibly fast-paced and demanding world of television news while still being able to carpool the children and work at their school. The decision was not an easy one for her: "It was like walking away from something that you love but you know it would eat you alive if you stayed in it. You wouldn't be able to raise your children. So it was like being an addict. It was trying to do something just a little bit."

Shriver believes that as a result of women in her position who established themselves in a major career and then started having children while still wanting to continue to work, the networks had to offer an option to keep them. Slowly over the years a few women have done job sharing. Two reporters with children were hired to make one full assignment reporter. This is not common and represents a significant breakthrough in the industry. For women in television, the choices remain open—whether to have children, whether to raise them themselves, whether to remain in this intensely competitive business. These are the choices an adult woman must be responsible for and try to be at peace with. It is never easy to have it all—a happy marriage, functioning children, and an active career. For so many it is an elusive goal based on the myth of the superwoman. Maria Shriver comments:

> I don't think you can be the biggest star in television, the greatest mother, the greatest wife. I don't think you can do all of those things. The best advice my mother gave me was that as you look back at

---

[3] Maria Shriver's fourth child was born on September 27, 1997.

your life, it's like a marathon, you'll have periods maybe in your twenties to mid-thirties where you were the best worker you could possibly be. Then you will have a period where you perhaps dedicate yourself to being a wife or a mother. Then you may have another chunk of time where you go back and have an effect on the world in other ways. When you look at your life in totality you might have been a superwoman, but I think we kid ourselves and set ourselves up for failure to try to think that you can have it all simultaneously.

Shriver has a small piece of paper glued on the front of her daybook that she has carried around for the last five years. It lists the qualities needed to succeed in a chosen career and the qualities needed to be a good mother. They are exactly the opposite, so she advises, "I don't think that you should come in and expect to be Barbara Walters, Betty Crocker, and Indira Ghandi in the same breath. And I, myself, thought that I could do that."

Maria Shriver's struggles become more meaningful when viewed in the totality of her heritage. She is part of one of the most famous families in American history. Her uncle was President John Fitzgerald Kennedy and as a Kennedy she has a role to play in everything from the Special Olympics to the Kennedy Foundation and the Kennedy Library in Boston, to helping the candidacy of those members of her extended family who are running for political office. She is married to Arnold Schwarzenegger, a superstar in his own right with a celebrity lifestyle. So she is busy juggling the roles of daughter, sister, cousin, wife, and mother. These individual hats are being worn simultaneously. She describes the dichotomy:

> I do find myself interviewing Hillary Clinton on Monday, working in the classroom on Tuesday, and covering the O. J. Simpson trial on Wednesday. During the final arguments for the Simpson trial, I was doing arts and crafts in the morning and by one o'clock, I was sitting at the trial listening to closing arguments. I looked down and I had glue on my hands and magic markers from the classroom. So sometimes it's great and sometimes it's a little bit disorienting.

The need for fundamental changes in our society to accommodate the reality that women are the childbearers and often require a more flexible work schedule was strongly advocated by Elinor Guggenheimer:

> I think that the marketplace doesn't reflect the needs of women and their lifestyles. It's my feeling that some day the marketplace, realiz-

ing the fact that having children and raising them is an absolutely essential part of the human life or there's no life—you can extinguish us like the dinosaurs, but women have to have children and they have to nurture them and help bring them up. I think the marketplace eventually may change enough so that women enter the labor force at forty instead of twenty, and at that point they start equally with the men in their twenties, so that they're not boxed out of key positions. Women do outlive men and maybe changes like that are in the future. I don't know what they'll be. But I do know that the marketplace today doesn't reflect the reality of life.

The television news business is notorious for divorces. The men who have had successful careers in broadcasting have paid a heavy toll in their personal lives as well. Sam Donaldson is candid about his life's choices:

I see a few exceptions of people who have been able to marry a very active aggressive pursuit of a career with a family and the pursuit of other interests, but I haven't been one of them. My work habits are now more regularized and frankly I'm not bucking for some other rung on the ladder. But in the early days of climbing, I did what I tell journalism students today. The way to succeed, you have to be very aggressive and you have to work very hard. I took all of the assignments offered and I thought nothing of canceling plans with my family, anniversaries, birthdays, dinner parties. My work was first, and my family life suffered because of it. I had a divorce because of it, I think. Married to a very fine woman, she was then, she is today, who finally got tired of living that way, for which I don't blame her. I wish I had had more sense about it. Although, it's worked for me. I'm married now to the love of my life, who's also a television reporter. Not only is Jan a wonderful woman, but she knows the business. She has to call up and say "I can't make it for dinner tonight." I have to try to understand. Although, it's galling to have the shoe on the other foot. But she understands when these things happen.

Donaldson reaffirms the necessity to make trade-offs and sacrifices in your life in order to succeed in this business. But he recognizes the way the responsibilities of motherhood have become more acceptable:

Women formerly had to try to pretend either that they weren't mothers or they were a mother but they only spend twenty minutes a day with their child. And so they must have felt very guilty. Today, I think

Sam Donaldson, ABC News

women are able to come out of the closet and confess they are mothers and they're going to take care of their children. At the same time, they are correspondents and they're going to do their work. One of the reasons they're able to do this is men have now come to understand that they've got to do more than just occasionally change a diaper and then be able to brag for the rest of their life, "Yeah, I changed a diaper, you know." They, too, have to cook dinner, take care of the children, spend their Saturday afternoons with children, rather than out on the golf course, so that their wife can spend her time someplace else.

Maternity leave is now accepted, whereas once a woman would try to come back within two weeks, now they take six months off, come back knowing there's a spot there. Not just a legal requirement but it's going to be there. I keep bringing up Ted because Ted Koppel and I are great friends and I like him very much. You remember in 1975 Ted took nine months off from his job here at ABC so that Grace Ann could go to law school. Now Ted still anchored the Saturday news, he did some other things from his home, but he essentially was not covering the diplomatic beat. I said to him often, it's marvelous not only were you willing to do that for your wife, that's fine, you get a gold star for that, but you felt secure enough not to worry that while you were gone some other shark would move into your beat and that management would say to you, "Ted, you know we've got X here who's been doing such a great job at the State Department, maybe you should be general assignment correspondent for awhile." Ted was then not the overwhelming success he is now. And he said to me, "I knew I was good and I knew that if I came back and they didn't want me here, they'd want me somewhere else."

The consequences of personal choices are often not known or appreciated until much later in one's life.

Richard Threlkeld has been a news correspondent for thirty years. His first marriage was a casualty of the demands of his job and the choices he made. "It wasn't CBS management that told me to get a divorce. It was me and it was me choosing to be gone 80 percent of the time while my kids were growing up. My wife and I became more and more estranged. Whatever regrets we have, we have. I don't blame the business. I think it's the human being who makes that kind of choice."

Threlkeld is now married to Betsy Aaron. On November 1, 1996, they both moved as television journalists to Moscow, he to become CBS Moscow correspondent and she to become CNN Moscow correspondent. Threlkeld has two daughters from his first marriage. Aaron was widowed during her childbearing years so has no children of her own. They have been together for nineteen years. The mutual love and respect they share is inspiring. He says, "She's a very, very special person, and we are very lucky that we found each other at just the right time in our lives. I know everybody says this, but we really are just one of those couples who fall more and more in love with each other every day and how fortunate it is that we are both doing the same thing and both love what we're doing."

Dan Rather, CBS anchor, has been married to the same woman for thirty-nine years and has two grown children. He reflects on the addictive nature of the news business and the effect it has on family responsibilities and relationships:

> I never did it perfectly and I didn't always do it well. Specifically, when I first came to CBS news. I was so proud to be here and so focused on the job. I had no idea about the traveling. The first year I worked with CBS news I think I was home thirty-one days out of the year. We made these decisions as a couple—we came to CBS. We were proud to be here. We wanted to succeed, to do right, to do well. But we had no idea what it would take to meet the standards. I got assigned to the civil rights movement. Dr. Martin Luther King was the story at the time. And looking back on it, I didn't try as hard for balance between work and family as I could have and should have. It's a common mistake. I believe people make it less today than they did then.

Tom Brokaw, NBC anchor, has a long-term marriage and three grown daughters. He credits his wife with bringing a wonderful equilibrium into their family life and for being totally unimpressed with the celebrity factor that is attached to his world. Brokaw admits to being worried about the fact that a lot of women in this industry have too little time for a personal life. He faults a society in which women are not yet able to determine their own personal agenda as much as they should:

> Men are still the ones who are likely to ask somebody out and ask them to accommodate their schedule around the man's personal and social calendar. Women are still, unfortunately, in a situation where they are socially at the beck and call of men to much too great a degree. This industry requires a lot of hours, a lot of unexpected departures, a lot of time away, when they don't know when they're going to return. So it's unconventional. Therefore, I worry a lot about the fact that a lot of women simply can't have the kind of social interaction on the outside of this business that I think would be helpful for them.

Walter Cronkite, the dean of television news anchors, has recently completed his autobiography and an eight-hour series of documentaries for the Discovery Channel. He spoke to me of his fifty-six-year marriage and how his legendary career impacted his family:

> I was fortunate enough to marry a newspaper woman herself, and she understood the demands of the business. We taught our children

that there were extraordinary demands of the business, that they couldn't count on my being there for every school appearance that they made. Although, I made most of them. I'm very proud of that. I made a great effort to be there when it seemed I should be there. I missed a lot of other opportunities to be with them. The evening news broadcast, coming at the time it did, I usually got home about the time they were going to bed. But I rushed home to be there for that occasion, to get them out of the bathtub and put them in bed, if I could. I don't see that the uncertainties of schedule necessarily made a lot of difference in our lives. The traveling salesman and the busy executive is constantly hopping a plane for some distant part of the world and suffers the same sort of indignities.

Walter Cronkite never admits having had conflicts arising out of the tension between work and home life. The breaking news stories, the assignments were "all perfectly understandable to us as to what was needed and what had to be done. I don't think either of us ever gave it a second thought."

David Brinkley, seventy-seven years old and a fifty-year veteran of broadcasting, stepped down as host of ABC's *This Week with David Brinkley* six months after I met with him in his Washington, D.C., office.[4] He was married for twenty-five years to a woman who did not work outside the home. "We didn't need her income" was the reason he gave. He credits his illustrious career with enhancing the lives of his four children. "They got to do and see all kinds of things that they would not have done or seen if I were a bank clerk, say. No, it's been very good for them. They get to travel and very few kids manage to meet Winston Churchill and Evelyn Chadwick, for example. It's been very good for my kids and they're all happy and successful."

Heather Allan describes her own personal struggles as well as the problems she faces dealing with reporters who have parental obligations:

The most difficult decision I ever made was leaving South Africa. That was very hard on a personal level. I ended a very long, steady relationship to come here. That was a career decision and I sacrificed my love for it. Up until that point, I had a fine time, but coming to Los Angeles was a huge decision for me. I left my family behind, my

---

[4] Having reduced his duties earlier, David Brinkley made his final on-air appearance on Sunday, September 28, 1997.

David Brinkley, ABC News

dad, my brother. I can't say I didn't have a life, but it pretty much did revolve around NBC for many years; I met my husband, oddly enough, at the 1988 Republican Convention. He's from New Zealand, he's a Kiwi, and he's a news cameraman and a very good one. I don't know how other people do it, but I don't think I could marry somebody who wasn't in the business. It's been a very good marriage so far and we're four years into it. But I was thirty-nine before I got married—and kids, I never particularly liked them and I never particularly wanted them. I get quite disgusted with the whole mommy track in this business because I think that if you want to have children that's your affair. But for God's sake, don't go around telling the world how hard it is to juggle and all of that jazz. I just feel that's your laundry and for God's sake, keep it in. It doesn't do the cause any good, quite honestly, to go off and have babies because, personally, I want to say that this is a full-time job and you pretty much have to give it your all and you can't do it part time. What I'm seeing is a lot of part time women who feel they can work part time and have babies part time. As a manager, it's a nightmare to have to deal with it. It's a nightmare.

In the workplace of the nineties, you find men and women both attempting to juggle the role of parenting. This is attested to by Linda Mason who comments on the major changes over the last several decades:

When I had my first child, I was very senior so they wouldn't send me out on day trips. But I never mentioned if I was up all night with one of the kids. They didn't hire me to be a mother. They hired me to be a professional. This went full circle when several years ago I was on the weekend news Sunday morning. I had two male producers at different times. One called to say he was going to be late, he had to take the child to the doctor before taking him to day care because the wife was working and neither wanted to stay home because the home care person hadn't arrived. I felt that's full circle. I've never done that. So it's a very different attitude.

Cokie Roberts remembers the difficult times she faced when her two boys, now twenty-seven and twenty-nine, were young. She and her husband Steven Roberts, a senior writer at *US News and World Report,* were forced to juggle two full-time journalism careers:

It was very hard. It was hard on me. It was hard on them and it was hard on my husband. It was the first time he really had to take on pretty much equal responsibility. I mean, men never take on totally equal responsibility because we're the ones who think up the problems and ask them to help. But we didn't have money. We needed my salary. We didn't have some fabulous nanny for day care. I mean, we were really struggling. I was on the road a lot through campaigns and it was very difficult for the children and for Steve because there were times when he couldn't cover a story because I was out, and times when it was inappropriate for me to go out because he'd been out.

We just constantly tried for balance. I look back on those years and I wonder how, in God's name, we did it. . . . They've grown up to be extremely lovely human beings. They like me, I like them. They like their father. They like each other.

It is important in a discussion about family decisions to legitimize women who are the primary caretakers of their parents and siblings. This responsibility often requires intense effort, time, money, and personal sacrifice. Roberts speaks of her own family experiences:

I also spent an enormous amount of my work time off taking care of my sister when she was dying of cancer. Women who are not mothers are still caretakers. They take care of their own parents, they take care of siblings. They take care of their mothers-in-law. Woman's primary role in life is to be a caretaker. Whatever else you do you do, you are also taking care. For women not to understand this is a terrible mistake. Then they just get stuck and resentful. At some point in their lives they will find that they are taking care of somebody. It's something they must do because there's nobody else to do it. And to me, the thing to do is to rejoice in it because it's by far the most fulfilling thing you ever do.

Nina Totenberg is legal affairs correspondent for National Public Radio. She also had a contract with ABC to do special reports for *Nightline*. Totenberg is married with three grown stepchildren. She has made the difficult and conscious choice not to have any children of her own:

I married a man who was significantly older than I am. And it was very clear that if I wanted children, I would have the primary responsibility of taking care of them and raising them. I, unlike Cokie Roberts, am not a superwoman. I don't think I can do everything. She also has a younger husband than I do. I was thirty-five when I married him and I already had a decent career. If I'd had a husband who really wanted children, we would have had children. But I didn't have a husband who really wanted more children. He already had three. So in the end I sacrificed that, I suppose, to my career. And, in truth, I don't have any deep regrets about that. I may, when I get older and there's nobody to take care of me. I think it was the right choice. I enjoy my sister's children. I like children very much. I guess, I would have liked to have had them but not at the cost of who I am, and who I am is a reporter.

But an event happened two and one-half years ago that has had a tremendous impact on Totenberg's life. Her husband fell on the ice and hit his head. He had three brain operations and had to learn to walk again. Then, a year later, a tumor was found on his lung. When he went into the hospital to have a lung cancer operation, he almost died and had to spend five and a half months in intensive care. Totenberg continued to work and to work hard, but acknowledges that it was not with the same single-minded devotion that she did before. Totenberg speaks of the enormous support she has received from colleagues, friends, and ABC. When her husband appeared to be stabilized, she went to Oklahoma City to cover the bombing story.[5] After she had been there two days she received a call from the hospital telling her that her husband had taken a terrible turn and that his blood pressure was plummeting, his heart beat was not regular. The nurse told her that she thought that this time he was not going to make it through the crisis. She made a reservation to return. The earliest plane out of Oklahoma City was at ten thirty in the morning and she would arrive back in Washington at five in the afternoon. She called Tom Bettag, the executive producer of *Nightline* at six that morning to let him know what had happened. She explained that in an hour she was scheduled to do an interview with the lawyer for Timothy McVeigh. Bettag told her not to worry about the interview. She responded:

> No, I've got to go to Oklahoma City anyway. I will do the interview, but then I have to leave. He said, "Fine," and he hung up and I hung up. Five minutes later he called me back and he said "I have chartered a plane for you. Just be there by 8:30." So, ABC probably spent ten thousand dollars for this fancy jet and two pilots, and had a car waiting for me at Dulles Airport. I was at his bedside by one o'clock in the afternoon. When I walked in I could see all the monitors start to change. And Cokie had gone there for me, and was sitting at the hospital so that he wouldn't be alone if he died. She had waited at the hospital until I got there.

The stories of cold heartless people in the news profession often are grossly exaggerated. Nina Totenberg's husband survived and is doing well. She told me she played tennis with him for the last three weeks

---

[5] The Oklahoma City Federal Building was bombed on April 19, 1995; 168 people were killed.

even though he is not really able to run at all and he wears a crash helmet "so that if he falls, he doesn't bonk his head again."

Phyllis McGrady was executive producer of ABC's *PrimeTime Live*. The role of caretaker fell hard on her shoulders when her mother had a heart attack in 1984. It became necessary for her mother to remain in the hospital for an extended period of time. She went to Roone Arledge, then president of ABC News, to inform him of her decision to take a leave in order to care for her ailing mother. McGrady describes his reaction to what was a controversial decision at the time. Arledge told her how hard these choices are that one must face in life. McGrady states:

> He talked to me about how he had always regretted that on one of the major Olympics, at a time when his father was really sick and he had visited his father beforehand and said "I'll see him when the Olympics are over and I'll try to take some time," and his father passed away. He said, "It was one of those things I've always regretted, that I hadn't been there, and I hadn't seen him." And he continued, "You know, these are decisions that one has to make in life and I think you are making the right decision. I don't love it, but I think you're making the right decision. I think you need to go and you need to take time and when you're ready, there will be many things that you can do here at ABC News."

People in management have not always been supportive of personal life decisions that impact adversely on time away from the job. In 1991, Susan King was an anchor for the six o'clock and the eleven o'clock news at a local station in Washington, D.C. She was a well-known face and a major star in the news community for many years. She had been married for over twenty years when she decided to adopt a baby. It became a big news story in itself. When she went to request three weeks off, she was told she could not have it. There was no maternity leave. She was shocked. She admits: "They were really very unpleasant." They refused to let her take any time off. But because the family and medical leave legislation had passed in the District of Columbia, they could not refuse. So Susan took nine days of unpaid family and medical leave. It was an experience that became a turning point for her: "That was an experience, having the boss say, 'Look, you're going to have a kid, but we don't have to support you.' Then I asked to help them craft an adoption policy so it wouldn't be discriminatory against those of us who didn't give birth. They just never responded. So it was pretty shocking to me because I'd always covered women's issues and saw this changing world and this kind of work and family stuff and realized how an employer could just make it real miserable for you."

Women usually pay a higher price for career success. But sometimes life deals a double barrel of crisis and tragedy. Virginia Sherwood is regarded by colleagues as a pioneer in the news business whose competence made it possible for many to follow in her footsteps. She was the only woman covering news for ABC when I first interviewed her in 1973. She was on her way to do a story on the return of the prisoners of war in Virginia Beach, and I was running through the airport in Washington, D.C., to speak to her before she left town. At the time, she was a divorced mother with three children. Several years later, she remarried and left the network to form her own consulting company. During the early seventies before leaving ABC, Sherwood was doing a story on gun control and how the gun lobby and the National Rifle Association were trying to defeat Joseph Tidings in Maryland. As she was working on this story her sixteen-year-old son was shot and killed by another boy, one year older, with a stolen gun. It was a devastating time for Sherwood and remains an open wound. She describes receiving a handwritten note from then President Richard Nixon: "It was a wonderful letter. Even though you don't like some things that happen, you love people for caring."

Five years later, Sherwood's second son, nineteen years of age, was also killed. He was going to school in New Orleans and was discovered shot in the house where he lived. The person responsible was never found. She emphasizes to everyone she coaches, the importance of always being honest and fair, no matter what the circumstances. As Sherwood recalled the horrific tragedies, she was overcome with tears: "You'll know what I mean by being honest, by being fair. When I can lose a son to a hand gun, a stolen hand gun, and I was doing that story and I had to do it. Not only did I have to interview both sides, I had to interview the head of the NRA. I still have a letter from him stating that it was the fairest interview he's ever had." A true testimony to a woman of courage and integrity.

The newswomen working on local television stations usually have a more defined work schedule and have less need for travel than those at the network. But the sacrifices and the pressures remain intense. Gloria Rojas worked in New York local television news for twenty-three years. When we met in 1973 she was a divorced mother with a young son. She remarried and now has three stepsons. Rojas feels her career made it very hard for her son and she paid the price in guilt. She gained a great deal of weight over the years as a response to the frustrations of her life. She went from 105 pounds to 175 pounds: "If you look at all the heavy guys there are on TV, weathermen, anchormen—all kinds of guys are heavy. I think I was the only fatty for females. . . . There were just too many conflicts. I had just too many things going on, my family, my child, my husband, my marriage, my stepchildren. There were just too many things that were negative."

Rojas is still haunted by some of the painful and draining moments:

I was at Willowbrook, that horrendous hospital and all those children lying in their filth. Geraldo [Rivera] had opened up that story and I was there and I got paged. My son had broken a leg on a ski trip with his class and they wanted me to go up there and pick him up. Here I was in the midst of all this and the immediacy of it felt greater to me than the pain of my boy who was on a junket. And I sent my brother to pick him up. Thank God I had family and I wasn't in some strange city. But to this day I think of a twelve-year-old wondering, "Where the hell is my mother and why am I not important." And when that happens week after week, you wonder what kinds of choices you are making. Everybody who works has to make them. But everybody who works doesn't have to make them all the time. I mean, a plane falls into the bay at Newark and you have to go. You may be in the midst of something very important to your family, but you go. And I think it hurts your children. But they have a lot of advantages out of it. I mean, my son had a comfortable childhood as opposed to if I'd been teaching I couldn't have sent him to camp, couldn't have sent him to college. He went to law school with no loans and he met a lot of interesting people. He had a lot of interesting experiences because we had the money to travel. But I'm making it up to him with my grandchildren because I feel a great deal of guilt. He's never accused me, but I feel that I shortchanged him because I felt my career was important and my career had uneven demands that I could never plan for.

Rose Ann Scamardella was a popular and highly paid anchor at WABC-TV in New York. In 1978, she became the first female in a man-woman combination anchor team that has become standard today on most stations throughout the country. She gave birth to a daughter,

Vanesa, when she was thirty-one years old. In 1984 when her daughter was three, Rose Ann walked away from her television career:

> I really wanted to be a mother, and I was at the height of my career, so mothering was very important. I realized that some people can, but I really couldn't do both, the way I wanted to. When I could juggle, when she was little and I was doing the eleven o'clock news or even when I was doing the five o'clock and the eleven o'clock, I lived near the station, so I would come home, have dinner, put her to sleep and go back. That was okay. But when they were asking me to do something where I would really have to choose between her and them, I chose Vanesa.

Except for the loss of her high-six-figure income, Scamardella has no regrets. "I was the Girl Scout leader, I ran the Christmas pageant, and taught catechism classes at church. I was on all the volunteer groups. I went to the Garden Club. That part of my life was really fun and I wouldn't trade it for anything. I had a Brownie troop for six years and we went camping and we did all of those things. So I was really available."

Scamardella now lives in Connecticut and teaches journalism at a prestigious boy's prep school. She brings in some of her old news tapes. She says her students have no idea what she did, but their parents still remember her. She gets a kick out of that. Rose Ann Scamardella was the woman on whom Gilda Radner based the *Saturday Night Live* character Roseanna Dana. She has a signed poster over her desk at home from Radner, "To Rose Ann from Roseanna Dana." The characterization was such a success, it made Rose Ann Scamardella more memorable and more marketable. Those memories have lasted and provide her with lasting pleasure.

Sally Quinn realized that it would be possible for her to have a child and a career during the time she took leave from the *Washington Post* in order to write a novel. Until then, she was traveling so much she had doubts about her ability to be a good mother. Her son Quinn was born in 1982. He was born with a hole in his heart and had open-heart surgery when he was just three months old. Since then Quinn has had continuing medical problems. He also has serious learning disabilities and attends a special school. For the last fourteen years, Quinn has been the primary focus of his mother's life. She is also involved in caring for her own mother, who has had a series of devastating strokes which have left her partially brain damaged. The combination of dealing with her mother's illness and caring for Quinn has put Sally Quinn's career on hold. She is trying to find the time to finish her latest book. She accepts it all simply as the hand she was dealt and feels very fortunate not to have financial problems. "All I can think about is people who are in my situation or worse who don't have the financial resources to deal with the problems the way I do. So it makes me feel really lucky that I can have the luxury and the time to spend time with my mother and my child and I don't have to go to work everyday and try to support the family and do all of that at the same time."

Sally Quinn emphasizes the need to decide what makes you happy and then just do it. She explains: "You want to have a good time. [Her husband] Ben has the same philosophy of life.[6] He loved being a journalist. He loved being editor of the [Washington] *Post*. He had a good time, and when he wasn't having such a good time, he quit. He retired and went on to do other things. He's still at the *Post*. He still does a lot of things with the *Post* and he enjoys that. He also has new interests and he's having a great time at that. We have a great time together and we have a great time with Quinn."

Sally Quinn strongly believes in the choices and options that are open to women and the need to assess them appropriately:

> I think that there are some women who are just meant to be incredibly high-powered career women and some women who are meant not to be parents and mothers. Some women were meant to have ten children, some women were meant to stay home. I think the most important thing for a woman is to try to figure out what she wants. . . . So many women are just torn apart by trying to have high-powered careers and trying to raise their children at the same time. No one's happy. The children suffer, they suffer, their husband suffers. Almost all women I know at some point in their lives, if their career is going fabulously well and they have children and a husband, you know that something is being sacrificed. Either the kids are getting short shrift or the marriage is getting short shrift. You can look at me and see where I decided to make the sacrifices and that is in the career. I think my husband is happy, I think my child is happy, and I

---

[6] Sally Quinn is married to Ben Bradlee, former editor of the *Washington Post*. He was finishing breakfast on the terrace of their Georgetown home when our interview took place.

guess that makes me happy. I would be miserable if I was doing brilliantly in my career and they were not happy.

With a strong economic base it becomes less of a strain to raise children because options for day care and specialized home care are possible. Yet, at every level, women in television news find it extremely difficult to balance their career with family obligations. The lifestyle often demands twenty-hour days and travel to every corner of the globe. For some it is hard, for others it is impossible. For most it is a conflict that creates frustration, tension, guilt, and exhaustion.

Kelly Lange has been the anchor for NBC4 news in Los Angeles for twenty-six years. She has the longest tenure for a woman anchor at the same station. Lange has been through two marriages and has one grown daughter. She began her broadcasting career doing traffic reports from a helicopter for KABC radio in 1967. She left for the airport every morning at four-thirty when she had a baby daughter to care for. Her meager salary prevented her from being able to hire a baby-sitter, so she took the child with her:

> I think I was the first woman who took her daughter on the job. I would just get her up in her pajamas and she'd still be sleeping. She'd sleep in the car and I'd grab a ducky or a book or whatever and we'd go in the helicopter. At some point we'd take a little break, go down to an airport and I'd get her an orange juice. Then when I got off the air, I took her to nursery school. Then I'd go do the rest of my job. So it's never, never been easy. I mean Helen Gurley Brown says we can have it all. I don't think so. I don't think you can have it all.

Women have chosen to conquer so many areas in their quest for opportunity and advancement in their careers that many failed to appreciate the full sacrifice that would be demanded in their personal lives. For some, the biological clock became a reality to be faced; for others, relationships were compromised and difficult to sustain. Many, many women in the television news arena are jokingly referred to as "the news nuns," those who are married to their career. But as stations and budgets are being downsized, as contracts fail to be renewed, as ambition and competition mellows, the need for personal fulfillment and a sense of balance takes precedence. The realization comes that true wealth is quality time well spent and serenity in one's life. More is not always better.

Judy Muller is divorced with two grown daughters. She is continually reviewing her options and evaluating her lifestyle: "People in this business are just driven. I see it all around me. I see women all the time, this job is their life. I don't think I want to be in that place. I don't want to end up when I'm fifty-five and no job because they decide I'm not what they want anymore and I have nothing else in my life. That's just not what I want."

The pride, pleasure, and pain of watching children grow and develop became a repeated theme for those who chose the role of motherhood. The responsibility remains an awesome one. The need to do the right thing in the face of maintaining career obligations and goals; the desire to contribute to the development of a healthy, well-balanced, happy and fulfilled human being while balancing the crucial career concerns and ultimately seeking the final measure of a successful life. Somehow, if familial obligations are not met, if children do not turn out right, the feeling is one of failure, failure in the most important role women can undertake.

Marlene Sanders is a widow with two sons and two grandchildren. She is one of the true female pioneers in television news broadcasting, one of only five women working in network news in the early seventies. (The others included Pauline Frederick, now deceased; Lisa Howard, a victim of suicide; Marya McLaughlin, retired and living in Washington, D.C.; and Nancy Dickerson who at the time of my interviews was recuperating from a serious illness but has subsequently died.) Raising their two boys was a shared enterprise with her husband. For example, as a young boy her older son Jeffrey Toobin got the mumps while Sanders was away on assignment in Vietnam. She never worried. Her husband took charge. As Sanders, at sixty-five, is looking for new career challenges, she takes pride in Jeffrey's success. After he was graduated from Harvard Law School, Jeffrey became a writer. He now works for the *New Yorker* magazine and is ABC's chief legal analyst. He dedicated his book on the O. J. Simpson trial to his mother, "the best journalist I know." Sanders believes her son chose his career as a result of being introduced to the news world through the experiences she was able to share with him. She says: "I'm very proud of him. I think he's an absolutely superb writer. He's a much better writer than I am." While acknowledging that her family was definitely inconvenienced from time to time, she never believed they suffered. Sanders admits to being a very strong person, physically strong, and very organized. "I always had things going well. I had good help. Everything was in order. There was

JOE PINEIRO/COLUMBIA UNIVERSITY

Marlene Sanders

no chaos. There were a lot of demands on me, but I'm a very high energy person and I never seem to weaken under the strain."

Sanders has been given difficult challenges in her personal life. She has a twenty-seven-year-old son who is severely retarded. He lives in a home and Sanders has not seen him in ten years. She used to make regular weekly visits with her late husband Jerry Toobin, who was very supportive during this whole ordeal. She does not blame anyone. She feels no guilt. She calls it just "bad luck."

Carole Simpson is married with two grown children. She takes great pleasure from the continuing achievements of her son and daughter. Her daughter was recently graduated, first in her class, from the Medical School of the University of California at San Francisco. Simpson describes how she sat in the audience while her daughter delivered an address on affirmative action and its importance. Tears of pride began streaming down Simpson's face as she watched her daughter receive a standing ovation. Her son, next to her, leaned over and said, "You can rest now, Mom. She does it better." It simply does not get more fulfilling than that. Whatever else brings her fame and success in life, Carole Simpson has experienced a defining moment of happiness.

The increasing power and prestige of women in the newsroom has made the role of motherhood a central issue in the development of workplace policy and acceptance. Parenthood has become a priority and the changing work environment has attempted an accommodation. Women generally do not want to be forced to make the choice between professional success and personal happiness. Women want to have the freedom to define themselves and to fulfill the whole of their identity. This primary objective, led by women in television news, very much remains a work in progress.

11
Salary
and
Status

From birth to age 18, a girl needs
good parents,
From 18 to 35, she needs good looks,
From 35 to 55, she needs a good
personality,
And from 55 on, she needs cash.

SOPHIE TUCKER (1884–1966)

Throughout the course of American history women have felt major financial constraints due to the bias of men in the workplace. They have traditionally been directed into jobs where the pay scale is poor and where a large supply of labor continues to force down their wages. In fact, as soon as women began to enter a field, there was frequently a major decrease in the wages and benefits that had been enjoyed by their male counterparts. Only through continuous pressure of legislation and changes in the economy, have strides been made by women in the labor force. But major disparities and inequities remain a glaring reality.

The 1997 population survey from Department of Labor's Bureau of

Labor statistics documents the disparity in earnings based on gender: the overall median weekly full-time wages and salary of men was $579 while women earned only $431. In the industry classification Editors and Reporters, the same source reveals that men earned a weekly median income of $769 compared with $606 for women. This is particularly significant since of the 257,000 people employed as editors and reporters in newspapers, radio, and cable, 51.2 percent are women. Although females compose the major population group, they remain an underpaid minority in the labor force.

Vernon Stone, journalism professor emeritus at the University of Missouri, has been researching the working conditions and pay in newsrooms since 1972 when only 12.8 percent of the television news force consisted of women. Stone first surveyed the nation's commercial news directors under a grant from the Radio-Television News Directors Association; in that year only two of the 398 who responded were female. Thus it was estimated that 3 of the total number of 630 news directors were female (00.5%). In 1994, 21 percent of the 369 who responded were women. Projected that meant 152 of the nation's 740 news directors were female. The trend toward an increase in the number of women who work as news directors across the country continues.

Journalism professors Lee Becker and Jerry Kosicki from Ohio State University conducted a survey in early 1996 and found that 24.1 percent of the nation's television news directors were women. The estimate, then, is that women were the heads of 205 of the 850 television news operations in the United States.

But this same research revealed that the salaries paid to the news staffs of the television and radio stations have failed to keep up with the average cost of living. According to Vernon Stone's research, it was reported that in 1994 the median annual salary for a television station's highest paid anchor was $54,875. A news director earned $48,625. Other annual staff salaries reported by Stone included executive producers, $37,335; weathercasters, $35,310; sports anchors, $30,875; producers, $22,965; and reporters, $21,915.

The Stone research also points up a widening gap between the highest and lowest paid positions in broadcast journalism. In the sixty smallest television markets, reporters are said to earn $15,850 while top anchors in the twenty-five largest markets receive a salary of $233,000. Those stations in the nation's five largest markets paid annual salaries in excess of $1,000,000. In New York and Los Angeles, the top two markets in the country, the salary paid to the top anchorperson exceeds the $2 million mark. The biggest gains remain with those who have already reached the top of the pay scale. Those who are about to enter the broadcast journalism field with a bachelor's degree can expect to earn a median salary of about $18,000 a year. The more popular the profession, the lower the pay.

As women began to enter and work in television news in ever greater numbers, the issue of pay equity became an ongoing battle that required courage, stamina, and a concerted effort by those who placed themselves on the front lines. But while things have improved for many, there is general agreement among the women I interviewed that economic equity is not yet a reality. Kathy McManus, ABC bureau chief in Jerusalem, succinctly states the problem: "I was underpaid for years. But you know, what are you going to do? You fight your battles and you try to blaze the trail for the next person. No, the next woman, not the next person."

The women's group at ABC headed by Carole Simpson brought the pay and equity issue directly to the attention of management and that effort resulted in significant change. The biggest discrepancy discovered was a major inequity in the pay of women producers. Carole explained: "We found that on average the men were making $90,000 a year. The women were making $60,000, having the same credentials for the job, having to do all the things that men were doing. It was a $30,000 disparity in pay. So we fought and got a pay equity study."

An outside firm was hired to conduct the pay-scale study because the women's group refused to accept an internal review. The year was 1987 and when the facts were revealed, management gave forty-five women and fifteen men increases in pay. In reflection Simpson states: "I'm quite proud of the women at ABC who supported me in that effort and of Roone Arledge who listened and responded and made a difference. There is a big difference."

This activism has made a difference in her own life: "I have suffered both race and sex discrimination. But the most discrimination I've suffered is sex; I have heard more often, 'You can't do it because you're a woman' than 'because you are black.' But you look at the business and until I began anchoring weekend news in 1988, you had a Max Robinson, you had an Ed Bradley, you had Bryant Gumble. But there was no black woman. I mean people say Oprah, Oprah, but that's a talk show, not a news division. So I'm still the only black female doing it regularly."

While Simpson admits that her activist work may have led to the anchor slot on ABC, she knows that is not the reason she has remained in the position. In her inimitable style, Simpson declares, "I would like to think that it's because I'm a good anchor rather than because I was a troublemaker and a noisemaker. Initially, maybe that's why, but I'm sure I would not have held on to it this long had I not been getting the ratings. They have found that in cities where there are large minorities—Seattle, San Francisco, Los Angeles, San Antonio, Oklahoma City—where people see somebody who's different than the white guy in a suit, it's very popular." So for Carole Simpson, her popularity in certain communities gives her the ratings base which translates into dollars for the station. With the diversity of the American population, economic sense must combine with common sense for meaningful results.

Robin Sproul, ABC's Washington bureau chief, was one of the women who received gender equity raises as a result of the pay-scale study. She remembers getting two raises at that time: "I said, 'How did I get it twice? How did I get that second one? Did you just not give me enough the first time?'" Today Sproul believes that equity has been achieved: "I can honestly tell you, there are probably some holdover people who may be skewed higher than they ought to be as there are in any company. But in the ranks of people coming up and the producers who have been here, since the last ten years, it is very equal."

Carole Black, president and general manager of NBC4 in Los Angeles, is the first woman to run a big-three owned and operated station in a large market. She tells of experiencing salary discrimination due to sex earlier in her career: "Once someone said to me at a company years ago, 'Well, he makes more for doing the same job, but he's got a family and your husband's a dentist.'" Black is very familiar with everyone's salary at her station and makes sure that she treats her management people equitably. She emphasizes: "My God, as a woman I wouldn't allow that. No way. You know it's not going to happen because I did grow up in that generation of people that had to work harder and do more and get a little less for it. So, I just think that if any woman is allowing that to happen in her own company, that it's a travesty."

Salary differentials based on sex definitely existed during the seventies and eighties and were experienced acutely by the overwhelming majority of women who were working in both local and network television. Jennifer Siebens, who started with CBS as a producer for the weekend news in January 1976 has remained with the network for over

Carole Black, News4, Los Angeles

twenty years. In December 1986 she reported to work as Los Angeles bureau chief and has held that position for more than ten years. In our interview, she discussed her own earlier experience with pay equity when she worked as a producer. During one contract negotiation, she discovered that a colleague of hers who had been in her class at Columbia University's School of Journalism was also a field producer at CBS on the *Evening News* with Walter Cronkite:

> I found out, in idle conversation one day, that he was earning thirty thousand dollars more a year than I was. I didn't even think to ask him, he just mentioned what he was earning. We were talking about contracts and this came out. I was flabbergasted. Now, he was one of their hero producers, but I was a "nuts-and-bolts car crash on any subject" producer which I regard as being equally crucial to a daily news broadcast. All right, I'm Walter's special projects producer. But I was one of the grunts and I was really good at it. I raised holy hell. They made up for it right away on the next contract.

Siebens was one of the few women I interviewed who was willing to discuss her salary level. She placed her annual earnings in the low six figures. She also admitted that salary differentials based on sex, in her opinion, are gone now. Of her own salary, she says, "I'm very well compensated. I have no complaints."

But one of Siebens' pet peeves concerns the superstars who earn millions of dollars a year and have a problem coping or complain about how hard they work: "I love all these superstars but, God Almighty, when anchormen grouse, or when prime-time stars grouse about having to do it one more time, or having to come in a bit early—you know, I can't tell stories out of school—But you want to slap them around and say, 'Get a grip. Look at your life and look at what real Americans do.'"

The woman who has been the highest paid in the industry for the last two decades is Barbara Walters. When she arrived at ABC in 1976 to become the first female co-anchor of a network news program, she signed a trailblazing contract for $1 million. It was a stunning figure in the industry. The flurry of publicity this generated changed the earning potential of leading on-air news anchors and created an atmosphere that helped salaries escalate into the stratosphere. She is the person that broke so many barriers for women, salary being among the most significant. Walters admits: "I didn't start out thinking I'm going to help other women, aren't I wonderful? But in breaking certain barriers because I had been there longer than many of them, it made a difference for them. Even the salary that was so publicized. Everybody went in after that and asked for more money. But the fact that it was a woman who did it initially and that a woman could, and that a network felt that a woman was important enough and valued enough to give it to her, helped all the other women and men." Barbara Walters's new contract, which was in negotiation when we spoke, is reported to be $10 million annually. This would make her the highest paid on-air news personality in the country.

David Brinkley acknowledges Barbara Walters's role in his own salary growth. In our interview just before his retirement from ABC, he told me: "I went all over the world covering television news. I didn't make any serious money. I made a living. But it wasn't a whole lot. By today's standards it was ridiculous. Barbara Walters was the first. I guess we're all in her debt."

In my conversation with the venerable Walter Cronkite, he attributed the huge escalation that occurred in salaries beginning in the eighties to "aggressive agents." He continued:

It coincided, of course, with the growing realization on the part of the networks that the news broadcast and public affairs broadcast were profit centers. When they became aware that this was not a loss leader but a profit potential, obviously, then the bidding went up for the talent that could deliver an audience. When Barbara Walters got the first million dollars to leave NBC and go to ABC to be an anchorwoman, which didn't work, as we know, at the time with Harry Reasoner. But when that happened, I was asked, by a lot of people, "Is she worth a million dollars?" And my answer was, "Compared to what?" Compared to a rock-and-roll singer, she's worth a lot more and they are appearing in the same medium. Compared to a high school teacher, she's not worth a million dollars at all. But that's a comparison that is not made. A comparison is limited to the medium in which they work.

A sixty-two-year veteran of news broadcasting in the Los Angeles market, George Putnam tells of an encounter with Walter Cronkite in the early sixties. Putnam, now on KIEV radio, created a legend for himself by continually changing jobs while he was working in local television. He was offered a hefty pay raise each time. KTTV and KTLA were literally located across the street from each other and he went back and forth between them with regularity. As Putnam explains, "They raised the money and I crossed the street and the ratings jumped. I advise people to do the same."

George Putnam recounts the time he was in San Francisco covering a story and met Walter Cronkite. They had a drink together at the St. Francis Hotel and Putnam alleges that Cronkite turned to him and said, "George, is it true that you are making between $300,000 and $400,000?" When Putnam answered, "Yes," Cronkite replied, "Well, I'd better go back and talk to someone. I'm only making $125,000."

When I repeated this story to Walter Cronkite during our interview, Cronkite said he did not remember it at all. He continued: "Honestly, I doubt very seriously it happened. I was never seriously concerned with what I made. It was always much more than I made with the United Press and I was very happy with it."

To understand the fluctuation over the years in the earning power of broadcasters, both women and men, it is instructive to look at the early days of television news. For example, when Bob Clark was hired by ABC in 1961 he was given a standard contract that Jim Haggerty was offering to people while he attempted to build up the ABC news organization. Clark remembers: "We were hired for basic salaries of $12,000 a year. But we were on a fee system, so you ended up earning $20,000 a year." Clark also speaks of the changes in the salaries of the anchors: "Frank Reynolds, who was the sole ABC anchor man at one stage, had come to Washington as a White House correspondent and was lured into going to New York to be the anchor in 1968 for $75,000 a year. Now that's a job that pays Peter Jennings, I don't know, $7 million a year."

This is in the same salary range that Dan Rather, Tom Brokaw, and Diane Sawyer, the network superstars, are reported to earn.[1] It is all based on personal contract, what the market will bear, and what their agents are able to negotiate. The major networks are Fortune 500 corporations with a mandate to make money. The fierce competition to hold top on-air news talent creates intense negotiating opportunities that agents and lawyers exploit to the advantage of their clients. Clearly, superstars bring viewers to a program and the corporations are able and willing to pay what is needed to keep their top talent satisfied within their own stable.

Virginia Sherwood remembers that when she left the network in 1975 the salary range for correspondents was somewhere between $35,000 and $75,000. In the current marketplace, these same people would earn from one hundred to several hundred thousand dollars annually. Sherwood remembers when Ted Koppel and Bob Clark and Peter Jennings were probably making $150,000 yearly. In those days the only people Sherwood named in the six-figure salary range were the anchors. But now, says Sherwood, a million is nothing new: "We don't think of it anymore. It just reminds me about something a friend used to say. They remind you of the days of Everett Dirkson who used to say a million here, a million there, and pretty soon you've got real money. Now he'd have to say a billion here and a billion there and pretty soon you're talking about real money."

A great factor in the escalation of star wages was the arrival of Roone Arledge, then president of the news division at ABC, in 1977. When he arrived he was determined to make his mark quickly and improve the acceptance and ratings of the ABC news operation. He had deep pockets and he successfully lured talent away from the other networks. His

---

[1] When Dan Rather extended his contract with CBS in November 1997 to run through the year 2002, his salary was raised to $7 million annually. Earlier in that year Peter Jennings at ABC and Tom Brokaw at NBC each renewed their respective contracts at an annual salary of $7 million.

strategy worked and as ABC's ratings went up, so did the salary scale. A legendary figure in broadcasting, Roone Arledge must be credited with building a formidable news division, one that boasts at the end of each evening news broadcast that more Americans still get their news from ABC News than from any other source.

Diane Sawyer remains one of Roone's top stars, and he remains the reason she came over to ABC from CBS. As one of the highest paid and most sought after women in television news, Sawyer does not experience nor is she aware of salary differentials due to gender. But she does admit that there is more interest in what women are earning: "We're just a newer presence at some of these salary levels. So maybe you don't always read what the men are making. You almost always read what the women are making."

The salary of most on air correspondents is usually kept confidential and most are reluctant to discuss it openly. An exception was Judy Muller who admitted to earnings in the low six figures for her work as ABC correspondent based in Los Angeles. While other people's salaries remain a mystery to her, Muller feels the superstar wage of $7 million and more that is being paid to Ted Koppel, Peter Jennings, Diane Sawyer, and Barbara Walters "is insane." She told me, "I think I would die if I were paid that kind of money. I'd feel what do I do every hour that's worth that. I mean, the pressure would be overwhelming."

Interestingly, some of the men who are today earning megasalaries have admitted they are slightly embarrassed by it—but they have no intention of giving it back.

In general, men are believed to still make more money in broadcasting than the women at the same station. There are always exceptions. It is said that Ann Martin in Los Angeles, anchor of the KCBS-TV news is the highest paid woman in that local market with a salary in excess of $2 million. But most women are still faced with a role that is evolving. Men have put in more years than women because of the fact that women's entrance into the field was barred and closed due to overt sexism. Also, women are not as comfortable demanding additional money. Their lack of years of training in these negotiating skills places them at a disadvantage. When agents enter the picture, it brightens.

Kelly Lange remembers the time her first agent, Michael Ovitz, put her job on the line in order to have her gain equal pay and equal billing. Lange was doing a ninety-minute talk show, *The Sunday Show*, that was done live all over southern California. She first did it with Tom Snyder, and when he left for New York, she anchored with Tom Brokaw. When he also left, Lange worked with a number of different men who served as her co-host. Then, Paul Moyer was hired. Her agent called to tell her that he demanded a "favored nations clause" in her contract. That meant that she would have to be paid the same salary and given equal billing. She was told by her agent, "The way they've got it set up now he's the number-one guy, you're the second banana. We're not asking for first banana or top money. We're asking for equal banana and equal money. What that means, Kelly, is unless I hear by close of business tomorrow that you got it, you don't go to work on Sunday." Lange told me that management got the call at ten minutes to five on Friday and said, "All right." She had an agent whose job it was to look out for her financial future and he helped to negotiate her breakthrough. Michael Ovitz was to continue to prove a formidable player in the talent and moneymaking arena for years to come.

Since Kelly Lange has remained at News4 Los Angeles for more than twenty-five years, she believes her salary never took "a major big jump." She feels that if she had gone to work for another station, it probably would have translated into more money. She does remember earning $10,000 a year on her first job in radio in 1967: "You always remember. I remember my take home pay was $157.40 a week."

Carol Jenkins has a similar career experience. She spent twenty-four years at WNBC-TV in New York before leaving to join Fox News. She never went through a monumental leap in salary. Jenkins states: "I had one of those steady twenty-five year careers where, just like any working person, there were incremental increases along the way. But part of that was because I chose to stay. The way you bargained was to go from shop to shop. I never did that."

Nonetheless, Carol Jenkins complained continuously of a salary inequity. She admitted that Chuck Scarborough, WNBC-TV anchor was making more money than she was. Jenkins categorically believes that with few exceptions, "There's always a man who's making more money than the top woman."

When Rose Ann Scamardella was hired as a street reporter in 1972 she was earning $18,000 a year. When she left in 1984 to spend more time with her daughter, her salary was in the high six figures. Scamardella credits it all to Barbara Walters: "When she got that million dollars, everybody's salary escalated. That's when the animals took over the zoo. We were all making really big bucks." She explains that first the WABC-TV local anchors Roger Grimsby and Bill Beutel started to make a great deal of money. Television news people followed the lead of talent with star power, as Rose Ann describes those with high recognition among viewers, and their demands for more money were met by management. In all monetary negotiations, viewer appeal is considered the prime prerequisite.

Extensive research is routinely done by television stations to find out how viewers feel about the reporters they see, their presentation, their voice, their appearance. These findings help management decide their bottom-line decisions about hiring, firing, and salary raises. Talent is bought and sold and contracted for. If a station's management feels that someone is needed on their news team and this person is able to garner the increased ratings that bring in additional revenues, there is the good chance that salary demands will be met. Since every on-air news talent negotiates a separate contract, the terms reflect whatever the agent can bring in and what the market will permit.

There is a disturbing trend that has affected several of the women I interviewed who have risen to the top of their profession only to find themselves replaced by younger, lower paid women. While on-air men also have been forced out as management looks for younger and cheaper talent in an effort to curtail costs and improve profits, there is a disproportionate number of high salaried women who have born the brunt of these decisions.

Maureen Bunyan was a pillar of WUSA-TV, Channel 9 in Washington, D.C., for twenty-two years. She was an award-winning journalist with strong community ties and had a loyal following of devoted viewers. Her salary was reportedly $450,000 a year. She was a staple in the market and well known and respected throughout the country. When new management came into the station, they wanted to remove her from anchoring the six o'clock and eleven o'clock evening newscasts and reduce her salary, reportedly by 25 percent. They told her that the chemistry was not there between her and her co-anchor Gordon Peterson. This team had been working together for seventeen years, an unprecedented tenure in a newscast. She decided to leave rather then accept their offer. She told me that many people do take a change in assignment and a reduction in salary, but "I decided that after twenty-two years, and twenty-six years in the business I wasn't going to do it for no good reason. And I wasn't given a good reason. But I knew what the reason was. The reason was a change in values and I knew I wouldn't be comfortable working with people whose values were so different from mine."

Bunyan was adamant that this was not a compromise she was willing to make. Her decision created national attention. Over fifteen hundred viewers called the station to express their displeasure. Hundreds of letters were written by irate people, for whom Bunyan had become almost a member of the family, saying she was going to be sorely missed. Bunyan explains some of the reaction:

> The reason I got so much attention was because I was considered to be at the height of my career, with one of the best jobs in local broadcasting. I hadn't done anything wrong. In terms of looks, I hadn't got fat or gray overnight. I hadn't committed any faux pas in reporting or asked the president of the United States any embarrassing questions. So professionally and personally there seemed to be nothing wrong. But I also did something that most of us in any industry and business don't do and that's to say, "Take this job and do you know what with it!" But that's my personality. So it wasn't that hard for me to do.

Maureen Bunyan is a beautiful, intelligent, and proud woman. She has set a standard by which other female journalists are judged. Barbara Bush, when she was first lady, said in an interview that Maureen Bunyan was the woman she most admired. The authority, credibility, knowledge, and respect Bunyan has earned over the years merit the accolades she has received. The changes being made in television news have to do with power, gender, and image. Bunyan is gratified that after twenty-six years she has been able to establish an identity as a complete woman who not only discharged her broadcasting duties with distinction but also through her strong ties to the community has made a significant impact.

Bunyan is saddened and disturbed that the news is no longer an independent entity and that the people who work in the news are no longer independent people. They have become part of the package. Demographics rule decisions. The quest for younger viewers dictates decisions about coverage and anchors. As news has become more of a business, the nature of the people running it has changed. The structure of news has become more of a corporate product. There is little room for people who wish to remain independent thinkers. For successful professional, authoritative women especially, the environment today is one in which they must fight to stay alive.

Maureen Bunyan

Susan King was another high-profile, experienced, anchor woman working at a local television station in Washington, D.C., WJLA, who was forced out of her position and replaced by a younger woman at a lower pay scale. In the summer of 1993, King's contract was up for renewal and they told her that she was important to the station but "we don't want you to anchor anymore." There was a decrease in pay that accompanied the change in assignment. As King puts it, "They made me an offer I could definitely refuse." At that time the union put in a grievance on her behalf that said what they were essentially doing was firing her. That case went to arbitration and, after two years, King won. When she talks about her experiences, King acknowledges that her efforts have helped many other women, including Maureen Bunyan: "Thank God I won my case or Maureen would have gotten screwed." She is pleased that her case set up a national precedent which says, according to King, "that you cannot dump individuals of long standing and status and offer them something clearly of lesser stature and claim that you are not un-doing them."

Susan King, now assistant secretary for public affairs at the Depart-ment of Labor, believes that her career reflects the trends that women have faced in broadcasting over the years. She started as a secretary be-cause desk assistant jobs were then only given to men. In 1971 she was working at CBS when they first put on a woman as a desk assistant. So women who were nowhere got into the system and began to prove themselves. They proved able to have authority and credibility and there was a period of growth where women were able to reach, on-air, into every rank of the business. King pointed to "women like Andrea [Mitch-ell], Lynn Sherr, Lesley Stahl, and Barbara [Walters], who is the god-mother to everyone, who proved that women can sustain and continue in the business." But then, points out King, there is another trend:

> Although there are those women I talked about, some of them have been pushed sideways and are not as prominent as I think they de-serve to be, Andrea Mitchell being one. Some others, like Maureen, who are put aside a little bit, for the trend that I'm fearful of is the credibility and the experience of women may not be as respected as male credibility and experience. The demographics will often mean new trends of women coming into the business to fulfill the sort of Ken and Barbie side of the business.

The push to dominance of demographics has resulted in the quest for the viewer between eighteen and forty-five years old. That's the name of the game in the industry today where good demographics can translate into tens of millions of dollars in advertising revenue. But there is evi-dence to suggest that in order to fulfill those set demographic needs, it's all right for the men to be older but the women tend to get younger. And even though men are not exempt from these same economic realities, the woman is usually the first to go. It is a sad commentary to find the credibility and integrity that experienced woman journalists have fought to have recognized are often minimized and devalued.

Rebecca Bell had been with NBC for over nineteen years, serving since 1970 when she was one of only sixty network correspondents employed by NBC News as an on-air journalist. Her first job was for WDSU-TV, an NBC affiliate in New Orleans; she was paid half of what a man was paid because, she was told, "you're a single woman and have no family and you shouldn't need very much." Only when the American

Federation of Television and Radio Artists intervened and told her boss "either pay her full scale or fire her" did her salary level change. And she remembers that her boss actually came very close to firing her.

In 1976, Rebecca Bell became the first woman NBC ever put on as its Paris bureau chief. For eight years she traveled all over Europe, Northern Africa, and parts of the Middle East and the Far East, covering and directing coverage of international news events. In 1984 she was made director of news services for NBC's 205 affiliated local newsrooms including their regional satellite networks and overseas facilities. In 1989, when General Electric bought the company, Rebecca Bell left NBC. In her words, "I was downsized and someone half my age and paid half my salary was brought in." Bell now says philosophically, "There are inequities in life. Nothing's perfect and that includes television news." A sad, but accurate commentary.

12
Mentors
and
Mission

I want to be all that I am capable of
becoming . . .
KATHERINE MANSFIELD (1888–1923)

As we chart the careers and contributions of women in television news,
it becomes evident that only through years of hard work and dedication have they been able to make a stronger presence felt in the industry. Most entered the field as the movement for equal opportunity for
women became a force for hiring. Their success permitted a new generation of women to follow in their footsteps and become a visible
role model for still others waiting in the wings. The advances made by
women mandated the need to persevere in the face of setback or success.
Every woman working in the television news world today knows the
transience that permeates the profession and the need to continually
fight to move ahead. But progress in television, as in society, comes very
slowly, and in waves. Those who are able to remain strong and pace
themselves for the long distance achieve a strong finish and provide the
impetus for the women who will stand on their shoulders in the years
ahead.

The seventy women and fifteen men in broadcasting who make up
the interview sample for this body of research were all influenced to
some degree by people who played key roles in their personal and professional lives. Their individual decisions and career paths were shaped

by those who preceded them. The mentors with whom they worked reflect a broad spectrum of diversity, sensitivity, and intelligence. Their words provide insight into their hard-won careers and offer inspiration to others still searching.

Diane Sawyer observes that there is no one person who most impacted her enviable career. She notes, however: "I'm a collector. I have like a necklace of pearls, each of them retrieved from a multitude of people I've met along the way." When I continued to press for a name, Diane mentioned the late Charles Kuralt as a source of inspiration and help.

Judy Muller also immediately named Charles Kuralt as her special mentor:

> Charles Kuralt is my idol. I think he's the best writer in broadcast journalism. I remember once I got a note from him. We knew each other. We were friends. But back then I was just in awe of him and I'd collect his scripts, because if I ever teach again I'm going to use these scripts to show the beauty of simple writing. He once wrote me a note saying, "I just heard your commentary driving in to work, and nobody ever takes time to tell each other these things, so I thought I would tell you that you are articulate, and eloquent." I put it in my scrapbook, this frayed little note from Charles Kuralt. I started to cry. I have an Emmy. But nothing will ever mean as much to me as getting that note. To me, I could have retired that day and said, "I arrived; the highest praise!"

Elizabeth Vargas, at the time of our interview, moved over to ABC to be the news anchor for *Good Morning, America*. She was thrilled to finally meet some of the people she had been watching all of her life, "emulating and admiring" them:

> I can't speak highly enough of both Diane Sawyer and Barbara Walters. I've been an enormous fan of theirs for a very, very long time. Their work is incredibly strong. They're just wonderfully talented, intelligent women. Diane, in particular, has been like a mentor, reaching out to me and making me feel very warm and very welcome after what was a very difficult decision to leave a network that I was very happy at, and take a big risk to jump across town to another network that was brand-new for me, where I didn't know anybody. They've both been really, really, really great.

Sylvia Chase, a twenty-five-year veteran of network broadcasting, has been a role model for women journalists through the years. But she credits Mike Wallace for being her own early role model. She also looks to Barbara Walters: "I believe her experiences at ABC were about as painful as they could be, and she was so incredibly public a figure that she couldn't hide. I know that she was in a lot of pain because she now talks about it. It was an awful experience for her. So when the going gets tough, I often think, 'Well you know, think about Barbara, she did it.'"

Barbara Walters is the single name most mentioned as the person women look up to for support and confidence. Carol Jenkins, another broadcasting veteran with twenty-five years of experience, holds up Barbara Walters as "a symbol that it can be done." Jenkins comments: "As you mature, she makes you believe that a career in television is possible. Barbara has done an extraordinary job of keeping that pipeline open. So while she hasn't had a direct effect, there's always something in the back of my mind that says, 'Barbara can do it. So the rest of us can try to!'"

The inimitable Ann Compton talks of a steady stream of influences she has felt. She begins with Barbara Walters: "I watched during the Camp David accords. She didn't get on-air much, but she never stopped pushing, hour after hour, day after day, calling people on the phone, trying to hammer a story out of what was basically two weeks of zipped lips. Nobody was saying anything. She was relentless." Compton also points to Helen Thomas of United Press International who "comes in earlier than I do every morning, leaves later than I do, and never, ever sits through a briefing without saying, 'But there's something I need to know.' People with real drive who refresh my sense of commitment."

Compton also looks to women in politics who have had to hold the line and break new ground:

> I think of Carla Hills, who was a cabinet secretary in the Ford administration. I still remember her standing on the stage in the East Room when she was sworn in, with her five little children including the littlest one in white organdy and the mary janes. When I saw Carla Hills a couple of years ago, I told her how I remembered that moment and how just looking at that I thought, "Well, there's no reason I can't do that." And she said, "That little girl in mary janes just graduated from Stanford Law School . . ." And there are political women like Lillian Carter, mother of Jimmy Carter, who raised four very different children. She raised them in the South, and her husband's dead, and her oldest son comes to Georgia to run the business and to run for governor; she goes and volunteers for the peace corps. I don't

think she made it to election night, the night he was elected governor; she was then sixty-eight years old. She wanted to go to India and work in villages—she was a nurse by training—immunizing children and families.

The women Compton admires most are those who have chosen to listen to their own voice and who accomplish things quietly and in incremental ways.

In my opinion, a role model is one who not only possesses traits of character and talent that are inspirational, but who also demonstrates the physical and professional characteristics with which one can identify. It was in the late fifties when Carole Simpson decided in high school that she wanted to be a reporter, and she knew no one who had done this before: "Of course the only reporters I had heard of at that time were Brenda Starr and Lois Lane." She also remembers that Lois Lane had Superman to help her. Carole's parents thought she was "crazy." She proved them wrong.

Carole Simpson has remained at the forefront of stories relating to the advancement of women in broadcasting. She has helped so many of her colleagues achieve a higher level of equity in the profession while never compromising her own standards and fierce determination. She continues to help young minority students with scholarship support and is a role model for women throughout the industry.

Pat Harvey has always been a strong admirer of Carole Simpson and she credits her with giving early support to her dream of being a journalist. Harvey explains: "I never met Walter Cronkite. I mention his name because my father was so concerned about me going into this business. I was to have been a teacher or an executive secretary or a nurse. His words to me were, 'Honey, you don't look like Walter Cronkite.'"

While Harvey admires Walter Cronkite greatly, since she is an African American woman, they obviously had few physical features in common. But Harvey thought she had a great deal in common with Carole Simpson:

> I met her in Saginaw [Michigan] covering George Bush when he ran against Ronald Reagan in 1980. I was more excited about meeting her. She just sort of took me aside and said, "Do you really want to get in and do what I'm doing?" I said, "Yes, more than anything." And she said, "You know, I've been up running with him since five o'clock in the morning. This is a grueling schedule." And I said,

"That's okay. That's what I want to do." So she sat down and had dinner with me and just talked to me about family, career, and how difficult it was. I admired her for that and still do. She will always have a lasting affect on me.

As anchor of KCAL news in Los Angeles, Pat Harvey knows that she herself is now the role model for many other young women who are aspiring journalists. She feels this is an important responsibility and gives freely of herself to meet this obligation and to pass on what help she can to those who are willing to work hard and make the needed sacrifices.

Gwen Ifill always looked for inspiration from those who proceeded her in the industry. She remembers that when she was a little girl, there was a woman on television whose name was Melba Tolliver: "I would see her on television wearing this big afro and giving the news, and I was just blown away. As a kid, I thought that was the coolest thing to see a black woman, who looked kind of like me, delivering the news. I think that always stuck in my head, and it affects me now. I know there are little girls who are watching me now and saying, 'Hey, look at that. I could do that.'"

Ifill's father was a minister and a civil rights activist who raised his daughters to believe they could do anything they wanted. As Capitol Hill correspondent for NBC in Washington, D.C., Gwen Ifill continues to prove that there is nothing she is unable to do: "The people I see who stumble the most are the ones who impose their own limits on themselves. I was trained not to do that."

Carole Black is concerned about the low self-esteem that prevents women from achieving their true potential:

Something happens about the age of eleven or twelve when women stop feeling good about themselves and start worrying more about how they look than about what they know and want to be liked rather than want to show how smart they are or study. It's very sad because I think there's a lot of talent that goes away. I would love nothing better than to figure out the way that young girls and young women can feel good about themselves and believe in themselves and feel that they can be all that they want to be and that it won't mean that they would be alone in life. Or it won't mean that they would be ostracized by guys. I would like to be that for women. I'd like to show them that they can be everything that they want to be, and that

Michel McQueen, ABC News

they should be their feminine self. They don't have to be like a man. They'll be most successful just being themselves."

The journalist that Michel McQueen credits with having the most influence on her is *Washington Post* columnist David Broder. McQueen considers him to be a "very kind man": "He has always managed to do his job in an excellent fashion without becoming a jerk. He told me once he's always interested in people from the high and the low. He treats everyone the same. It's very important in journalism to be open to people. Journalism is about people and what happens to them in their lives." McQueen feels it important to always remain open to new people and not become "a mole." The other person Michel McQueen holds up for admiration is Ted Koppel. She says he is aware that his wealth serves to distance and separate him from the vast majority of people, yet he works to reduce that chasm. McQueen candidly continues: "One of the things that irritates me about being a minority is that minorities are constantly aware that they are black. But white people aren't aware of being white." She believes that white people choose not to be aware of the way in which their sensibilities affect their world view. They tend to think they are the human beings and "we're black." She says, "You're white as well as human and I'm human as well as black." Ted Koppel, McQueen believes, "recognized that he is his own particular combination of experiences and views, and that that shapes who he is and what he is in a way that I think a lot of people who are wealthy, male, and privileged do not do." McQueen found it characteristic of his priorities that Ted Koppel chose to hold a town hall in Israel after the assassination of Yitzhak Rabin rather than remain in Washington to attend a megaparty that Disney, the new owners of ABC, had decided to give. McQueen declares: "I was so proud. I find it inspiring to be around him."

The person Maureen Bunyan looked to for inspiration and guidance in her career was Mal Goode, the first African American man hired as a reporter by any of the television networks. He was hired by ABC in New York in the sixties. By then, he was in his middle fifties after a long career as a journalist in New York and Pittsburgh working for black newspapers and radio. He covered the civil rights movement and he also covered the United Nations for ABC. Bunyan describes his influence:

> He was a personal friend of mine and just had incredible integrity. He also was a mentor to many young people and shared his expertise. He was a fighter. He would tell you stories about what was done to him that would just make your hair stand on end. Names he was called by his colleagues. Camera crews that refused to work with him because he was black. Hearing his stories would always give me more resolve when I felt upset or down in the mouth. He had a habit, for years and years, of calling me every Friday afternoon. He'd be in his office at the United Nations or at the radio station where he was working. We would chat and I would tell him this is what happened to me this week and Mal would say, "Don't let the bastards get you down." And I'd pick myself up and get going again. So, spiritually, he was really a tremendous support.

Rose Ann Scamardella gives credit to the late Roger Grimsby for being her strongest mentor. Roger was the anchorman for WABC-TV's

Eyewitness News and was acknowledged as the person who held the whole news team together. Scamardella comments, "He was very bright, very good at what he did. He was the anchorman when I was there. He was almost cruel to us, like we were the children, the reporters. I had to work very hard to be accepted by him because he thought I was just hired because I was an Italian woman and I wouldn't do my job. So I think working hard and learning from him, almost to get his acceptance, was important to me."

Betsy Aaron speaks highly of Av Westin, who as early as 1973, when he was an executive producer at ABC news, prided himself on giving opportunities to qualified women who were working at the network. Aaron now the Moscow correspondent for CNN, says of Av Westin, "He gave me a chance. He said to me, 'Work hard. Be better and I'll give you the opportunity. I won't pull the plug on you unless you screw up.' And I could talk over story ideas with him. I think he was just really a good boss." That is high praise from a fine news woman who has survived working for certain men who would not fit that same assessment.

Heather Allan has high praise for the man who hired her. His name is Martin Fletcher, a Tel Aviv correspondent. Heather says, "He was very influential in my early days." Former NBC News president Larry Grossman is the other man Heather refers to as impacting her career in a positive way. She believes that Larry Grossman was "an exceptionally good and kind person and was good to everybody. He was a very well loved person and he was just a good soul."

While not a mentor for her career, Heather Allan heaps high praise on Andrea Mitchell. She's a big fan. Allan describes the need for women in television to be bigger, better, and stronger and she believes Andrea Mitchell is all that and more: "I think she's just astounding and I don't think they can put her down. I know a lot of women that work here feel the same way about her. We root for her daily, every time we see her on. She's what it should be."

When I spoke to Andrea Mitchell, she was equally ready to give accolades and thanks to the mentors in her life. Mitchell speaks first of Judy Woodruff and John Palmer who were the senior NBC correspondents when she first went to the White House: "They were both superb reporters and both understood television very well and I learned different things from each of them. I also learned the generosity of spirit they basically displayed toward me. So I hope that I have been as giving to younger people as they have been to me."

Mitchell also speaks highly of her professional relationship with Sam Donaldson. She admits to learning a great deal from watching him work: "I learned the level of intensity that Sam brings to everything is quite extraordinary. That was quite a lesson." No longer covering the White House or Congress for NBC as she had been doing for eighteen years, she was given the title of chief foreign affairs correspondent for NBC, focusing on the intersections between politics and foreign policy. This transition in her career, Mitchell explains, was the result of NBC's agenda "to develop and promote the career of a very young and exciting young anchor man, Brian Williams, giving him the platform for the White House beat, which has worked out very successfully for everyone." By expressing the benefits and the challenges of her new position, Andrea Mitchell gives testimony to her strong spirit, independent strength, and unfailing ability to accept what is given to her and to give back her best in return. She remains an exceptional role model for women who aspire to make a lasting contribution to the world of television news.

Susan Zirinsky arrived at CBS in 1972 "as a sort of child." She was still in college and her first job was part-time, working weekends. Twenty-five years later Zirinsky reflects on the two people who have had the greatest impact on her career, Dan Rather and Lesley Stahl:

> Lesley was a partner for many, many years because we did the White House for a long time. It was a growth experience for both of us. We were soul mates for a long, long time. Out of so many women that I've worked with, she represents the best of the best. She is always curious. She is always hungry. There is passion to a good story that is the same today as it was twenty years ago for her. And Dan is the same way. Maybe we're just a club for excessives. Dan on the road, on a good story, is fantastic. Dan is tireless in a war. He will do anything from cook the soup for everybody, to carry the bags, to help write radio, to everything. The pressures or the rigors of what he has to do in New York seem to fade away and he becomes invigorated on the road. It's a different Dan than most people know.

Susan Zirinsky wants, above all else, to serve as a mentor to people. She finds great satisfaction from seeing other people succeed. While she continues to experience deep disappointment from the fact that she was not made executive producer of the *Evening News* in 1991, Zirinsky loves the business, loves what she has been doing. The ability to overcome setbacks and disappointments is a true measure of a person's enduring success. Susan Zirinsky, hailer of helicopters and taxis, has continually proven that with persistence, patience, passion, and determination she is capable of achieving solid career heights.

The leading men in broadcasting have a diverse and interesting set of influences that they credit for enabling them to achieve the high level of success and distinction in their respective careers.

David Brinkley considers his high school English teacher his most important mentor. He describes how one day she told him, "David, you ought to be a journalist." This was when he was a junior in high school in his hometown in North Carolina: "I was writing things and letting her read them. She became my tutor. When she said that to me, it was the first time it ever crossed my mind. I owe her a real debt." Legions of broadcast news viewers and professional colleagues share that appraisal.

Dan Rather also credits a former teacher with providing him with the influence and skills that contributed to his long and distinguished career: "Professor Hugh Cunningham, he was my college teacher and he was tremendously gifted. He taught journalism, but basically he taught life." Rather also spoke of Edward R. Murrow and the legacy he provided: "Professionally those were among the two greatest."

Tom Brokaw remembers those people who were there in the early days. He first came into the industry thirty years ago and the names of John Chancellor, Reuven Frank, and David Brinkley rise to the top of his list of men who helped establish the standards and quality of excellence that broadcast journalists point to with pride and that he found inspirational in his own career climb.

Bob Mulholland, former president and chief operating officer at NBC, now retired, speaks most highly of the impact of Reuven Frank: "With his standards in many ways, Reuven invented quality in network broadcast news. With the attention to writing and detail and picture and just quality reporting, quality journalism." David Brinkley when speaking of Reuven Frank told me, "He is the man who invented television news as we know it." Many other lions of news echo that evaluation.

Among the men who shepherded and guided the career of Sam Donaldson is Howard K. Smith: "I admired him, watched him, and listened to him." Donaldson continued, "Do I admire Cronkite? Yes! And do I admire my idol, David Brinkley, with whom I've worked now for almost sixteen years? You bet!"

But Donaldson saves his highest praise for Roone Arledge:

Behind Roone's back we all grouse about things that he does or doesn't do and his idiosyncrasies. But the fact is for people like me and Ted Koppel, Peter Jennings, and many others, Roone Arledge made us. At the very least he gave us an indispensable item. He gave us an opportunity to show our wares on a major level. He did more than that. He backed us. He created conditions under which we could flourish and think. The three of us that I just named had been at ABC a long time before Roone Arledge came to the news division. We did good work, excuse me for being arrogant if you will, but who knew it? Roone came and gave us the where-with-all and the positions. I mean, Roone said that Ted Koppel should substitute for Frank Reynolds when Frank wanted the night off for his birthday during "America Held Hostage." Roone made Ted Koppel the anchor of *Nightline*. Then Ted demonstrated why Roone was right, of course. He's the best in the business doing that. But without Roone, Ted would be just a very fine aging diplomatic correspondent. Not what he is today.

The willingness to give credit, thanks, and accolades to colleagues and to those who preceded them in the industry provides the men and women working together in television news with the awareness that they do not stand alone in their triumphs and tribulations. For the many who aspire to join them, they serve as a guiding force for the future. This is a formidable responsibility, yet one that is acknowledged and embraced by the best of the best.

"Goodnight and good luck."

13
Milestones
and
Millstones

Because of their agelong training in
human relations—for that is what
feminine intuition really is—women
have a special contribution to make
to any group enterprise.

MARGARET MEAD (1901–1978)

As we look back over the last quarter century in the history and development of television news broadcasting, certain changes have contributed to a dramatic difference in the way news is gathered, transmitted,
and received. The first and most fundamental has been the result of improvements in technology.

As Walter Cronkite describes it, "The most dramatic change has
been the technological advances that we've made from the film process,
which was very slow, and the equipment, which was very large. To get
proper film, the negative had to be developed and then printed into a
positive film. It was a comparatively slow and cumbersome process. We
moved on to videotape and then to miniaturized equipment and finally
to satellite transmission which has made a major difference, of course,
in television coverage."

Satellite technology has permitted us to have instantaneous news coverage whereas in earlier days journalists were prisoners of the daily deadline. Technology led to significant changes in programming. Sam Donaldson explains:

> Instant satellite technology allowed a Ted Koppel, along with others, to invent a *Nightline* in which, at the outset, it's basic format difference was the ability to link around the world a single conversation of people. Before the technology, there could not have been the program. The programming that allows, whether it's CNN or us, to bring you instant live pictures from Bosnia or wherever there is news, that drives the programming. CNN could not exist in my judgment if it had been in existence during the Vietnam War. It would not have the impact because it was all on film and it all had to be processed and shipped on airplanes, with a few exceptions, to San Francisco or Los Angeles. CNN's advantage now is that it's on the air all the time and instantly can go places. Therefore, its reporter Peter Arnett can broadcast from Bagdad. We didn't do this in Berlin. We couldn't do it from Berlin. Never mind the question of whether Adolf Hitler would have allowed that, whether we would have allowed that. It's moot. Couldn't do it. Could do it now.

Richard Threlkeld also believes the satellite revolution changed the skills that were required in the field. He states: "Like the change from silent films to talkies, an awful lot of correspondents who were good with the written word and were very, very good reporters simply couldn't talk well or intelligently on television live. So the skills now require that, in addition to everything else, you have to be able to talk well, intelligently and succinctly on live television."

The overwhelming majority of the newsmen and women who I interviewed for this book have expressed deep concerns about the current standards and practices that exist today in their profession. Some are merely disturbed, others feel baffled and frustrated, a few are angry. Sheila MacVicar has a particular interest in foreign affairs. She speaks with passion and eloquence of what she sees around her:

> It drives me nuts, absolutely nuts, that American networks are convinced that the American public is completely disinterested in things that happen beyond its own borders and that there is no public service demand on networks to basically tell people about some extraordinary things that happen overseas and elsewhere. Yes, I am speaking in an American election year. Yes, I know that makes a difference,

that America is more inward looking historically during presidential election years. But, I look at things that Americans and networks are willfully ignoring. I think that they are not going to understand the world of the new millennium. I think that they are going to fail to understand the aspirations and dreams and goals of a whole bunch of people who are out there, who ultimately could perhaps threaten American security. And that I think is, in the most basic way, the reason we need to be paying more attention to what's going on out there. I also think that American ignorance about issues and people and places beyond its own borders never fails to astonish me. I think that in my time at ABC, that ignorance, through us, has increased. I look at the things that we don't do—that we are not telling Americans about. And that's my frustration.

Christiane Amanpour also expresses deep concern about the continuing tendency to give less significance to international news. She views CNN as an exception but speaks candidly about the fact that there is the focus on looking inward and not giving international news the attention it once enjoyed:

> International news, foreign correspondents used to be the creme de la creme of our profession. It was considered a major reward, way back when, to receive a posting to a foreign bureau. Now it's rapidly becoming the wilderness. And certainly, in the early 90's it was worse. I think the balance is being redressed now. People who closed foreign bureaus are now starting to open them up again. But I think that the importance attached to international news is diminishing. I think that's not only a shame but a danger. I also think that when a president comes in and professes that his major contribution will be to domestic affairs and professes not to be frightfully interested in foreign affairs . . . but all of the crowning achievements of many presidents and all of the major blunders and failures, often revolve around foreign affairs.

There has been an outcry from serious journalists who continue to struggle with the need to maintain journalistic ethics and standards in face of the enormous ratings pressure and the public's increasing appetite for the quick, the easy, and the tabloid.

Jennifer Siebens emphatically declares that there is nothing that makes people in the business weep more than the scandalous stories:

Dan [Rather] called it the Hollywoodization of the news. But I think that oversimplifies what's going on. I don't think we do enough analysis any more. I don't think we look sufficiently at real issues. You know, the collapse of education, the collapse of law enforcement, the inability of governments to lead their people, be they local, state, or federal. These are profound issues for this country. I have to say that in Walter's [Cronkite] days some of the news was pretty boring. Elvis died and Walter barely wanted to deal with it. Just out of touch. So the good old days weren't so great either. Walter was a world wire service guy and some committee would issue a report 30 minutes to air and he'd want to do a story—the UPI instinct. But I think the culture of the tabloid magazines—and during the O. J. trial, the pressures were on all networks. That was a story that had so many naturally sleazy elements. And we get dragged into a subject. How far do we go into things we would normally never look at and then get pushed by ratings and by the public's apparent want for it. But I think at CBS there's a course correction now underway. We're trying to sort our way through this as we hit the year 2000.

The sensationalism and the herd mentality give rise to deep disdain and creates an uncomfortable arena for news people who respect their profession and understand that its basic responsibility is to serve the public. Judy Muller wants to see the return of the separation between news and entertainment. She wants to try to get back to where all editorial decisions are made by hard-core journalists who ask the key questions:

> Will the public be served by this information or are we just looking to up our ratings? Is it gossip or is it news? Should we do this? Nobody takes the time anymore to reflect because there is no time. The competition is so fierce. But I think you could be a standout organization if you were the only one, for instance, who didn't report Richard Jewell's name.[1] Now maybe we had no choice, but I think we do. Yes, we were told by the FBI that he's a possible suspect. But, we don't report possible suspects unless there's hard-core evidence. We are not tools of the FBI. I think that would have been really classy. But, nobody did it. So, I don't think it's possible to separate news from entertainment and I despair over that.

---

[1] Richard Jewell was a prime suspect in the 1996 summer Olympics bombing. He was hounded mercilessly by the media but never charged with the crime.

On March 11, 1998, in a speech delivered to the Radio-Television News Directors Foundation (RTNDF), Roone Arledge spoke with candor about the unacceptable journalistic practices that have "terrorized innocent victims." He referred to the fact that "47% of the people in this country think journalists don't care about the people they cover." Arledge proposed that ABC take the lead in finding a cure for the "feeding frenzy" that victimizes people involved in a sensational news story. He believes it will not only help the victims caught in the press coverage, but it would also help journalists "get some of our respect back."

Heather Allan wants to see more serious news presented. She believes that what is put on air is "trivia":

> It seems to me that we have never come to grips with the really big issues that are facing this country. We never really look at Mexico, for example, and why people are coming across the borders. Yet, there is a reason that there's an illegal immigration problem here. But, nobody really wants to look at it. And I guess when you put it on, people turn off. So I'm not sure where the answer is. I just wish that we could do a better job of it because I believe Americans would have a better idea of why things happen. I don't think we do a good job of explaining anything. For example, Bosnia, we never bothered to go to Bosnia. For a whole year we never went to Bosnia. Then all of a sudden the American troops were going to Bosnia. So you send all the anchors to Bosnia and you show here are the troops in Bosnia. You haven't explained to anybody why they're there and why they're probably doomed and why it's probably a futile exercise. Nobody really looks at these things and nobody will give you time to do it.

Allan believes the old adage that if people get the government they deserve, they also get the television news they deserve.

Judy Woodruff wants to eliminate the unnecessary emphasis that is placed on the ratings:

> I understand we're a business. I understand that we don't make a lot of money on the news side and that there are cost restraints on what we do and that we're expected to hold up our end of the profit and loss sheet. But, we're not in the donut making business. We're not selling tires. I mean, we are imparting to the American people information to help them make decisions about how they go about living their daily lives. How they go about relating to their communities. What they should believe about their government at the state, local,

national, international level. How they should vote. We are giving them important information day in and day out and that's a big responsibility. If we are just looking at ourselves as another business to make a profit and we tailor this industry so that we've got all the bells and whistles and the glitter, then we're off mission. I worry about that.

Deborah Potter explains her frustration with the news she sees:

I'd like to be able to turn on my set and figure out what happened today. Sometimes I feel as though I'm wading through stacks of stuff that have nothing to do with my life. I'm talking in particular about local news. I would like to see a move away from the mindless coverage of crime. I love news. I think news is important. I want my children to know what's going on in the world, and I cannot sit and watch local news with them. This is devastating to me. It's even so bad we can't even listen to the local radio news because it's one crime after another. We all know why we do it. It's easy to get but it doesn't inform anyone.

Potter would like journalists to do a better job of covering politics in a way that provides useful information for people who have to make up their minds and cast a vote in November rather than spend so much time on superficial issues.

Bob Clark believes that there has been such a condensation of news that today we really just have a headline news service:

I can recall a time when a New York executive producer came down and told us we were going to have to handle Washington stories in two and a half minutes. We just couldn't have anymore of these three and three and a half and four minute stories. Now, of course, a lot of things are down to a minute ten or a minute and twenty. It is the shrinkage of sound bites from twenty-five or thirty or forty seconds down to like four or five seconds, where sound bites are used as exclamation points or just attention grabbers. That's the way TV news goes. That is not to say that you can't package a good honest television report in a minute fifteen seconds, but it's very difficult and it makes it much more difficult to handle a serious Washington story responsibly.

The commercialization of news has distorted its mission and eroded its standards. There is a moral obligation and responsibility that journalists have to inform the public in the best way possible. Without the civic role of journalism, one has lost sight of what remains crucial to a functioning democracy.

Richard Threlkeld looks back to the early founders of the networks:

I think people like General Sarnoff at NBC and Bill Paley at CBS did feel, most of the time, in those years an obligation that this beast called a television network had made them a lot of money, had made them rich and made them famous. At the very least, they had to give something back. There's no sense today, in management, at any of the networks or at any of the cable channels that sense of giving back, that sense that there is a higher duty out there than to just make money, which is to inform people. You can do it at a relatively modest cost, but they're unwilling even to pay that and that's too bad.

Since news is viewed as merely another profit center, and no longer seen as a public trust, the idealism brought to television news in the pioneer days failed to live through this period of increased ratings pressure and competitiveness. While Bill Paley took immense pride from the success of the CBS news operation and from the giant contributions that were made to his network and to the history of broadcast journalism by the likes of Edward R. Murrow and then Walter Cronkite, today's owners do not possess that same sense of identification and pride. There is no longer the willingness to accept the special mission of journalism. The old school that established broadcast news as the arena to provide meaningful information and to make the world a better place has been replaced by corporate greed and the need to make more and more profits for corporate big-wigs and shareholders. It is a sobering reality that affects all of us and the future of our society.

Walter Cronkite believes that in the years ahead we will see a return of solid news and a growing dissatisfaction with what he labels "the entertainment/infotainment aspect of the evening news." He understands, as few others can, the strengths and the limitations inherent in the medium:

I think that tunnel vision is an inadequate form of communication of news in the first place. It [TV] shows us where the news is made and who makes it in better form than any other medium. It's got a great advantage in that regard. But the time limitation is an absolutely major hindrance to a full reportage as television should be able to give. A half hour isn't nearly enough time. An hour still would be inade-

Walter Cronkite, CBS News

quate, probably, to really adequately cover the complex world in which we live today. The complex nation in which we live, even complex cities in which we live. There are so many issues which need a vastly greater treatment than television is able and willing to give them. People need to go to print. Even our newspapers are following television's trend of shorter stories and featured treatment to a degree that one has to go to magazines and books to get all of the information they need today. I think it's a shame to spend that half hour of news time with a lot of feature stories when there is so much news it ought to try to cram in.

The cult of celebrity that has engulfed the television news profession is another area of disappointment and frustration. At one point the job of journalist was chosen by those individuals who were interested in covering history as it was being made and reporting it. The fundamental purpose of broadcast journalism should always be to give people a condensed version of the truth as best and fairly presented as possible.

Al Ittelson expresses his thoughts with searing frankness. What would he most like to change in television news?:

The bullshit. The phoniness and self-importance of the people who front the profession and run it. I think that kind of haughtiness and self-importance runs through the profession. When we're doing the best, we're not the important person. The story is important and it should be told with as little involvement of the storyteller, except in the beauty of telling the story. I'm afraid that's the biggest hole and the softest part of journalism. I think it's because it is not based on serving the public as much as it is on impressing the public.

Phyllis Haynes was not optimistic that corrective action was possible from within the industry itself, no matter how great the frustration or the concerns:

In an era of downsizing, in an era of the disposable newsperson, in an age when Disney takes over a network, you are talking about people getting angry. What a joke! It's too late for that. The only possible way to change television news is through the consumer. If the consumer gets annoyed enough, then there will be changes. Unfortunately, the consumer is being anesthetized by the glitz and the glamour. I think that the only thing that is going to create change are community action-minded people. Like the parents who got out there and tried to force the networks to have children's programming. Change from within where people can be fired at the drop of a hat, in a takeover environment, is a joke. If anything, we need to fortify our union strength. I can't believe I'm saying this because I've always been one for fairness and didn't want to see any stronghold. But, boy, when I see how disposable the communication industry people are, they ought to be grateful that there is an AFTRA.[2]

David Brinkley told me just a few months before he retired from ABC that, in spite of the industry shortcomings, there is much to be pleased about. As he looked back at the contribution of television news over the decades, he said:

> I am pleased at the fact, and it is a fact, that we have made the American people better informed than they ever were in history. Better informed, I'm talking primarily about this country, but I believe it applies around the world. We have given more honest, factual information to more people than anyone in the history of the world. I don't mean we at ABC, but we in the television industry. If you are willing to make a small sacrifice, you can learn more than great scholars learned in the past. We lay it up for you, make it easy, make it visual, give it to you in full color and in hi-fi sound, and it's all there. Not on the nightly news every night, but over a period of time, over the television programs, the various programs. There's almost nothing that you won't know about.

A comforting analysis if true, a call to action if not.

---

[2] American Federation of Television and Radio Artists is the union governing on-air television broadcasters.

14
Advice
and
Admonition

My will shall shape my future. Whether I fail or succeed shall be no man's doing but my own. I am the force; I can clear any obstacle before me or I can be lost in the maze. My choice; my responsibility; win or lose, only I hold the key to my destiny. ELOISE MAXWELL

Today, with the intense competition for existing positions in the broadcasting profession, the need for proper planning and an appropriate understanding of the realities of the marketplace remains crucial. The star-driven, glamour-seeking young people who seek journalism careers because they desire early fame and fortune have a misguided understanding of what is needed for success. These false ideas of glamour can only lead to disappointment, rejections and ultimate failure.

Most leaders of the television news world today are competent, caring and conscientious journalists who take pride in their profession and work tirelessly to ensure that the important information crucial to a functioning democracy is presented to the viewing public. The women and men at the forefront of the broadcasting industry have deep reservations about the motives and training of some of the young people who seek entrance into the tumultuous and changing atmosphere of their chosen and time-honored profession.

Andrea Mitchell admits to having little patience for people who come to her and say, "I want to be an anchor." She explains:

> That is not a career goal. Tell me you want to be a journalist and I will do anything that I can to help guide you to a reasonable path. But, don't start out thinking you want to be an anchor. The best anchors, as Brokaw, Rather, Jennings, and Jim Lehrer have proved time and time again, are the best journalists. These are people who can handle breaking news, who can anchor conventions, who can cover politics, who can anchor a debate, and do an informed interview without having somebody whispering in their ear what the next question ought to be. So get it all learned. Get the foundations learned, building block by building block. And don't think that you can just leap to the top of celebrity without having done the fundamentals.

Mitchell worries that with the present trend toward the tabloid qualities of television, with an increasingly blurred distinction between regular newscasts and tabloid magazine shows, a misunderstanding of what abilities are required to do the job became rampant: "Tabloid magazine shows, like *Hard Copy* and *Inside Edition,* and all these others, have misled a lot of people who are consumers of these tabloid shows into thinking that they can graduate from school and become a reporter. That's not what reporters do."

The most respected and revered living journalist, Walter Cronkite, declares:

> My advice is be a journalist first. Be a news person first. Know how to collect news, how to gather news, how to report news, how to be sure that you're being fair, honest, impartial. And let the medium in which you work, let that come almost by accident. You ought to be capable of being a print reporter or a broadcast reporter or an Internet reporter. We don't really know what the medium will be as we turn the corner into the next century. A person who really deserves to be a journalist would be able to operate in any medium. There are too many young people in the communication schools, so called today, who will have their hearts set on being "anchor people." Good gracious, it drives me crazy to go to a university campus and have a beautiful young thing or a handsome young thing, come over to me

and I say, "What do you intend to be?" and they answer, "I intend to be an anchor." That's *not* what you're supposed to intend to be. You're supposed to intend to be a journalist, in my mind.

For Tom Brokaw, the least meaningful aspect of television news is the celebrity side of it. His advice: "The most important part is that you know what you're doing, that you bring to this business intelligence and ability to express that intelligence either in written or verbal form, and that you seek gratification for work well done, not by recognition in the streets."

Diane Sawyer wants to say to young people interested in a career in television news today to love something substantive:

> Stop worrying about how you look on camera, and stop worrying about which markets to go into. Find something you are so curious about that you have to know everything about it. So passionate about that you have to tell other people about it. Someone wrote to me once that you know you are in the right career when the world's greatest joy meets your greatest joy. Look for the thing you want to change the world, which also fills your heart and soul, because I don't think one without the other sustains very long. If you love learning about something and you think it's important to tell people about it, then that will take care of your career.

David Brinkley places his emphasis for success on the ability to learn the English language as perfectly as possible:

> Read good writing, not necessarily news writing, but writing of any kind and see how beautiful the English language is when it is well used. Learn to use it well. If you really want to make a long time, life time career of journalism in any form, print or broadcast, again the tool of our trade is the English language and if you can't do that, you're like a plumber without a wrench. You cannot do the job you are supposed to have to do. And if you can do it outstandingly well, if you can do it effectively in a way that reaches people, the audience, you're halfway home.

Sam Donaldson despairs about the inadequate knowledge of history that he confronts among young people who seek to forge a career in television news:

> You know it's interesting about kids today. In one sense in computer literacy, statistical analysis, things that I didn't know anything about,

they're terrific. In another sense, though, they're clearly not learning history and English literature like I did in my day. One day there was a very bright, young woman (she was a desk assistant, she graduated from a college in Ohio, very bright, we all liked her) and while I was reading *Time* magazine, Man of the Year, I said to her, "They printed the list of all of the men of the year and I know every one of them. We'll just try you on some. I don't expect you to know all of them, you're 22 years of age." I said, "The first man of the year was Charles Lindbergh. Have any idea who he was?" "No," she said, "I never heard the name." "Well, that really doesn't surprise me. He died in 1974. From about 1940 on, he was sort of a non-person because of his opposition to our involvement in the second World War. But," I said, "he was the first guy to fly the Atlantic and he was a huge hero. I mean, in 1928 that was the only name you would have heard in this country." So I tried her on another name. I was kind of bold. I said, "Joseph Stalin." "Nope." "Well," I said, "that does surprise me," and I explained to her who Joseph Stalin was. Now I'm really bold. So I looked at her and said go for broke, "Harry Truman." She said, "Yeah, Harry Truman, he was vice president of the United States." I said, "That is correct, but that is not the answer that I'm looking for." I said, "Henry Kissinger." "Oh, he's somebody's press secretary." I said, "Okay, good-bye." So I have been using that test ever since.

For Lynn Sherr, being a reporter is, in her words, "one of the great things you can do in this world." When she talks of helping the next generation she returns to a key aspect of the job and its meaning: "I kind of like the simple word reporter because I like what it means, which is you are reporting, for as corny as it's about to sound, it means you are out there to tell the truth. And I just don't think there's anything more important. I think that's why I'm here. I'm here because I like to tell the truth. I like to get to the bottom of something and I want to tell you what it's all about."

Sherr admits that she does not want people whose interest is just for the glamour and the money, although she is not prepared to give any of it back since she basically gets to do what is most important to her, which is to tell the truth. She continues:

So I want people interested in this business to care about the truth, to care about the facts, to understand the difference between facts and hype. To understand the difference between facts and opinion.

Cheryl Gould, NBC News

And also to understand that being at the network is certainly the top of the pyramid. But, you can learn to be a reporter at your weekly newspaper in the middle of the country, at a cable station. Reporting is a transferable skill and it requires exactly the same consciousness to cover a state legislature as it does to cover the White House. And it requires exactly the same skills to go out and cover a space shot as it does to cover a meeting of the local chamber of commerce. These are all skills that you've got to learn and hone at the lowest level before you can move up. So I say, figure out what you want to do and if you want to be famous, maybe you should go into the movies first. But, if you want to be out there to tell the truth and if you want to be out there to contribute toward democracy, I think that's what we're doing. And I think it's very important."

Cheryl Gould articulates many of these same feelings and concerns. She believes the most crucial concept is to be true to yourself and not to lose sight of the important values:

The journalistic and ethical standards must always be paramount and not the glamour and the show biz side of things. Unfortunately, I think that has preoccupied young people more than it should. Women and men are coming into television news more interested in how they get to a six-figure salary or how they get to an anchor position. So much of what I see on air, particularly local news, is so entertainment-value oriented that it dismays me because these are the people who are entering our pipeline. That pool is what we're drawing from for correspondents and field producers. I worry that the same kinds of reasons are why people of my generation entered the noble field of journalism, I worry that it has lost a lot of its cache and it's a different field. I want to tell young people, get a good liberal arts education. Think and read and be interested in the world around you and from that will come more of a journalist than if you learn how to look into a camera and read a teleprompter.

The need to write, to know history, to acquire a broad-based education is a repeated request among those acclaimed and admired journalists who are working in television news today. Cokie Roberts has serious words of advice for those who plan to enter this profession:

> Please go get a good liberal arts education. We do not need people who know how to cut tape. We can teach you to cut tape. We need people who know something. We need people who know something about history, who know something about government, particularly if you're going to cover politics, who know something about economics, and who know something about the English language. It's just so frustrating to get these smart, interesting kids who can't write anything—and they've got a Master's in Communication. Sorry, go write an English sentence for me and come back. The necessity to read and write needs to be driven home with incredible force. You can know all kinds of stuff and if you can't communicate it by clear writing, what good is it? Nobody will be able to understand what you're talking about.
>
> So, that is the first thing we need, and then the second thing is not to turn up your nose at any job. You're not going to start as Dan Rather. Some of them think they will. That's less true of this generation than it was with the kids ten years older than they are. These kids are much more realistic. But you need to go ahead and take the desk assistant job, the production assistant job, or, if what you really

want to do is be on the air, go out into the boonies where they will teach you everything.

And then, work much harder than any of the men of your acquaintance. And don't get all bolixed up in, "It's not fair." Life's not fair. But also, and I couldn't mean this more, don't let the work get in the way of family. You can always work. There's only a certain period of your life when you can have children. There's only a certain time when that mother of yours is sick. Those are the things. The clichés are true. You don't lay on your death bed thinking about the story you didn't cover. You can always do another story, always do another job. You can never recapture those moments.

Joanna Bistany warns of the need for sacrifice as you climb the career ladder and the necessity for women, especially, to be aware of the choices they will be called upon to make:

It's a very hard profession, a very competitive profession. I think that you can do extremely well in this profession and still have a life. However, if you want to make it to the top, whether it be an executive producer of a major show, an anchor of a major program, or senior manager, then it takes a toll on your personal life and there is no way around it. There comes a point where you can't do it all in terms of making it to that next step. And I think that we do young women a disservice to let them think there's no price to pay. There is a price to pay. It just depends on whether or not you're willing to pay it. And I would say the same for men, as well. I mean, there are nights when you don't get out of here until 7:30 or 9 o'clock and then phone calls at home. I talk to a control man on *Nightline* almost every night at midnight. If you have kids, that's tough. It's very tough to balance that, male or female. But, I have not deluded myself into thinking that men have become the primary care givers to children. So, since most of the burden still falls to the woman in the relationship, they're the ones who more often have to make a tough decision.

Bistany does not hesitate to pinpoint the sacrifices that a high-powered career demands, especially as a woman in a male-dominated environment. She states:

I basically chose my career over a personal life. I made a conscious decision when I did it. Don't forget, prior to this, I was in the White

House and prior to that I was on a presidential campaign. All of which means 7 days a week, 15 hours a day. I came here and I realized the only way I was going to make my way up was (a) to learn and I had to do that on my own, and (b) that I'd better make myself so bloody indispensable to the guys at the top, that they wouldn't dare want to let me go—instead they'd want to let me have more opportunity—and, as a result, I put in enormous numbers of hours. I volunteered to do everything.

It used to kill me when these young kids would come up and I'd say, "Can you set up an editorial lunch?" and this twenty-three-year-old says, "I don't do lunches." Oh, give me a break. I think when I was breaking into this, I volunteered for everything. I mean, we'd be in a meeting, I'd be the only woman, you know senior management. It would be Roone and David Burke and the meeting would be going through lunch. Everybody would look at me and say, "Well, are we having lunch?" And I would sit there and I would call my assistant or one of their assistants, and say, "Can you get us some lunch up here?" I did that for a while. Then I felt that I'd reached the level where I'd paid my dues. I had proved myself in my professional capacity and so I finally said, "Is your finger broken? You're next to the phone. Pick it up and use it. I'm not asking you to go out and bake some bread. Just call your secretary." I didn't mind doing this because I knew I had earned my stripes and earned the respect and affection. In a way, you almost had to be a little bit like a guy.

Bistany also expresses deep concern about the change she sees in young people. They do not seem to possess the necessary drive that she regards as mandatory for a successful career climb in this business:

I notice a change in the young women and in the young people in general. A lot of the young women, unlike ten years ago, don't want to work this hard. Just don't want to do it. A lot of them come in and don't have drive and ambition. A lot of them are a little spoiled. I mean they were the baby boomers' kids. The baby boomers have done quite well, you know, a good portion of them. And they have other interests in their lives. Some of them, they don't need it. They don't have a need for whatever it is to have to do that extra mile. Maybe it's because now some of the barriers have been broken down that they don't feel that challenge of having to go through that brick wall to get to the other side.

The seductive nature of television news, where you are often given a front seat on the major breaking stories of the day, often prevents a person from seeking and achieving a balance and satisfaction in their personal lives. Time and years quickly fly by and many who have sacrificed everything for their career then look around only to find themselves alone and holding an Emmy for comfort. Even worse, many lose their jobs along the way or end a career never having achieved their desired goals.

When I asked Jeanne Meserve, a former ABC Washington bureau correspondent, who left after eight years and is now an anchor/correspondent for CNN, what advice she would give to young people who are planning a career in television news, she was the sole person to answer, "Don't do it!"

What are her reasons? Meserve replied:

> I think it's a cruel business. The judgments that are made in television are so personal and they are so subjective. It goes to the very core of your ego. And unless you have an angel sitting on your shoulder, you are bound to be wounded and wounded badly somewhere along the line in this business. I think there are more sane ways to make a living. Plus the demands. They own you, and they should for the money they pay you at the network level—they should. But, it means you make great compromises when it comes to family and personal life. And in my old age, I have come to value those things more.

It is crucial to understand just who you are because the choices we make in life flow from that information. It is imperative to be true to your beliefs because we base our key decisions on them. We must be secure with this belief system so that we retain responsibility for what happens to us as we continue to struggle with the difficult options that confront us on our selected career path.

Rebecca Bell headed NBC's first Paris bureau in 1976. Now retired, her advice is candid: "If you're going to go into it for some idea of financial gain or glamour—all of those things are there, but, it's not going to help you through those 18-hour days and war zones. But, if you love it, go ahead. If you don't, you're going to have a lot of problems because it's a very demanding and very consuming occupation."

One of the true women pioneers in television news, Marlene Sanders also warns young people to carefully examine their motives. She succinctly states, "I have been working with students for a long time and I think a lot of them have illusions that they're going to make a million dollars a year as anchors. If that's what they want, they should instantly do something else."

Susan King started in 1970 with NBC as a "glorified secretary" and then went to CBS where she worked with Walter Cronkite in another "glorified secretary's job." But after 20 years of accomplishments that took her to ABC News in Washington and finally to the anchor position at WJLA, she warns that broadcasting demands that you "give it everything you have." She continues, "To get started you'll probably have to bleed, and they'll make you bleed. Be persistent. Work as hard as you can and have no illusions. It may not be a long-term career. It's probably worth it. I have absolutely no regrets from my career. I love the business of journalism. I think it is the people's trust. And it can be a fascinating way to be a player in your society and never compromise your values. I think true talent and quality does survive."

Linda Ellerbee has a direct and definitive piece of advice for young people to remember: "Learn that the worst thing they can do is fire you, and that there are many worse things in this world. One of the worst is not being able to look at your own reflection in the mirror on the way to work because you are at work doing things that you believe to be intellectually inferior or morally wrong."

Ann Compton walked up the White House driveway on December 2, 1974, and remained ABC's White House correspondent for more than 22 years. She came to Washington, D.C., and started as the number 3 person on ABC's White House team behind colleagues who Compton states have been and remain very supportive. But her start was at a local television station in Virginia where she remained for 4 years. She remembers crying when she left. She called herself a big fish in a very small pond. Compton always gives young people the same advice: "I think you have to earn your stripes and you shouldn't come straight out of journalism school and expect to anchor a local news broadcast and then become White House correspondent for ABC. You have to kind of earn it step by step. And I think my advice to most of the women I have spoken to is don't let your reach exceed your grasp. Learn what you need to learn. Learn it well. Do it well and look for opportunities when they open."

Eleanor Guggenheimer, looking back over her long and distinguished career, believes the most helpful career advice deals with the need for women to retain their own unique characteristics: "Don't try to be a man. We have men in there already. We need women. I think we had a lot of women who felt that they had to become men. I mean, operate like men. I think we have special contributions to make and they're important. I would also say that there's nothing wrong with using being a woman. That doesn't mean going to bed with the boss. That means looking attractive and being feminine."

Pia Lindstrom left WNBC-TV in New York City after 23 years in a variety of roles including being teamed with Melba Tolliver in the mid-seventies thereby becoming the first all-woman anchor team in the number one market in the country. Lindstrom reasoned they were put together "one black, one white. I suppose they thought that was like book-ends." She recalls that when she first began in the news business she, and the other women who started with her, felt they had to work twice as hard. They could never refuse an assignment, get mad, use bad language, or get fired. Lindstrom contends that there is still a double-edged sword hanging over women. The problem remains how to maintain authority, and not have people say, "you're a bitch." Lindstrom declares,

> Women are not accustomed to being team players. They don't know how to take a punch, throw a punch and then be pals. To use the sports metaphor, men are used to going out on the playing field, huddling with each other, hitting each other, kicking each other, spitting at each other, and then they come back and they all go off and have a good time and slap each other on the back. They're all so used to arguing and fighting and pushing somebody up against the wall, then a day later they're all out having beer. They can do that. Women are not socialized that way and we may not even have that nature instinctively.

Lindstrom points to Margaret Thatcher as a woman who epitomized the ability to be authoritative—someone who was able to take the punches and give them out as well. Lindstrom believes that success in a male-dominated career requires power and determination. It is necessary to understand how to dominate people without having them hate you: "Or let them hate you, and you don't mind as long as they do their job. It requires not being loved." Women face conflicting ideas about how much they should be liked and admired and how attractive and feminine they must be. It is necessary for women planning to enter the world of television news broadcasting to come to grips with this conflict

Pia Lindstrom

and duality and to decide how to effectively deal with the issues that inevitably emanate from it.

These conflicts were discussed by Wendy Takuda who acknowledges that so many of the cultural traits that were deeply ingrained in her youth are directly in opposition with what she is required to do inside a newsroom. Takuda believes that younger women today are being trained more effectively than those of her generation. She recounts the story of her daughter, Maggie, 8 years old, who plays softball. In the first game she was in, Maggie struck out. Wendy, who never was in team sports, was shocked and upset to see the parents of the other team cheering. Then the coach looked at Maggie and said, "No big deal, you're up next inning." At first Takuda was worried that they were going to hurt her daughter's feelings. When the coach simply allowed her to know, "you come up again," Takuda acknowledged:

> She's going to be so much better prepared for the business world than I am. I'm so grateful she had this training. My husband, Richard said to Maggie, "I don't care if you strike out, no big deal. But, don't strike out standing there. You strike out swinging." I mean, think about the analogy in life. He trained that little girl. "You go out there. You go ahead and strike out. Striking out is no big deal. But you never get to first base unless you swing." And I think about me sitting out in the newsroom and the times I'll be sitting there worried I might make a mistake or I might hurt someone's feelings, like it's the worst thing in the world. When we were growing up, the toys that we were given to play with—you play house, nurse, make people feel better. Don't hurt anyone's feelings. If you're going to say something mean, don't say it. This so ill prepares you for the business world. Business is business. You're not doing it to hurt feelings.

Carole Simpson regularly endows six scholarships for young people and commits additional time to help all of the desk assistants who are working in this entry level capacity at ABC. She tries to take them under her wing. But she is concerned and depressed about a lack of commitment she sees needed to keep up the pressure to make things better:

> Whether they're white males, white females, black, whatever, I like all of the young people coming into the field and I try to spend time with them and talk to them about it. But, they take everything for granted. These little young women that are very attractive now and very naive and very innocent, who are starry-eyed and think the world is their oyster and the sky's the limit, do not know that some day they're going to turn 35 and they are not going to be quite as cute and innocent. They're going to be mature. They're going to have their own ideas. They're going to feel strongly. They're going to have talents and skills that they're going to want to use and all of a sudden it's whoa! And you try to tell them this, that you've got to be vigilant. You still have to work harder than the men. You still have to make more sacrifices than anybody, and they don't believe that. They see women on TV and they think everything's terrific and don't know that it's still tough behind the scenes to get women in decision making capacities. Even our women vice-presidents that we have here, none of them has line responsibility that can really fire people. So there are

vice-presidents and there are vice-presidents. So we tell them how important it is to be watchful of what's going to happen and not forget the big chill, which they're going to inevitably get. You try to tell them. But, it's disappointing that they don't know what we went through.

Michel McQueen urges young women who are planning their careers to be open to the possibilities. To be open to diverge from the path. The results, she feels, can be terrific even though it can be uncomfortable at the time. A 1980 Harvard graduate, McQueen started as a summer intern at the *Washington Post* immediately after finishing school. In 1987 she went to the Washington Bureau of the *Wall Street Journal*. But, she found the unexpected can often lead to significant benefits when she turned down a CBS offer to be the number three reporter covering the White House. The other networks immediately interviewed her and she finally made the switch to television and ABC News late in 1992. McQueen's advice is to know who you are, and what you want to be: "I am more interested in journalism than I am in being famous. That's just who I am."

McQueen asserts that you must be accurate, be excellent, and have a strong work ethic. She says, learn to read, write, and listen carefully: "The advice is no different whether you're white, black, or green. I think, if you are a woman and if you are of color, the sad and unfortunate reality is that you must be prepared to have challenges to your competence that you probably would not have if you were a man. The people who question you—there's that little moment of hesitation where people will wonder whether you can do that job. And you just have to demonstrate that you can."

The learning never stops. It is important to remember that news is a 24-hour business so you must love it and be dedicated to it. You must be disciplined and willing to work hard, take risks and persevere. Al Primo talks about the advice he gives to his clients: "Television is constructed in such a way that the pitfalls and the hazards that you need to climb over to succeed are so enormous that most people just say, 'to hell with this, this is not worth it.' Those who stay with it are the people you see every night on television. So the trick is to stay with it if this is what you really want." Perseverance remains a litmus test for success and survival.

Dan Rather offers two pieces of advice: "The first thing to get yourself is a gut check, a heart check. Do you love it, or at the very least, do you believe you can come to love it? Because, to do it well, I think you have to have a passion for it." The other significant piece of advice that Rather gives is to "dedicate yourself to constantly doing better." He firmly believes you must devote yourself to a lifetime of improvement in order to achieve a true full measure of success.

To do well in broadcast news, it is important to learn a lot about the world. Learn other cultures. Do not limit your view of the world from your singular spot. Understand that the whole rest of the world matters. Develop a more general perspective.

Rita Braver states: "Get a good education. Be smarter than you think you need be. Know about more things than you think you need to know about. Develop interests beyond yourself and remember, your job is to tell the world about interesting stuff. It's not about you."

If your burning desire is to be a serious journalist (and no one I spoke to is interested in anyone who merely wishes to be famous or on television), the need is to be talented, tenacious, willing to take risks and make the personal sacrifices that this lifestyle routinely demands. It remains crucial for you to be fair and accurate and to provide the correct information. People will be making their decisions based upon what they hear from you. It is the basis of our democracy. That is a fierce responsibility to carry with you. But, if you accept the challenge and follow your dreams, the world of television news can prove to be among the most exciting and satisfying professions.

15
Wishes
and
Whispers

The future belongs to those who believe
in the beauty of their dreams.

ELEANOR ROOSEVELT (1884–1962)

By sheer force of increased numbers combined with the talent and the
passion to succeed, women will continue to be a significant presence in
television news broadcasting into the twenty-first century. Only through
a strong partnership of women and men working side by side can the
richness and diversity in our society be represented.

The fierce competitiveness of the industry creates a culture of stress
and insecurity. While it is tough for most to survive, women who ascend
the broadcast news ladder definitely must pay a higher price than their
male counterparts. So, it is interesting to question and reflect on their
choice of things most desired for the future.

In my interviews, I asked each newsperson what they most wished
for themselves as we enter the new millennium. Their answers reflect
the wide spectrum of personal and professional lifestyles that are represented by the aggregate of those who live and work in the demanding
and unforgiving world of television news. The responses reflect the candor, sensitivity, and courage with which this unusual group of individuals face the future.

As we review some of their "wishes," we gain important insight into their individual personalities, their priorities, and their reservoirs of strength.

Barbara Walters: "I ask those kinds of questions and I can never answer them. Good health. I mean, that's the most important thing. To have good health and to have my daughter healthy and happy. Everything else is secondary."

Diane Sawyer: "I think it would be that I finally get a decent backhand and, as a friend of mine said once, that I always remember the difference between glass balls and rubber balls, and never let the wrong one drop."

Christiane Amanpour: "I would like to go to outer space. I think it would be a great trip and it would be a great foreign story."

Connie Chung: "My one wish is that I can work on my obsessively neat and compulsive behavior. I cannot. I want so much to get over this affliction that I have, which is to have everything organized and in it's place; with a little one-year-old, you know that's an impossibility."

Rebecca Bell: "To learn to listen. To not be so consumed with my own opinions that I don't take time to listen to the opinion and ideas of those around me. And to try to give back because I have been so fortunate."

Katie Couric: "Oh my gosh, such a heavy, deep, and real question. That I continue to be fulfilled in my job; that I continue to make women and men proud of the job I am doing—and that my daughters don't become juvenile delinquents."

Dan Rather: "I want to be a first-class, world-class journalist."

Sally Quinn: "Just to be happy and healthy. I would like to continue writing. I sort of picture myself at age ninety being a nicer Alice Roosevelt Longworth."

Gloria Rojas: "Well, I never wanted an Emmy, but I sure as hell would like a Pulitzer."

Andrea Mitchell: "It's never to be bored. To always be interested and challenged and excited about what I am doing. Personally and professionally, to always be learning."

Lisa Myers: "Oh, gosh, that's impossible. That is just too cosmic."

Ann Compton: "I am a tactician. I can get through the basic logistics of this theater of warfare, but don't ask me what happens in the next millennium because I'm not a strategic planner. My goal is to keep this job until my last kid's out of college or medical school."

Bob Mulholland: "That I live to see another three hundred channels added to my television set and all of them presenting news, or half of them presenting news that sounds better—to be able to turn on my television set and not shout back at it."

Carole Black: "To lose ten pounds! My wish for myself would be to continue to have the tremendous enthusiasm that I feel toward life and the excitement I feel every day I wake up."

Deborah Potter: "Oh, I'd like to live long enough to be a grand-mother."

Betsy Aaron: "Not to spend the rest of my life in Chechnya. Time to use all the experience I've had. To do a really good job because the world is changing and I feel so lucky to be part of this."

Walter Cronkite: "To live to see the next century. I suppose I have no aspirations—just to keep on enjoying it is all."

Theresa Brown: "Some personal happiness. I've always said I was unfulfilled, unhappy. I always felt exploited in television. I did have a successful career for a time. But I never felt good about it."

Bettina Gregory: "I just want to be peaceful and serene and accept whatever comes. I often say, you can not control the cards you're dealt in life, but you can play the hand as well as you can."

Ted Kavenau: "I was always an outsider and I love nothing better than to be able to pinprick people with a blow to the ego or pinprick people in power who have bloated egos. So, I'd like to be able to get back and do that again."

Sheila MacVicar: "That I live happily and travel lightly."

Kelly Lange: "I want peace on earth and I want that to be reflected within my own soul. I don't need another car. I don't need another new suit. I'd like peace of mind."

Marlene Sanders: "I would like to be able to use what I've learned over the years, somewhere, put it to use. I certainly don't want to go anywhere and play shuffleboard."

Nina Totenberg: "That I continue to be successful and that I continue to lead a happy personal life as well."

Dave Marash: "Let me keep doing *Nightline,* as I say, let them carry me away in a box, pry the microphone out of my hand."

Kathy McManus: "To get out of here without getting another disease. Frankly, in the last year, I've had meningitis, hepatitis, and mononucleosis. So my goal would be to leave here codeine free and go on to the next thing, whatever that is."

Cokie Roberts: "I want my children to marry the people they're dating and have grandchildren soon."

Elizabeth Vargas: "That I will find that balance of personal and professional happiness."

Melba Tolliver: "Oh, that I live a long, happy, healthy, contributing life. Did I cover all the bases?"

Linda Shen: "I wish I could act on my social conscience more effectively than I have in the last twenty-five years."

Lynn Sherr: "I think, given what I've been through, the simplest wish is good health for my family and for the people close to me."

Susan Zirinsky: "I think I'd like to learn to appreciate life a bit more and not live so much through the experience of historical events and perhaps have some historical events of my own."

Lisa Stark: "That I'm able to balance my two lives. Basically, that I'm able to be a good journalist and a good mom. Obviously, I'm not one who believes that you don't have to make compromises. But I'm hoping that the compromises won't hurt either my child or my job."

Gwen Ifill: "I wish personal happiness, satisfaction, and awareness of how blessed I am."

Al Ittelson: "First, I'd like to hit the lotto. I'd like to feel secure without having to depend on other people."

Linda Alvarez: "I guess my current wish right now is to grow old doing my job. Older, not old. George Burns said we all have to grow older, but we don't have to grow old. I don't want to grow old doing my job. I want to keep a fresh outlook on the changes around us."

Sam Donaldson: "To stay alive. I've got melanoma, child. That's an easy one to answer. I say to Steve Rosenberg, the chief surgeon who takes care of me, I don't want to see you in synagogues. I don't want to see you at the movies. You stay in that laboratory. You work, send out for a cheeseburger once in a while. Keep working on the gene therapy."

Maureen Bunyan: "To get there intact and get there with specific tasks and direction."

Sheilah Kast: "That big question gets a big answer, I mean, I hope that my life means something, has meant something."

Michel McQueen: "I don't know why I'm telling you this, but I try never to lie because my real goal for the next century is to have a very strong family life. That's really my ultimate goal because I feel that is the only thing that endures."

Virginia Sherwood: "Just living life to its fullest as long as I can, helping as many people as I can and having as much fun as I can."

Paula Zahn: "I guess to feel that same sense of awe and satisfaction I feel at the end of most days."

Rose Ann Scamardella: "A long life and many grandchildren."

Tom Brokaw: "That I get done all that I want professionally, which is to finish a book that I'm engaged in. To keep television news central to the mission of the networks, and to continue to have a life with my family that is as rich as it is now."

Marjorie Margolies-Muzvinsky: "I guess for me that I can continue to try to make a difference. I think as we look at the new millennium we realize that we've got to get more women in positions of power, at the economic table, at the judicial table, at the legislative table. We've got to level the playing fields in many areas."

Betty Rollin: "Oh, to stay alive for a spell, given my cancer history, and that's for my husband and for myself, I really wish for numbers."

Kathy O'Hearn: "I would like to either meet someone that I could mate with or marry. And, I still have a little inch of time to have a child. I would love to have a child. I don't feel driven to have a child. I won't have a child on my own. But I feel I've done single very successfully. I feel like I've taken wonderful care of myself and my dog, and I want to give back to someone else."

Richard Threlkeld: "To live as long as I possibly can."

Amy Entelis: "To get to tomorrow, because with my kids and their demands, I don't get to think too far ahead. But I really love what I do. I had the luxury to create my job. It didn't exist before I did it. I got to put my own stamp on it. I did it supported by a terrific new organization. I don't know what would be better than this."

Judy Woodruff: "I don't have a wish for myself. I'll be all right. I guess my wish would be for the men who are making decisions about electronic journalism of the next few decades. Always keep in mind the journalistic mission of these news organizations. That they never forget that's the most important thing we're doing here, and we're not just another business."

Linda Ellerbee: "When you've had cancer your current goals and aspirations are pretty simple. Right now, I want to see 2000. My one wish for myself is that I can just keep on. Lucky Duck Productions is the best thing that ever happened to me. We produce for all these different networks, and I sell my shows to them. I don't have to work for any of those guys ever again."

Cheryl Gould: "That I'm able to maintain this very delicate balance of professional demands and parental and spousal demands and that I am able also to keep up the standard that I hold so dear to our profession. That television news not descend into the area that I don't want us to go into. But that we maintain the kind of standards that I entered the business for. I want to be able to feel proud about what we put on the air every day. That's my goal. To feel that we're making a difference as journalists, and that I'm making a difference being in this field. And, that I'm also able to be a good friend and a good mother and a good wife and a good colleague."

Michelle Norris: "I want it all. I want a successful career in television, but my family is very important to me. I want to have a family."

Jennifer Siebens: "To survive."

Judy Muller: "Well, I'm a recovering alcoholic so I try not to go too far into the future. I try to go one day at a time. I got sober when I was on the verge of losing everything if my drinking continued. This is a killer business and if you are alcoholic it will kill you. I knew I wanted to live and I made the choice to be present, conscious, and sober. So when people say 'what would you wish for in life?', I wish to get through this day without a drink and be completely present for my loved ones."

Jackie Judd: "I guess my wish would be that books like yours wouldn't have to be written in the twenty-first century."

16
Legends
and
Legacy

They talk about a woman's sphere as
though it had a limit;
There's not a place in earth or heaven,
There's not a talk to mankind given,
There's not a blessing or a woe,
There's not a whispered "yes" or "no,"
There's not a life, or death, or birth,
That has a feather's weight of worth
Without a woman in it.

KATE FIELD (1838–1896)

Television is a dominant force in American society. As a news medium, it remains vital to the functioning of a free society. Through its ability to present a dramatic narrative television is capable of touching the soul of its public. It has been a witness to history as it unfolds, bringing popular and unpopular subjects alike into U.S. living rooms. In a national survey conducted in January 1997, 80 percent of those polled view the role of the news media as crucial in a free society; 88 percent of those surveyed spend at least one half hour on a typical weekday obtaining news.[1]

The portrayal of women on television remains a dynamic force that shapes and influences attitudes and behavior about gender roles and reflects the position women hold in American society. Positive role models remain relatively rare in television, a medium that generally creates and reinforces the second-class status of females. The women who are now working successfully in television news provide role models of vision and leadership. The presentation of issues that affect men and women equally, when discussed on a platform that elevates and empowers women, serves to enhance their position and influence in our highly diverse and complex society.

The portrayal of women in prime-time television drama predominately features characters that are weak, emotional, vulnerable, sensual, seductive, ditsy, and the object of men's romantic fantasies. The stereotypical bird-brain roles depict women as kooky housewives, secretaries, club "girls," lovable widows, nosy nurses, and brassy assistants. The message reinforced daily is that women need not be taken as seriously as men.

Sadly, the overwhelming weight of cultural behavior lies behind these sex-role stereotypes: men are strong; men are heroes. Women are beautiful; women are goddesses. Men focus on work; women focus on love. Billions of dollars are spent annually in a vain attempt to achieve the idealized image of the sexual madonna. These roles serve to dehumanize all of us and especially to limit the impact and potential of women in society.

The communications world must recognize women as an indispensable resource if it is to fulfill its responsibility to the people it serves. As individuals, women must recognize and strengthen their inner reservoir of ability and commitment in order to achieve their personal goals and realize their full potential. Together, as women, we can demand nothing more; as fellow human beings, we must accept nothing less. We must work diligently, to overcome the sexist legacy that continues to impede our democratic republic.

---

[1] A national survey commissioned by the Newseum and developed by the Newseum (an interactive news museum), the Roper Center for Public Opinion Research, and the Freedom Forum Media Studies Center, conducted in January 1997.

Katie Couric, NBC News

Katie Couric understands the acute need to present herself in a prominent and accomplished way:

> I think that I consider myself a feminist, and a fairly strong woman, who feels very responsible to make sure there is parity on the program, and that I'm not delegated to the fluffy features; because, if I were, I would never have taken this job in the first place. I think the time was right for a strong woman in this role. So I think it's been fortuitous that my personality and my desire out there is not for someone who is stringent or overbearing, necessarily, but for someone who feels that she is representing women. I think that in very subtle ways the role of the women on programs like this can really set the tone for the country. I don't mean to sound self-important, or as if I am overreaching or overestimating my importance personally. But I think it can send some very clear signals out to women about equality, and about the need for their voice in the public arena.

When television provides women with a status of respect and distinction, the palette of opportunity increases and a wider range of desirable qualities become viable. The feminine-associated values of community and cooperation augment the masculine values of individualism and competition.

When Bryant Gumbel left the *Today* show, in January 1997, after serving fifteen years as anchor of the nation's leading morning television program, Matt Lauer was named as his replacement. He was brought in immediately as co-host with Katie Couric. The transition between hosts was smooth and provided Matt with a title that made each gender coexist equally. Couric encouraged that decision. In the months prior to the move, she expressed her feelings to me: "I think it is in Bryant's contract that he is anchor and I'm the co-anchor. As far as I'm concerned, if two people are doing the same program, they're both anchors. Or they're both co-anchors. I imagine that because I've been on the show and because I have some seniority, my role may increase. But I think in the ideal world, the man and the woman doing the show, or the woman and the woman, or the man and the man, would be equal partners, and I am basically an extremely egalitarian person. I think that would be the best scenerio." Couric proved herself true to her convictions when put to the test.

The difference the presence of women makes in political coverage and on the campaign trail is acknowledged by Nina Totenberg:

The first time I saw more women on a campaign plane than men was the Ferraro campaign, when there were definitely more women. Of course, they weren't just assigned to the Ferraro campaign, because it was partly a convergence of events. More women in the profession, a woman candidate for national office, and the desire to cover her with women as well as men. I traditionally do the vice-presidential stories. I go out with each vice-presidential candidate for a few days, and then I do sort of a profile of his or her campaign. In 1984, when I went out with Ferraro and Bush, and then in 1988 when I went out with Bentsen and Quayle, the transition was happening.

What was interesting to me was that you could feel there was a palpable difference in the atmosphere on the campaign plane when there were mainly women as opposed to mainly men. When there were mainly women, it was much less stratified. In other words, people tended to eat in huge groups, to invite cameramen to eat with them. There was not some elite little group of columnists who ate dinner, four or five of them alone, and then the *New York Times* and the *Washington Post* eating alone. Everybody ate together. It was a much less stratified group. It was just the reporters and techs on the plane. That was the difference. And the second difference is, when you're covering a campaign like that, there really is no reason to be wildly competitive because you're all getting, more or less, the same stuff. It struck me when they were mainly men, there was still enormous amounts of competition when it was totally unnecessary. By 1992 those differences seemed to have disappeared and the female approach seemed to have won out.

Women have been fighting fiercely to place a female face on the world map of journalism. News women have proven that they possess as much brainpower, as much competency, as much reliability, as much toughness, as much intelligence as the men, and often times even more. But when women are selected for prominent positions based on looks rather than qualifications, the stigma of "fluff" and "shallow" only degrades further the role that women play. It leaves a lasting impression that is difficult to overcome, and it only serves to reinforce the regressive forces that promote sexism in the United States.

In 1977, Joan Lunden was selected to anchor WABC-TV's *Eyewitness News* in New York, the nation's number-one television market. In a newspaper interview, she was quoted as saying she was not an avid newspaper reader: "I was very bad at keeping up with current events.

That is why I said, 'What in the world would I do in the news business?' I was not the kind that always watched the news business."[2] The news director assured Lunden that should be of no concern. He told her: "Well, for one thing you could be an anchorman." Joan went on to discuss her early preparation for this career: "A lot of people pooh-pooh this, but I was in a lot of beauty contests where I had to get up and perform in front of people and answer questions in front of an audience. I was in a lot of dance recitals. I danced all my life from the time I was two years old, doing little ballet things and acrobatics. I marched in parades all my life as a majorette. I ran for junior prom queen and senior princess and everything else."[3]

Joan Lunden ended seventeen years as co-host of *Good Morning, America* on September 5, 1997, the longest-running morning news host on network television. Named as her replacement was Lisa McRee, the former anchor of KABC-TV in Los Angeles, and a communications graduate of the University of California, San Diego. In an interview with the *Los Angeles Times,* McRee talked about her new position: "It means the greatest challenge I ever had. I just want to go and do a good job, to go and really work hard."[4]

During the early seventies there was a general hiring ferment that resulted in the largest visible influx of women in the history of broadcasting. The original reasons for this increased opportunity came as a direct outgrowth of pressure and legislation. The passage of Title VII of the Civil Rights Act of 1964 made job discrimination on the basis of sex illegal. But the biggest push came in 1971 when the Federal Communications Commission added coverage of women to its equal employment opportunity rule, which had originally applied only to racial and ethnic minorities. A growing number of women reporters began to appear on television news. Around the country, news stations felt the need to hire at least one woman and one black. Often a black woman was found to satisfy the required tokenism in one fell swoop. Some of the women hired during this rush to redress past iniquities were programmed for failure; others struggled, gained the needed survival skills, and succeeded. Several remain today the true trailblazers for women in television news.

---

[2] Robert Scheer, "TV Forges an Anchor of Fluff," *New York Post,* June 10, 1997.
[3] Ibid.
[4] Jane Hall, "Lisa McRee Leaving for 'GMA'," *Los Angeles Times,* September 6, 1997.

Of the thirty women I first interviewed in 1973 for my seminal study, fifteen (50%) are still active in broadcasting, five (16%) are retired (each of these women was *forced* out due to age barriers or salary adjustments set by management), two are teaching, two have their own businesses, one is in government, one is a writer, and two are deceased.[5]

A racial breakdown reveals that six (20%) of the original sample were African American; two were Asian; two were Hispanic. Two-thirds of the women, the overwhelming majority, were white. The muted voices of minorities in the newsroom continues to require accelerated opportunities and forced change. Ann Medina recalls her entry into the news profession and the misguided attempt to bring in women who were also members of racial and ethnic minorities: "My Spanish surname helped make me a triple whammy. When I was hired by the NBC network for their training program, their minority training program, even though, probably I could be characterized as a full-fledged WASP in many minds. They figured I was a woman, I had a Spanish surname, those were worth points, and they also figured I was Jewish, which was worth a point. So, I was a triple whammy."

Twenty-three years later my interview sample grew to seventy women, which is reflective of the increase in the number of women now working in newsrooms throughout the country. The racial breakdown shows fifty-two, or 74% of the women in my new sample are white, eleven (15%) are African American, four (6%) are Hispanic, and three (4%) are Asian. This comparison offers a strident commentary on the old models of behavior that continue to exist in the newsroom. The repressive forces that promote racial prejudice still flourish. The prism through which the critical events of the world are presented must include the diversity which is part of our culture. Whatever forces continue to resist and slow the ability of all of America's voices to be heard must be challenged on every front. Genuine integration of newsrooms in the United States must become our shared priority. The economic base of the news industry and its survival demands it; the future of our democracy depends on it.

The minority women who successfully work in television news have experienced all the indignities and racist insensitivities that are a daily reality in mainstream white America. Whatever their internal battles, they recognize the need and responsibility to serve as a mentor and a role model. Few in broadcasting have made so conscious a commit-

---

[5] Only two women from the original sample of thirty were not located.

ment to the struggle for advancement of minorities in news as Maureen Bunyan. Her perspective is valuable:

> I do believe that we have a responsibility to use our talents, and I also believe we are on this earth to make some kind of positive experience. Life is not all fun and games, but in whatever field we happen to find ourselves, I feel compelled. Having come to this country, having had an immigrant experience in my family background from Aruba and Guyana, I also have a little twinge of seeing the United States as a political entity and a social entity. It is very much different here than any other country in the world. So I appreciate the power that Americans have, and I see it from a little different perspective, so I don't take it so much for granted. I also feel that, as a minority person in a majority society, I have a special responsibility and I may not always fulfill it, but I have to keep trying because I've benefited from being in this country at this particular time, at this particular place, with whatever circumstances my family brought here. I've been a beneficiary, so I believe that I have to help others benefit. I don't consider myself a goody-two-shoes, but this is the synergy of life that I see in our particular time. I feel, as a woman, very strongly about this at the end of this century. We talked about going into the next millennium. Women have opportunities that we never had in the history of the world, to say nothing of the history of this country, or the history of the last few decades. Opportunities to be complete people and not to be limited by gender or social role or what other people think or by politics. And I'm just happy to be alive at this particular moment. If this were 1896 we wouldn't be sitting here, Judy. Who knows where we would be. You know, we're in our fifties, we'd be grandmothers sitting at home taking care of our grandchildren and sewing socks or God knows what, baking bread. So we have got a particularly exciting experience in our lives and I don't take that for granted.

If the goal is to bring excellence into the newsrooms of America, then the objective of diversity must be assiduously pursued and promoted. Without the inclusion of distinctly different talent and expertise, the profession will never achieve its full strength and potential. The phenomenal acceptance and success of stars such as Oprah Winfrey and Bill Cosby have failed to create a range of leadership positions for people of color. Skin color casts a deep shadow throughout the nation and continues to allow racial divisions to create chaos in our lives.

In 1973, only two of the correspondents I interviewed made over

$51,000 annually, while another two made less than $20,000 each year. At that same time Barbara Walters reportedly earned nearly $400,000 annually at NBC for her work both on the *Today* show and her syndicated program, *Not For Women Only*. She then commented to me, "I get paid more than many men working here, but less than a man in a comparable position."

In 1976, Barbara Walters left NBC for ABC to become the nation's first evening news anchor. Her salary of $1 million set a new record and began an escalation of salaries among star anchors and correspondents which continues today. What is most noteworthy is the fact that Barbara Walters has continued to top the salary scale and that her reported $10 million salary is the highest in the news business. With a syndicated broadcast, with four specials a year through her production company, in the entertainment division, and having two nights a week of the news magazine *20/20*, it seems safe to assume Barbara Walters is the highest paid woman in television news. Dan Rather signed a new contract for a reported $7 million, the same salary Diane Sawyer, Peter Jennings, and Tom Brokaw each command. These superstars' enormously high salaries are based on their perceived value to the station as well as their recognition and acceptance by viewers and by competition. The tip of the pyramid in broadcasting is occupied by women who have equaled or exceeded the men they share the spotlight with.

Star anchors are the highest paid people in broadcast journalism. The number-one television market in New York finds anchors earning in excess of $2 million. In the country's smallest markets, the top anchor may earn as little as $12,000.

The median salary in the United States for news anchors in 1994 was reported to be $40,000 a year. On average, the sixty smallest markets paid $22,000 for a typical anchor.

The salary floor is low in broadcast journalism because of the large number of people who clamor for entrance into the profession. The downsizing that is rampant in corporate America has led to a diminished opportunity for many to realize the level of earning power of those who preceded them. The seventy who make up the research sample for this book have achieved a prominence that has led to economic success and substantial parity with men. The average annual earnings for the women correspondents was in the low six figures. There was no single complaint concerning compensation, except by those women who were asked to take salary cuts by management in order to retain their on-air positions. The ugly fact remains that while men as well as women face cutbacks and demotion, women experience it first, more deeply, and in greater numbers.

The prodigious salaries that are being paid to television celebrity figures in the news business pale when viewed in a larger context of super stars. Michael Jordan, the icon of basketball heroes, reportedly signed a $36 million contract in 1997 for one year of playing. Steven Spielberg, the producer and director, is reported to have earned $313 million in 1996. Oprah Winfrey is said to earn over $100 million annually. It is reported that her new two-year contract calls for $200 million to $300 million dollars with additional stock options.

The television industry can well afford the huge salaries it pays to keep its stars and their agents happy. The television Bureau of Advertising predicted that in 1998, total television advertising will climb between 6 percent and 8 percent to between $47.2 billion and $48.1 billion. The 1998 Superbowl sold out its available advertising spots at the cost of $1.3 million for each thirty-second time slot. But newsroom profits typically are not reinvested in higher pay for the average working person who toils twelve and fourteen hours a day and contributes to the station's continued profitability. These unsung heroes must learn to be satisfied with gratifications other than money. In 1994, the median pay for entry-level reporters in the small and medium-small markets was reported to be between $16,000 and $18,000 a year.[6] Shared wealth is not a concept that is practiced in America's newsrooms or boardrooms.

In my 1973 study of women working in television news, the median age of the newswomen was thirty-four years. Fifty percent of the women interviewed were in their thirties, 30 percent were in their twenties, and 16 percent were in their forties. The only woman older than fifty working on air was Pauline Frederick, who, after twenty years as NBC's United Nation correspondent, was about to retire at the mandatory age of sixty-five. This dean of women correspondents was then earning approximately $40,000 a year.

Today, the ages of the seventy newswomen who compose this study range from thirty-seven to eighty-five years of age. The majority of the women (44%) were in their fifties; 35 percent were in their forties; 10% in their sixties; and 10% were in their thirties. Only one woman in her

---

[6] Verson Stone, "Television News Salaries," press release, University of Missouri School of Journalism.

seventies was still working in news management, while one woman of eighty-five was now heading a social policy agency. These findings give credence to the fact that women, once accepted in the field and considered as assets to their station's success, are able to sustain their career span over an ever expanding time frame and remain leaders of the television news world. While physical characteristics play no small part in fulfilling the norms of broadcasting, older women are allowed to be seen with greater frequency. But make no mistake: The women who are getting older do not look older. Indeed, to my eye, some of the women whom I met look even better today than they did twenty-three years ago. Still, women in broadcasting are seen as old long before their male colleagues. David Brinkley was seventy-six when we met and he was then appearing with regularity on his weekly news analysis program. The most senior woman on air today is Barbara Walters. We met in her sixty-fifth year and she was happily and deservedly enjoying her most acclaimed year in television. But she does not expect to remain as long as some of the men.

As for the future, Walters commented:

> I have a new contract with ABC to keep doing what I'm doing now for as long as this contract goes on, and then, who knows? I mean, television is changing. There are all kinds of other programs. I'm not sure that I want to keep working at this pace at the expiration of this contract because I'm not only doing two 20/20 programs every week, but four specials a year, and now I am the coexecutive producer and appear in my own daytime television program called *The View*. I have three different offices and staffs. So, I don't think I want to keep working at quite this pace. Nor do I want to go out feet first. I have a very strong private life. I like to have time to smell the flowers, and I want time to smell them a little more. It sure doesn't look that way now, but it's a lovely thought.

Of her legendary career, Walters says she considers she has been blessed. She acknowledges working very hard but that the work has been challenging, fascinating, and exciting. Looking at the level of her achievements, one must agree that she lives a demanding but truly fulfilled professional life.

One of the most respected and visible war correspondents of her generation, Christiane Amanpour is among the youngest in our sample of newswomen. She was thirty-eight years of age at the time of our interview and after signing her 1996 contract with CNN, she became the

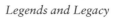

CRAIGE SJODIN/ABC NEWS

Barbara Walters, ABC News

first reporter at the cable network to earn in excess of $1 million annually. It is estimated that she will also be paid up to $500,000 a year for five or six appearances on CBS's *60 Minutes*. Her coverage of the war in Bosnia has won her an Emmy. She is also the recipient of a George Foster Peabody Award, a George Polk Award, and a Courage in Journalism Award. Her colleagues at CNN consider her among the "hottest reporters" in American television. With her ability, authority, and passion to reach an international audience, Amanpour is a serious journalist whose qualifications justify her enviable position.

The single issue that is most indicative of the emerging and changing roles embraced by women in television news over the last two decades is marriage and motherhood. In 1973, 53 percent of the newswomen were single and never married; 23 percent were divorced. Three of the thirty women I then interviewed had children at home from an earlier, failed marriage. All of the single women I spoke to were convinced that marriage would have substantially altered their careers and slowed their professional advancement.

An analysis of the current group of women who are successfully working in the broadcasting profession shows a strong and continuing commitment to their obligations as wives and as mothers: forty-one (59%) were married, fifteen (21%) were single, twelve (17%) were divorced, and two were widows. Forty-eight (69%) of the women in this sample had children at home: thirty-nine were birth children, eleven were adopted, and seventeen were stepchildren. One woman was responsible for raising eleven children, two from birth, five adopted, and four stepchildren. There was nearly universal acceptance of the belief that a nurturing family life was of critical importance to a woman's happiness and fulfillment. But these responsibilities weigh heavily on the shoulders of women whose profession extracts an enormous commitment of time and energy. The newswomen share continuous stress and guilt as they divide their energies and abilities between uncompromising demands. Some manage to achieve a more compatible balance than others; no one is spared the strain.

Those women journalists who had made the conscious decision not to marry often expressed serious misgivings. I sometimes sensed an edge of bitterness at the sacrifices made on the altar of professional success. Nearly every younger woman I spoke with who now works in television news has plans that include a family life. Certainly, there is no one style of living that is appropriate for every person. Marriage and motherhood are not necessarily mandated for all women. The key is choice, and the freedom to make that choice. However, it is imperative to know what options exist and what sacrifices are realistically required by the major decisions we make. While reaching for the best that is in each of us, it is important to recognize that it is acceptable not to have to do it all—and certainly not to have to do it all at once.

Margaret Mead, the anthropologist, once described the dilemma facing the ambitious woman as having to choose between being a "loved object" and an "achieving individual." It's time for us to realize that there will always be those who love us for what we are trying to be, just as there have always been those who have loved us for not trying to be anything at all.

It is interesting to compare the lifestyles of the men I interviewed for this study. Only one of the fifteen men in this sample was no longer married. Half (50%) were in marriages that had lasted between twenty-five and fifty-six years. This stability speaks volumes about the accepted historical roles of men as the breadwinners and professional successes and women as the caretakers of hearth and home. Actually, many working women miss having a "wife" to take care of them and put that request high on their personal wish list. One newswoman revealed that in her home, shared responsibility meant lifting up your feet when the vacuum went by. A great strength that women usually possess is the ability to laugh at themselves and not take themselves quite as seriously as men do. Certainly, this characteristic helps smooth out some of the rougher spots that confront us in life. When you are a woman and you marry a man who is more successful than you and he makes more money than you do, the world congratulates you on your choice. Whereas, if you are a man and you marry a woman who is more successful than you and she makes more money than you do, the world asks how you are coping. The difference in societal expectations remains rigidly fixed.

The focus and direction of television news in recent years has caused concern and consternation among broadcasters who worry about the eroding journalistic standards that pervade news programs. The tabloid nature of the news stories undermines credibility and devalues the profession. The focus on ratings and sensationalism makes veteran news correspondents uncomfortable, and does a major disservice to the viewing public. The balance between substance and sensationalism seems to be lost.

Linda Ellerbee remains an outspoken critic of the television news industry:

> As long as the people who make television (most of them) think they are much smarter than the people who watch television, they will always be giving you something other than their very best. They will be giving you what they think you need, or what they think you want to see, or what they think you don't want to miss. Whatever it is, it's not their very best. And so we have developed this subspecies of humans called TV anchors and reporters, who do horrible things like stick the microphone in the face of some mother whose child has died on TWA Flight 800, and ask her how she feels about it. Or who starts to explain stories to you, and you discover they have no historical context in their minds, that they have no idea, that for them nostalgia is last week. It's very hard to watch television as a producer now and not want to strangle some of the people you see delivering the news. They are calling themselves reporters. Now, there are good ones— there are some good ones. But they're not being rewarded for being good at what they do.

Always aware of the differences in the news divisions of the networks, Ellerbee acknowledges that over the years, changes were allowed that have been calamitous to the news profession:

> The main thing that was different is that when I began, the president of the news division's primary job was gatekeeper and defender of the faith. He was the one who puts his hand up and said to the rest of the network and to the advertising community, "No, you will not tread here. This part of the network is the rent and pay for being able to make lots of money on the public airwaves which you do not own. The public owns. We are the rent you pay, and you may not play in these fields." It went from that to the bringing in of consultants, many consultants. The more frightened a man is, the more consultants he will hire. From consultants came the blending of the news divisions, the entertainment division, the sports division, and the advertising community. The people who get screwed are the audience because television news today is mainly grade yellow.

Women who have spent their whole professional lives in television news review their accomplishments and appraise their dedication. They evaluate the sacrifices they have been called on to make and seriously contemplate their choices for the future. Norma Quarles has spent over thirty years in broadcasting. We spoke three weeks after her return to CNN from brain tumor surgery. After facing a life-threatening experience, it was time to step back and discover what was really important to her:

> I have enjoyed the business. It meant so much to me, the ambition. When you're young and you look, and you say I have this burning desire to do this, to make a contribution. And certainly, I thought that we were going to change people's lives. We're talking about television. This was a fairly new industry then, and I thought, oh, we would have a tremendous impact on how people see things, on how people accept different races and nationalities. I mean, I had a dream of really being able to make a difference. In hindsight, I wonder how much difference it all made. Did we make any inroads? Were there any changes? Are there influences that we had on people's lives? Did we make life better for people? I don't know. Sometimes I look at it and I say, people call it an idiot box. Here I was so caught up, and I thought it was so important. Do I still think it's so important? I don't know.

What is known is that individuals of credibility and courage can, and must make a difference. It is now time for the women and men who have labored lovingly and with passion to enhance the value and integrity of journalism, to stand tall and refuse to pander to the greed and short-sighted values of businessmen who dilute the responsibility of the profession in the unending quest for ratings and greater profitability. The stakes are too high to place at risk an informed citizenry that remains the lifeblood of our democratic system of government.

While there is general agreement that women now populate newsrooms across the country in larger numbers than ever and occupy significant leadership positions on air (and, to a lesser degree in the managerial boardrooms), the fact remains that television news is still dominated by men, white men. Women still have to move faster, jump higher to keep pace or to prove themselves worthy. Women today are taken more seriously; they cover the president, not just the first lady; they cover floods, not just the Red Cross shelters; they are in war zones facing danger and death, not just reporting on the feeling of the families of victims at home. But, while women have risen in executive ranks to the level of vice president, they rarely have authority in financial decisions, or a final

ANCHORS AND CORRESPONDENTS

Network	Total No.	No. of Men	No. of Women	% Women
ABC News	98	61	37	38
NBC News	93	63	30	32
CBS News	69	49	20	29

voice in hiring or firing. Without this critical authority over bottom-line decisions, the victories that have been won remain hollow. When women are fully integrated into these top-echelon positions, there will be a significant decrease in the sexist divisions and practices that are still pervasive. Only then will women reach a level of parity in the world of television news. It is of interest to look at some current statistics. The three major networks provided me with the total number of anchors and correspondents each employed in 1997 and the breakdown by gender, as shown in the table above.

Broadcasting is big business, and it is reflective of what occurs in the rest of society. As women grow in stature and occupy leadership roles in corporate America, as well as in the various branches of government, their relative strength will be felt in newsrooms across the country. The basic operating principle in television, as in all industry, is that the higher women climb, the more resistance they encounter. Power is coveted. Those who are in control want to stay in control. Those at the top go to great lengths to assure the status quo. In 1973, while admitting to me that a glance around any newsroom revealed that broadcasting was a white-male bastion, Ted Kavenau felt there was no need to change things: "It would bother me if I was a woman. But I'm not a woman. I'm a man. If I'm on top, I don't concern myself that much with those below." That sexist state of mind continues to flourish today. So, in spite of major gains for women over the last quarter century, in spite of a history of talent and achievement, there remains a legacy of prejudice and repression.

When a woman is placed in an elevated position of authority, it does not automatically ensure that she will then serve as a positive influence and strengthen opportunities for other working women. Marlene

Sanders refers to women who fail to lend a needed hand to support other women on their staff as "Aunt Toms."

Many newswomen I spoke to related experiences in which their strong advocacy of a story or point of view was regarded as "bitchiness." If a man argued or disagreed, it was viewed as standing up for his convictions and therefore a virtue. Women seem always to be held to a higher standard of conduct, and are often forced to walk a tightrope in the continual quest for acceptance and support.

Certain women and men have personalities and work ethics that create problems for those around them. Kathy Christensen was the first woman to be named as executive producer of a network evening news program. It was viewed as another breakthrough for women in television news. However, she became unpopular among several ABC producers and correspondents. She especially experienced problems with women. Several newswomen told me that they were ready to refuse to work with her anymore. She was considered abrasive and condescending in her interactions. Since my interview with Christensen she has been removed from this position. But, whether the reason was corporate politics or poor job performance, the ability to be able to demote or fire someone for cause should not be affected by gender or race. People deserve the respect and rewards that accrue to those who have proven competence. Equality in the workplace must be based on merit and professionalism. Reverse discrimination is equally unacceptable and demoralizing.

Women working in television news today are standing on the foundations built by those pioneering women who struggled and fought to achieve recognition and acceptance. They all bear the emotional scars of those sexist battles. Many have made more personal sacrifices than they care to admit. But these same women became the role models and mentors for the next wave of women trying to climb higher on the ladder of success. While there have always been extraordinary women with talent, strength, and perseverance, their accomplishments do not necessarily translate into broad-based acceptance of women generally. The pioneers may have cleared the path, but it remains a rugged trail, and the journey for those trying to follow is still long and frustrating.

Only as television news continues to recognize women as indispensable will it be able to fulfill its responsibility and realize its abundant potential. Let us hope that the twenty-first century will ensure that men and women, working together, become the operative model for the broadcasting profession. Enrichment of our country through cultural and gender diversity in the newsrooms of America is required for news to effectively reflect the aggregate view.

An informed citizenry is the blood and sinew of a democracy. Television is the most powerful instrument invented to date for the delivery of information. When women stand shoulder to shoulder with men, when minorities are truly represented in the process, when the corridors of decision and power reflect equality and diversity, then—and only then—will the profession of broadcast journalism reach its crucial goals. When excellence trumps gender, the way will have been cleared to achieve these ideals in the new millennium.

17

Notable and Quotable

Errol Flynn died on a seventy-foot yacht
with a seventeen-year-old girl. Walter's
always wanted to go that way, but
he's going to settle for a seventeen footer
and a seventy-year-old.

BETSY CRONKITE

The nine-month research process produced indelible impressions that made this period of discovery especially meaningful. These interview experiences touched my life in a way that was deeper and more emotionally riveting than I anticipated. I shared feelings and events that will always remain treasured memories. Together they form a mosaic that provides a richer context and understanding of the women and men who briefly shared a part of themselves with me.

• Connie Chung with a picture of her newly adopted son Matthew, saying she knew every mother believes her child to be the most beautiful in the world but in Matthew's case, "it is absolutely true."

- Sally Quinn revealing that the mezuzah on the doorway of her Georgetown house was given to her by Art Buchwald after their home had been robbed. It was to provide protection. It worked.
- Pia Lindstrom declaring that her late mother, the legendary actress Ingrid Bergman, once asked how she knew what to say on air without a written script.
- Melba Tolliver taking me by New York subway to join her in a yoga class after our interview ended.
- Maureen Bunyan arriving at the Washington, D.C., restaurant where we were to have lunch only to tell me that her father was taken to the hospital, gravely ill, and she would be unable to do the interview. She wanted to come in person to let me know. Her father died later that day.
- Cokie Roberts on the couch in her office skillfully working on needlepoint during our entire interview. She showed me, proudly, a picture of her family. When our interview ended, we walked together to the washroom where we met Ann Compton and Carole Simpson in an impromptu high level "women's room" meeting.
- Dan Rather excusing himself during our interview to take a phone call from Peter Jennings. When he returned he commented how nice it is when your competitors are worthy men who never "hit below the belt."
- Gloria Rojas reminding me that we had once been students together at Herman Ridder Junior High School in the Bronx.
- Sheila MacVicar revealing how female foreign correspondents often took off their bulletproof vests and washed their underwear in the coffee pot, the only place that contained hot water.
- Sam Donaldson apologizing for the big mess that was in his office, papers and books thrown around everywhere. But his was an organized mind at work, even admidst the superficial chaos.
- Tom Brokaw admitting that he was conditioned to work well with women because of a strong mother, a successful, supportive wife, and three independent daughters.
- Bob Zelnick writing on his release form that scholars such as myself should "spend more time worrying about the *quality* of the journalist we are putting on the tube and less about the *sex* of that journalist."
- Susan Zirinsky recalling that immediately after her marriage ceremony she left her new husband to meet producer James Brooks. They spent the next four hours developing the model for the female lead in the film *Broadcast News*.
- Marlene Sanders inviting me to join her for dinner when she learned I was alone in New York.

• Betsy Aaron telephoning from Moscow to tell me that she was stopping in Amsterdam on her way back to New York and would have to reschedule our interview.

• Carol Jenkins speaking about her adopted son, one of Mother Hale's crack cocaine babies she had first met on a story, saying she will always be grateful because her career had given her this child.

• Judy Woodruff arranging to meet me in San Diego where she was covering the Republican National Convention for CNN. There I experienced the circus atmosphere that surrounds our democratic process—and decided that the live pig walking the public sidewalk wearing a top hat was more impressive than the myriad of stuffed elephants dressed in American flags.

• Av Westin declaring that a prime prerequisite for a woman's on-air success was "good hair!"

• Barbara Cochran stating she was the second woman in her newsroom to get pregnant in the more than one-hundred-year history of the *Washington Star.*

• Christiane Amanpour revealing for the first time that she wanted to go to outer space.

• Diane Sawyer being called out of town or out of the country on four different occasions requiring a reschedule of our interview. She and her secretary were always gracious and apologetic, while reassuring me that "it will work out," that "it always does." It did!

• Betty Rollin admitting that at the age of sixty she still "doesn't know what she wants to be when she grows up."

• Cheryl Gould acknowledging that she gave birth to her son Jacob at age forty-two, "just in the nick of time," and that he is truly the light of her life.

• Kelly Lange sending me an autographed copy of her novel *Trophy Wife* that reads "Here's to the hard-working women—you, me, and my Devin in *Trophy Wife.*"

• Ted Kavenau deploring the "acting" that he sees daily on television news. He labels the newspeople "phonies."

• Ann Medina faulting her lifestyle, which took her to difficult war zones and deserts for over ten years and caused her to go through menopause at the age of thirty-seven. With no family history of early menopause, her condition stymied her doctors. She blames it on the physical stress of her job.

• Maria Shriver saying her interest in television news started during the 1972 political campaign when her father was the Democratic candidate for vice president and she spent most of the time traveling on his plane—but in the back where the press sat.

• Judy Muller describing how ABC hired a consultant to help improve her on-camera image and the only suggestion given was that she wear scarves. She never did—and emphasizes that she never will.

• Walter Cronkite remembering that there was only one person of "female gender on television news" when he began. He was referring to Pauline Frederick—and that's the way it was . . .

INTERVIEW SCHEDULE

Asterisks indicate individuals also interviewed for my first book, *Women in Television News* (Columbia University Press, 1976).

*Aaron, Betsy. September 27, 1996; New York City, New York
Allan, Heather. August 1, 1996; Los Angeles, California
Alvarez, Linda. July 30, 1996; Los Angeles, California
Amanpour, Christiane. October 9, 1996; Paris, France
*Bell, Rebecca. September 10, 1996; Bethesda, Maryland
Bistany, Johanna. June 19, 1996; New York City, New York
Black, Carole. December 27, 1996; Los Angeles, California
Braver, Rita. May 21, 1996; Washington, D.C.
Brinkley, David. May 24, 1996; Washington, D.C.
Brokaw, Tom. June 10, 1996; New York City, New York
*Brown, Theresa. April 9, 1996; Los Angeles, California
*Bunyan, Maureen. May 24, 1996; Washington, D.C.
*Chase, Sylvia. June 11, 1996; New York City, New York
Christensen, Kathy. June 12, 1996; New York City, New York
*Chung, Connie. June 13, 1996; New York City, New York

Clark, Bob. July 24, 1996; Washington, D.C.

Cochran, Barbara. May 22, 1996; Washington, D.C.

*Collins, Pat. June 10, 1996; New York City, New York

Compton, Ann. May 21, 1996; Washington, D.C.

Couric, Katie. June 14, 1996; New York City, New York

Cronkite, Walter. September 13, 1996; New York City, New York

Donaldson, Sam. May 26, 1996; Washington, D.C.

Ellberbee, Linda. August 13, 1996; The Berkshires, Massachusetts

Entelis, Amy. June 18, 1996; New York City

*Frank, Reuven. June 11, 1996; New York City, New York

Gould, Cheryl. June 14, 1996; New York City, New York

Gregory, Bettina. May 21, 1996; Washington, D.C.

*Guggenheimer, Elinor. August 5, 1996; New York City, New York

Harvey, Pat. August 21, 1996; Los Angeles, Calfornia

*Haynes, Phyllis. June 17, 1996; New York City, New York

Ifill, Gwen. July 30,1996; Washington, D.C.

*Ittelson, Al. November 6, 1996; San Diego, California

*Jenkins, Carol. June 17, 1996; New York City, New York

Judd, Jackie. May 23, 1996; Washington, D.C.

Kast, Sheilah. May 23, 1996; Washington, D.C.

*Kavenau, Ted. November 6, 1996; Secaucus, New Jersey

King, Susan. August 2, 1996; Washington, D.C.

Lange, Kelly. August 1, 1996; Los Angeles, California

*Lindstrom, Pia. June 10, 1996; New York City, New York

MacVicar, Sheila. August 16, 1996; London, England

*Marash, David. May 20, 1996; Washington, D.C.

*Margolies-Muzvinsky, Marjory. April 19, 1996; San Francisco, California

Mason, Linda. June 19, 1996; New York City, New York

McGrady, Phyllis. November 26, 1996; New York City, New York

McManus, Kathy. November 22, 1996; Jerusalem, Israel

McQueen, Michel. September 9, 1996; Washington, D.C.

*Medina, Ann. October 22, 1996; Ontario, Canada

 Meserve, Jeanne. July 29, 1996; Washington, D.C.

 Mitchell, Andrea. May 20, 1996; Washington, D.C.

*Mulholland, Bob. July 24, 1996; Naples, Florida

 Muller, Judy. September 6, 1996; Los Angeles, California

 Myers, Lisa. September 30, 1996; Washington, D.C.

 Norris, Michelle. August 1, 1996; Washington, D.C.

 O'Hearn, Kathy. June 14, 1996; New York City, New York

 Potter, Deborah. August 27, 1996; St. Petersburg, Florida

*Primo, Al. December 11, 1996; Old Greenwich, Connecticut

*Quarles, Norma. June 13, 1996; New York City, New York

*Quinn, Sally. May 20, 1996; Washington, D.C.

 Rather, Dan. June 11, 1996; New York City, New York

 Roberts, Cokie. May 22, 1996; Washington, D.C.

*Rojas, Gloria. June 13, 1996; New York City, New York

*Rollin, Betty. June 10, 1996; New York City, New York

*Sanders, Marlene. June 11, 1996; New York City, New York

 Sawyer, Diane. September 26, 1996; New York City, New York

*Scamardella, Rose Ann; August 5, 1996; Lakeville, Connecticut

*Shen, Linda. April 19, 1996; San Francisco, California

*Sherr, Lynn. June 17, 1996; New York City, New York

*Sherwood, Virginia. July 24, 1996; Angel Fire, New Mexico

 Shriver, Maria. October 23, 1996; Los Angeles, California

 Siebens, Jennifer. July 25, 1996; Los Angeles, California

 Simpson, Carole. June 16, 1996; New York City, New York

 Sproul, Robin. May 23, 1996; Washington, D.C.

 Stark, Lisa. September 19, 1996; Washington, D.C.

 Stone, Karen. July 17, 1996; New York City, New York

 Takuda, Wendy. August 1, 1996; Los Angeles, California

 Threlkeld, Richard. October 19, 1996; Winsted, Connecticut

 Tolliver, Melba. June 12, 1996; New York City, New York

 Totenberg, Nina. August 5, 1996; Washington, D.C.

Vargas, Elizabeth. August 23, 1996; New York City, New York

*Walters, Barbara. June 18, 1996; New York City, New York

*Westin, Av. July 15, 1996; New York City, New York

Westwood, Helen. July 19, 1996; Washington, D.C.

Woodruff, Judy. August 10, 1996; San Diego, California

Zahn, Paula. August 5, 1996; New York City, New York

Zelnick, Bob. May 26, 1996; Washington, D.C.

Zirinsky, Susan. August 9, 1996; New York City, New York

BIBLIOGRAPHY

Auletta, Ken. *Three Blind Mice: How the TV Networks Lost Their Way*. New York: Random House, 1991.

Brinkley, David. *A Memoir*. New York: Knopf, 1995.

Alan Carter. "Black by Popular Demand." *Emmy*, February 1997, p. 29.

Craft, Christine. *Too Old, Too Ugly, and Not Deferential to Men*. California: Prima Publishing & Communications, 1988.

Cronkite, Walter. *A Reporter's Life*. New York: Ballantine Books, 1996.

Dates, Jannette L., and William Barlow, eds. *Split Image: African Americans in the Mass Media*. Washington, D.C.: Howard University Press, 1990.

Ellerbee, Linda. *And So It Goes: Adventures in Television*. New York: Putnam, 1986.

Faludi, Susan. *Backlash: The Undeclared War against American Women*. New York: Crown, 1991.

Flanders, Laura. *Real Majority, Media Minority: The Cost of Sidelining Women in Reporting*. Monroe, Maine: Common Courage Press, 1997.

Foote, Joe S. "Women Correspondents' Visibility on Network Evening News." *Mass Communication Review* 19, nos. 1 and 2 (1992).

French, Marilyn. *The War against Women*. New York: Summit Books, 1993.

Gelfman, Judith. *Women in Television News.* New York: Columbia University Press, 1976.

Graham, Katherine. *Personal History.* New York: Random House, 1997.

Gunther, Marc. *The House That Roone Built: The Inside Story of ABC News.* Boston: Little, Brown, 1994.

Hunter-Gault, Charlayne. *In My Place.* New York: Farrar, Straus & Giroux, 1992.

Lont, Cynthia M., ed. *Women and Media: Content, Careers, Criticism.* New York: Wadsworth, 1995.

Madsen, Axel. *60 Minutes: The Power & the Politics of America's Most Popular News Show.* New York: Dodd, Mead, 1984.

Marc, David, and Robert J. Thompson. *Prime Time, Prime Movers.* Boston: Little, Brown, 1992.

Matusow, Barbara. *The Evening Stars: The Making of the Network News Anchor.* Boston: Houghton Mifflin, 1983.

Meyers, Marian. *News Coverage of Violence against Women: Engendering Blame.* California: Sage Publications, 1996.

"The New Look of TV News." *Newsweek,* October 11, 1976, pp. 68–81.

O'Dell, Cary. *Women Pioneers in Television: Biographies of Fifteen Industry Leaders.* Jefferson, North Carolina: McFarland, 1997.

Paisner, Daniel. *The Imperfect Mirror.* New York: William Morrow and Company, Inc., 1989.

Bob Papper, Michael Gerhand, and Andrew Sharma. "More Women and Minorities in Broadcast News." *Communication,* August 1996, pp. 8–15.

Rather, Dan. *The Camera Never Blinks Twice: The Further Adventures of a Television Journalist.* New York: Morrow, 1994.

Robertson, Nan. *The Girls in the Balcony: Men, Women, and the New York Times.* New York: Random House, 1992.

Sanders, Marlene, and Marcia Rock. *Waiting for Prime Time: The Women of Television News.* Chicago: University of Illinois Press, 1988.

Savitch, Jessica. *Anchorwoman.* New York: Putnam, 1982.

Sterber, A. M. *Murrow: His Life and Times.* New York: Freundlich Books, 1986.

Trotta, Liz. *Fighting for Air: In the Trenches with Television News.* New York: Simon & Schuster, 1991.

Verne, Cary. "Beyond Today." *Los Angeles Times Magazine,* January 2, 1997, p. 2.

Wolf, Naomi. *The Beauty Myth: How Images of Beauty Are Used against Women.* New York: William Morrow and Company, Inc., 1991.

Ziegler, D., and A. White. "Women and Minorities on Network Television News: An Examination of Correspondents and Newsmakers." *Journal of Broadcasting & Electronic Media* 34, no. 2 (Spring 1990): 215–223.

INDEX

(Page numbers in italics reference illustrations.)

Index

Index

Northridge earthquake, 122–123, 132 n.1
Not For Women Only, 238

Ober, Eric, 38, 58
O'Hearn, Kathy, 48, 61, 98–99, 147, 228
Ohio State University, 174
Oklahoma City bombing, 163, 163 n.5
Olympics bombing of 1996, 202 n.1
Osgood, Charlie, 90
Ovitz, Michael, 181–182

Paley, Bill, 205
Palmer, John, 195
Pauley, Jane, 134, 145
Peterson, Gordon, 183
Pfeiffer, Michelle, 44–46, 50
Phil Donahue Show, 32
Pickford, Mary, 47
Pinkney, Charles, 99
Pitt, Brad, 35
Plastic surgery, 31–32
Politicians. *See* Women politicians; and specific politicians
Potero, Juan, 121
Potter, Deborah, 93, 204, 226
Presley, Elvis, 202
"Pretty quotient," 40
Priebke, Eric, 116
Prime News Service, 27
Prime Time Live, 14, 17, 25, 72, 88, 129, 164
Primo, Al, 27, 66
Primo Management Service, 27, 66
Putnam, George, 179

Quarles, Norma, 121–122, 245
Quayle, Dan, 234
Quinn, Sally, 67, 167–168, 168 n.6, 225, 250

Rabin, Yitzhak, 194
Racism, 94–109, 175, 236–237
Radcliffe, 125
Radio and Television News Directors Foundation (RTNDF), 95, 203
Radio-Television News Directors Association, 5, 141 n.1, 174
Radner, Gilda, 167
Rather, Dan: advice to aspiring journalists by, 222–223; as anchor, 78–80, 91; on competition, 250; deepest desire of, 225; on family life, 157–158; on Hollywoodization of news, 202; in-

terview with, 3; on perceptions of women, 16; photograph of, *81;* and role models, 196, 197; and salaries, 180, 180 n.1; as writer, 50
Ratings, 203–204
Reagan, Ronald, 116, 127, 149–151, 191
Reasoner, Harry, 75–76, 79, 82–83, 179
Redford, Robert, 45
Resnick, Faye, 81
Reverse discrimination, 14, 173–187, 247
Reynolds, Frank, 180, 198
Rivera, Geraldo, 166
Roberts, Cokie: advice to aspiring journalists by, 214–215; on ageism, 33; and Brinkley roundtable, 129; on family life, 161–162; future goals of, 226; and Oklahoma City bombing, 163; on perceptions of women in broadcasting, 13–14; photograph of, *15;* on sexual harassment, 59; and sisterhood support, 133, 134; "women's room" meeting with, 250
Roberts, Steven, 161
Robinson, Max, 175
Rogers, Ginger, 27
Rojas, Gloria, 41, 42, 107–108, 120–121, 137, 165–166, 225, 250
Role models, xvi, 188–198
Rollin, Betty, 40, 50–51, 146–147, 228, 251
Roosevelt, Eleanor, 30, 90, 224
Rosenberg, Steve, 227
RTNDF, 95, 203

Sadat, Anwar, 113, 116
Salaries, 91, 173–187, 236, 237–239, 242
Sanders, Marlene, 36, 91–92, 170–171, 171, 217–218, 226, 247, 250
Sarajevo, 114–115
Sarnoff, General, 205
Satellite transmission, 199–200
Saturday Night Live, 167
Savitch, Jessica, 32, 51, 51 n.2
Sawyer, Diane: advice to aspiring journalists by, 211; age of, xii; as foreign correspondent, 25–27; influence of, 14; journalistic contribution of, 116; photograph of, *26;* and role models, 189; and salaries, 180, 181, 238; scheduling difficulties with, 251; on sexual harassment, 70; and sisterhood support, 134, 137–139, 140; on stamina, 48; wishes